The Rise of the Therapeutic Society

The Rise of the Therapeutic Society

Psychological Knowledge & the
Contradictions of Cultural Change

Katie Wright

Washington, DC

Copyright © 2010 by Katie Wright

New Academia Publishing, 2011

All rights reserved. No part of this book may be reproduced or transmitted in any form or by any means, electronic or mechanical, including photocopying, recording, or by any information storage and retrieval system.

Printed in the United States of America

Library of Congress Control Number: 2011921073
ISBN 978-0-9832451-2-4 paperback (alk. paper)

New Academia Publishing
P.O. Box 27420, Washington, DC, 20038-7420
info@newacademia.com - www.newacademia.com

Contents

List of Illustrations	vi
Preface & Acknowledgements	vii
Abbreviations	x
Introduction	1
1. The Therapeutic Society & Its Discontents	13
2. Modernity, Medicine & the Problem of "Nerves"	49
3. The Legitimation of Psychological Expertise	87
4. Cultural Diffusion of the Analytic Attitude	127
5. Therapy: Inside the Talking Cure	177
6. Reflections on the Therapeutic Turn	217
Notes	227
Bibliography	255
Index	270

Illustrations

Nervous Sufferers Read This	61
Electro Galvanic Suspensory Belt	62
Parisian Agency Company: Men Be Manly	63
Cassell's Tablets: Remedy for Neurasthenia	78
Ardath Cigarettes: For Jumpy Nerves	79
Whisky Lets Your Nerves "Stand Easy"	80
Fishaphos Nerve Tablets	81
Nervy? Sanatogen Nerve Tonic	84
Home Study Course in Applied Psychology	133
Inferiority Complex Eradicated For Ever	134
Trapped by the Harsh Laxative Habit	138
Harley Schwadron Psychiatrist Cartoon	141
Would You Like to be a Counselor?	145
Help for Parents	169

Preface & Acknowledgements

Since the publication in 1966 of Philip Rieff's classic treatise, *The Triumph of the Therapeutic*, the West's fascination with the psychological has been a subject of ongoing scholarly interest. In the wake of his brilliant, if at times impenetrable, study of "faith after Freud," stands a now voluminous literature that extends Rieff's analytic frame in a variety of directions. In light of these debates, this book offers an account of the rise of the therapeutic in Australia, where its presence is evident no less than in other parts of the West. Beyond telling an Australian story, however, the book has a theoretical purpose that transcends national boundaries. My hope, therefore, is that it will appeal both to those already familiar with debates about the therapeutic, as well as those interested in the spread of psychological knowledges and changing ideas about the self and emotional life in Australia and beyond.

In the face of its pervasiveness, the therapeutic is a daunting object of study, one I suspect that leaves those who endeavor to investigate it acutely aware of the impossibility of coming to grips with its many and varied dimensions. It is both omnipresent and ephemeral, finding expression in a multiplicity of ways at different times and in a variety of locations. I have tried to capture something of its disparate historical development by focusing on some of the key institutional sites and processes involved in its emergence. I have also tried to bring to bear upon my analysis a central dimension of the therapeutic society that is too often overlooked: people's actual experiences of therapy.

That the initial ideas for this book developed into this volume was made possible by a number of people, all of whom I owe a debt of gratitude. I extend my warmest thanks and deep appreciation to the people interviewed for this project about their experiences of therapy and counseling. Their willingness to share intimate and personal experiences of very difficult times in their lives provides a most valuable insight into the complexity of the therapeutic. Although material from their interviews appears only in one chapter, it was these initial discussions that convinced me of the need to develop an alternative account of the therapeutic turn. I also offer special thanks to Stephanie Dowrick, Amanda Gordon, Antony Kidman, and Peter O'Connor, for sharing their insights and experiences of providing psychological support to others.

Many of the ideas that shape this book arose from discussions with Kerreen Reiger, and her encouragement and critical feedback from the early stages of the project to its completion has been invaluable. John Carroll also provided advice along the way, and from a more skeptical standpoint than mine, challenged me to think critically about the place of therapy in modern society. A number of other people kindly commented on drafts and for insightful and constructive suggestions, I thank Sean Byrne, Julie McLeod, Josh Switzer, and Brenda Tait. In addition, I thank James Wright for help in preparing the images for publication. Thanks also, of course, to my friends and family for their support and encouragement: Montana Sue Watkin and John Wright especially. I should also like to acknowledge the institutions which enabled me to complete this project: the Sociology Department at La Trobe University where this research began, and the Graduate School of Education at the University of Melbourne, where it was completed.

Parts of this work have appeared elsewhere in somewhat different form and I extend my thanks to the editors and publishers for allowing me to republish revised versions of the following: "Theorizing Therapeutic Culture: Past Influences, Future Directions," *Journal of Sociology* 44 no. 4 (2008): 321-336; "Engendering a Therapeutic Ethos: Modernity, Masculinity & Nervousness," *Journal of Historical Sociology* 22 no. 1 (2009): 84-107; and 'Therapy Culture' in *Reflected Light: La Trobe Essays*, edited by Peter Beilharz and Robert Manne, 302-312 (Black Inc: Melbourne, 2006).

I am grateful for permission to reproduce the artwork appearing on the cover: "Street Scene" by Charles Blackman, 1960, oil on masonite. Collection: Art Gallery of Ballarat, The William, Rene and Blair Ritchie Collection. Bequest of Blair Ritchie, 1998.

Preface and Acknowledgements   ix

I am also grateful to those copyright holders who have given permission to reproduce images used in the text. While every effort has been made to trace and contact copyright holders for all of the illustrations used in this volume, it has not been possible to determine copyright in all cases. For any omissions I apologize to those concerned.

This book is dedicated to my children Jake, Molly, and Brigid, whose good humor, encouragement, and patience kept me going, and to my husband Sean, who has lived with this project for as long as I have, and whose friendship, support, and scholarly insight made its completion possible.

Abbreviations

AAAS	Australasian Association for the Advancement of Science
AAPP	Australasian Association of Psychology and Philosophy
ABC	Australian Broadcasting Commission
ACER	Australian Council for Educational Research
ADHD	Attention Deficit Hyperactivity Disorder
AFL	Australian Football League
AIIP	Australian Institute of Industrial Psychology
AJPP	*Australasian Journal of Psychology and Philosophy*
ALP	Australian Labor Party
APS	Australian Psychological Society
BPS	British Psychological Society
CBT	Cognitive Behavioral Therapy
NRL	National Rugby League
MJA	*Medical Journal of Australia*

Introduction

Like the citizens of many other Western societies, Australians are fascinated with emotional and psychological life. Popular culture and social policy alike reflect a widely held belief that talk is therapeutic and that speaking about problems helps to resolve them. Character traits and behaviors are routinely evaluated through a psychological lens: we talk of people being in denial, repressed, and having anger management issues. We indulge in retail therapy to lift our mood, engage life coaches to help us succeed, and consult therapists for mental health problems, relationship difficulties, and personal tribulations. In times of disaster, trauma counselors are dispatched along with emergency service personnel. Helplines and support groups assist people in crisis, while psychiatry, clinical psychology, and a range of other therapeutic interventions are funded by the state. From concerns about rising rates of depression and ADHD, to celebrity confessions, misery memoirs, and footballers talking about their feelings, social and cultural life in Australia is marked by a concern with psychological wellbeing. As in the United States, Britain, and elsewhere, the therapeutic has clearly triumphed.

The privileging of psychological discourses and the prominence of counseling as a remedial life strategy are emblematic manifestations of the therapeutic society. Yet the therapeutic extends more widely than concerns with psychological selfhood and the individual in therapy. It encompasses a multifaceted spectrum of discourses, social practices, and cultural artifacts that discursively and institutionally pervade social and cultural life. It takes a clinical form in which individuals either voluntarily seek—or are coerced into seeking—assistance from psychiatrists, psychologists, psychotherapists, and counselors. Culturally, it finds expression in the spread of psychological ideas and therapeutic motifs in popular culture, as well as through discourses and practices that have been normalized through the institutional fabric of organizations.[1]

Through an analysis of its emergence in Australia, this book examines the rise of the therapeutic society and explores its legacy for sociocultural, political, and personal life in the globalized West. The historical shifts considered in the pages that follow reflect widespread changes that have taken place throughout Western societies. The book, therefore, not only throws light on Australian developments. It also provides the basis for theorizing the therapeutic more generally, and for examining questions of broader significance: What does it mean to live the good life in an age of therapy? Have ideals of reticence and self-reliance been dethroned by a culture of emotional expressiveness and help seeking? And has the rise of the therapeutic society ushered in a more compassionate and caring era, or have we simply become fixated with self-esteem and hooked on feeling good?

The book brings together historical research, social theory, and phenomenological accounts of therapy to offer an alternative perspective on the therapeutic turn, one that challenges orthodox accounts and raises new questions about gender, suffering, and struggles for dignity and justice. A principal aim of the book is to illuminate and historicize the therapeutic society through an examination of key institutional sites and cultural carriers that fostered its emergence. It seeks to elucidate the processes whereby over the course of the twentieth century, Australia's public and political spheres, no less than intimate and private life, were transformed along therapeutic lines. Put another way, how it was that by century's end, the renowned "she'll be right" attitude had given way to an unreservedly therapeutic sensibility, with psychologists and psychiatrists in Australia comprising almost twice the per capita rate of the United States—a country often assumed to be the vanguard of "therapy culture" in the West.[2]

While it may appear self-evident that a sociocultural phenomenon as multifaceted as the therapeutic will have wide ranging consequences, its apparently inexorable rise has aroused significant disquiet amongst social analysts and cultural commentators.

According to the prevailing view, vulnerability characterizes contemporary selfhood and victimhood confers privileged status to those who claim it. Confession and depression are regarded as symptoms of a sick society in which consolation has replaced political change and transcendental meaning has given way to self-improvement. Twenty-first century faith at best refers to the feel good revivalism of evangelical religion, but more often a belief in the power of therapeutics or pharmaceuticals. With meaning pursued on the therapist's couch, or through the banality of reality television, hollow chit-chat, self-help books, and endless rumination, modern society and selfhood are regarded by many as being in a state of steady decline.

The rise of the therapeutic has thus been widely regarded as an insidious development. The gloomy prognosis of cultural and personal decline delineated by Philip Rieff four decades ago both demarcated the terrain and set the tone of things to come. Christopher Lasch famously identified a "culture of narcissism," while more recently Frank Furedi bemoaned the pervasive emotionalism of "therapy culture."[3] Following Lasch, accounts of social control feature prominently alongside narratives of cultural decline. Feminist critiques of both therapy and the therapeutic society, for example, implicate psychological knowledge and therapeutic authority in the social control of women.[4] Though a more ambivalent reading is refracted through a Foucauldian lens, in the final analysis the therapeutic is largely reduced to a beguiling apparatus of subjection, with "psy" knowledges underwriting the government of subjectivity and social life in advanced liberal democracies.[5]

Social theoretical critiques of the therapeutic society traverse divergent intellectual traditions—from the cultural conservatism of Rieffian sociology, to neo-Marxism, studies in governmentality, and radical feminism. Yet through them all runs an abiding concern about the cultural shift towards interiority. The conceptual origins of this book arose from my engagement with these issues. As insightful and compelling as many existing accounts have been, I was nagged by a concern that the contradictoriness of the therapeutic has, for the most part, been unacknowledged or downplayed, and consequently that the ascendancy of the psychological and emotional realms was not as bleak a development as much social theory has suggested. Seeking to ground these issues in the sociohistorical context of the emergence of the therapeutic society, and in people's everyday experience, the research developed largely into an empirical project, albeit one driven by theoretical concerns.

During the early stages of the research it was through interviews with people about their experiences of therapy that the complexity of the therapeutic first presented itself. Stories of emotional angst suggested that a therapeutic worldview offered a means of framing and articulating experience, and as such provided people with a resource for managing uncertainty and difficult situations.[6] The messy reality of everyday life, which is largely neglected in theoretical analysis, problematized for me what might have otherwise been convincing readings of the therapeutic turn. As the research progressed, the possibility that the therapeutic might operate not only in repressive ways but also in emancipatory ones emerged as a neglected yet significant issue. It became increasingly evident that premises upon which dominant analyses rested became questionable in the light of inquiry that was open to differences in the experiences of women and men, and to the ways in which the rise of the therapeutic society and changes in the gender order were interconnected.

Theoretical and empirical concerns thus intersect as I trace the contours of the therapeutic society historically—how it arose and was legitimated in Australia—and develop an alternative framework from which to consider its implications. To capture its disparate strands in an inquiry grounded in the sociohistorical but driven by present concerns, my methodological approach follows Michel Foucault's exposition of the genealogical project. Rather than a search for truth or historical linearity, a major thrust of genealogical research involves the problematization of the present, and an examination of the past in light of present concerns. It is a mode of inquiry that aims to disrupt common sense by looking at what is familiar in a new way.[7]

In the face of the preponderance of social theory surmising its pernicious effects, the book aims to defamiliarize assumptions about the therapeutic turn. Therefore, while I draw on Foucault's approach to critical history and his delineation of problematization, I do not begin from the premise that there is something inherently wrong with what I am calling the therapeutic society. My interest, rather, lies in exploring its manifestations in various domains of social, cultural, and personal life at different points in time, in order to look anew at how we have come to understand the therapeutic, both theoretically and in everyday life.

My analysis, moreover, is concerned less with uncovering the operation of power in the governing of modern subjectivity than it is with throwing light on the contradictory consequences of sociocultural change. In the face of excessively negative theorizing, this entails, among other things, shedding light on the ways in which psychological knowledges and therapeutic dispositions have engendered new concerns with emotional life that in turn have given rise to new concerns about suffering. Particularly in relation to suffering in the private domain, and forms of injustice hitherto unacknowledged, this development has had major implications for gender relations, and in moving towards a more just society.

Historicizing concerns about psychological and emotional life throws light on the many factors at play in the emergence of therapeutic discourses and practices. Conceptually, I have delineated a number of key dimensions and central processes. These include: the destabilization of gender and the self; the legitimation of psychological expertise; professional therapeutic intervention into private life; the cultural diffusion of psychological models of reflexive selfhood; the ascendancy of the emotional realm; and, the disruption of the boundaries between public and private life. Though all may be understood as critical, they assume varying degrees of significance and take different forms of expression during different historical periods.

An examination of the therapeutic society grounded in the context of its sociohistorical development reveals that many aspects of social change have been propelled by an emancipatory impulse of progress. The individual became knowable, suffering was accorded new forms of recognition, and therapeutic strategies were developed to deal with the alienation of modern life. Yet in the process, the therapeutic has been bound up with the contradictions of modernity itself, ever inseparable from consumer capitalism, mass media, bureaucratic rationality, and professional self-interest. This complex picture is further illuminated when consideration is also given to the experiences of those who best exemplify the spirit of our therapeutic age: people who have sought psychological assistance and experts who provide it.

In the chapters that follow I examine a number of historical developments that demonstrate how therapeutic concerns and psychological knowledges arose within particular sociohistorical locations, often in response to emergent social and personal dilemmas. Suffice to say, the therapeutic society did not "arrive" out of nowhere during the last decades of the twentieth century with the spread of therapy and counseling. The seeds had been sown earlier with the diffusion of psychological knowledges and therapeutic strategies in diverse spheres of social, economic, and cultural life. Its strands can be traced through developments in medicine, in the economic sphere, and in the educational sector, as well as in professional practices and in the wider dissemination of therapeutic discourses.

Before Freud, therapy, or even psychology, had any significant cultural impact, discourses and practices associated with "nerves" were engendering a distinctly therapeutic ethos and recasting ideas about the self in critical ways. Concerns about nervousness captured the public imagination, and the increasing prevalence of nervous disorder in the late nineteenth century fostered the belief that the "stresses and strains of modern life" were damaging to individual health. Both in the medical arena and at the popular level, discourses of nervousness generated new conceptualizations of the self that challenged dominant models of personhood.

That nervousness was understood not just as a problem of women, but increasingly as an affliction of the male population, became especially important to the ascendancy of the therapeutic. For as men were subject to diagnoses of the contemporary equivalent of depression and anxiety, established views on mental health were disrupted, and prevailing views about gender—especially dominant ideals of masculinity—were challenged. The destabilization of taken-for-granted selfhood characteristic of this period was further intensified with the outbreak of World War I and the profound social and psychological consequences that followed. Yet while there was significant consternation about the emotional and psychological cost of modern life, at the same time, new hopes of cure were also emerging.

During the interwar years, yet more complex representations of the individual emerged as selfhood increasingly came to be framed in psychological terms. Though notions of nervousness persisted, the institutional spread of psychology was promulgating a conceptualization of the individual as calculable and knowable. The "scientific" analysis of self and behavior thus pushed the therapeutic in another direction. Psychology provided a discursive scaffolding which made possible the measurement and classification of individual differences. The reach of psychological ideas to normal populations was therefore fostered, with opportunities for the dissemination of psychology's broadening repertoire of knowledges of the individual into fields where those knowledges could be usefully applied.

At the same time, psychological and psychoanalytic ideas spread at the cultural level, underpinned by these institutional developments. In the popular media, psychoanalytic ideas fermented as models of reflexive selfhood were diffused, first during the interwar years with the influence of Freud, but increasingly by the mid-twentieth century as the technical rationality of institutional practices yielded to more therapeutic approaches. As emotional and relational dimensions came to the fore, the therapeutic also found expression in the advent of counseling for problems of everyday life. Psychological knowledge and therapeutic techniques went at least some way to providing strategies with which to manage the difficulties faced by ordinary people in an increasingly complex world.

Insofar as the interplay of gender and the therapeutic is concerned, the destabilization of the self, particularly the masculine self, has been of central importance. While this can be traced to the popularization of male nervous conditions in the late nineteenth century, the therapeutic continues in a variety of ways to challenge dominant notions of masculinity. Indeed during the late twentieth century, the therapeutic not only became more diffuse and multifaceted, but it increasingly assumed an emotional, humanistic, some might say feminized hue. It is through exploring these changing cultural dimensions and associated institutional practices that a central impulse of the therapeutic becomes evident, one concerned with the articulation of—and with attempts to remedy—

experiences of suffering. This is apparent in the early period through the discourse of nerves and becomes more explicit in the latter part of the twentieth century, for example, in public revelations of personal distress and in the growth of counseling and therapy.

Given the enormity of the terrain, the account I establish is far from exhaustive. What I hope it offers, however, are some new insights into the therapeutic turn and an alternative way of thinking about its ramifications. Specifically, I begin from the premise that the undermining of cultural authority, which Rieff's incisive analysis revealed was central to the "triumph of the therapeutic," has had uneven and contradictory consequences. While Rieff's Freudian-inflected account found the breakdown of paternal authority particularly troubling, an alternate view of psychosocial development and gender relations invites a different reading. I do not approach this, however, in the way that has come to characterize feminist readings of both therapy and therapeutic culture—that is, to interpret the elaboration of the "psy-complex" as the social control of women, both through professional intervention into private life and normative constructions of femininity.

Rather, with an eye to elucidating the multiple ways in which gender and therapeutic culture intersect—and the largely overlooked issues around gender and suffering—I examine the emergence of a discursive space for the recognition of emotional aspects of life that have traditionally been regarded, and dismissed, as feminine. A somewhat different picture emerges when the weakening of cultural authority is understood as part of a reconfiguration of the cultural-symbolic logic of gender, a reconfiguration that involves shifts in the demarcation of public and private life, in normative prescriptions of masculinity and femininity, and in levels of social acceptability regarding suffering. The opening up of the private, the legitimizing of the emotional realm, and the speaking of the hitherto unspeakable, I argue, has engendered more complex consequences—particularly for women and marginalized groups—than dominant accounts have thus far suggested.[8]

The interpretive context for my analysis of the therapeutic society is elaborated in Chapter One, which provides a critical overview of the main strands in the history of debates about the therapeutic, and a discussion of the theoretical issues pertinent to my analysis. From conservative sociological critiques of moral decline to concerns about capitalist control, analyses of disciplinary discourses, and feminist objections to therapy, I question assumptions implicit in dominant approaches, notably those concerning the importance of traditional authority, the sanctity of private life, and the rise of the confessional. While theorization of the therapeutic over the last four decades has offered valuable insights into this cultural turn, their limitations became apparent in view of a critical reading of gender and authority. By examining presuppositions of the individual and the social that form the basis of these analyses, and by drawing on social theoretical traditions that offer a more ambivalent reading of twentieth century cultural change, I develop an alternative framework for theorizing. In the chapters that follow, this perspective is explored through empirically grounded research that pays heed to the struggles of ordinary people in dealing with changing social conditions.

Moving from the theoretical to the historical, Chapter Two examines the discursive construction of nervousness. Anxiety about the "stresses and strains of modern life," advances in medical and scientific knowledge, and a developing consumer culture intersected in late nineteenth century Australia. In the context of significant social upheaval, the problem of nerves formed a juncture of medical knowledge and cultural discourses, one in which dimensions of gender, class, and consumerism came together in an emerging therapeutic ethos. The chapter explores how the increasing prevalence and recognition of nervous disorder destabilized accepted ideas about the self, especially the male self, a process that intensified with the outbreak of World War I and in its aftermath. Related developments in the field of psychiatry are also traced, especially those associated with emerging ideologies of treatment and prevention—first physical and then psychological—that saw the bifurcated categories of madness and sanity disrupted.

From changing medical and cultural discourses of nerves to the ascendancy of a scientific discourse of the self, Chapter Three examines psychology as the formal foundation of the therapeutic society. During the early decades of the twentieth century the institutionalization of psychology laid the basis for a new understanding of the self—one in which the individual was comprehensible through scientific knowledge. Psychology's articulation of the self was compatible with the notion of the liberal subject as rational and controllable, and the public sphere was constructed as a domain that could be improved by psychometrics and workplace testing. The chapter charts the professionalization of psychology in Australia and traces how emerging psychological knowledges were applied in the spheres of education and work—long before clinical psychology or counseling had any significant impact. The discussion reveals how psychology legitimized a new approach to the individual, one that was secured first through the development of a scientific project, but which later found expression in a new emotional and relational orientation to private life.

While psychology in education and industry was primarily drawn upon as a "science of the self," Chapter Four explores how psychoanalytically informed ideas resonated at the broader cultural level. An examination of the model of reflexive selfhood disseminated through the popular media reveals how psychoanalytic and other strands of psychological knowledge both reinforced and destabilized important dimensions of the gender order. At the institutional level, the emergence of marriage guidance during the postwar years represents a significant historical moment in which the advent of professional intervention for problems of private life paved the way for the variety of therapies and counseling modalities that emerged in subsequent decades. The nexus of professional self-interest and public education is explored through the marketing campaigns of the Australian Psychological Society, and through reflections of prominent Australian psychologists and therapists who straddle the roles of private therapist and public expert. The opening up of a new discursive space—what is commonly referred to as "confessional culture"—is then considered as enabling a public concern with suffering and a politicization of private life.

Chapter Five takes therapy itself as the focus and examines stories from individuals who have received psychological assistance, and reflections from those who provide it. Phenomenological accounts of both therapists and clients offer insights into quintessentially modern dilemmas. Interviews suggest that therapy cannot be reduced simply to self-absorption and narcissism, nor should its development be read in terms of the proliferation of "victim identities." Rather, therapy may be more usefully understood as a strategy to deal with fundamental dilemmas of modern life, from problems of mental health to a range of other difficulties arising from, or exacerbated by, various aspects of social change. The destabilization of the gender order and shifts in personal and working life emerge as central concerns, as does an important question, notably one neglected in debates of therapeutic culture: how to live with dignity.

The concluding chapter returns to questions of evaluating and theorizing the rise of the therapeutic society. Following an examination of disparate social, cultural, and institutional knowledges and processes, as well as accounts of individuals' own experience of therapeutic practices, the book suggests an alternative reading of sociocultural change. Rejecting dominant interpretations of moral collapse and cultural decline, it closes with an argument for greater recognition of the complex and contradictory dimensions of the therapeutic. In particular, I suggest that recognition of emotional suffering, made possible by the therapeutic turn, has an important part to play in moving towards a more just society. Indeed, I argue that acknowledgement of suffering and struggles for human dignity and social justice constitute central dimensions of the therapeutic project—ones that so far have been largely overlooked. A more complex and indeed ambivalent interpretation of cultural change is called for, one that acknowledges how the privileging of the psychological and emotional dimensions of selfhood has led to the exposure of widespread experiences of suffering, and has challenged a set of gendered arrangements governing both public and private life.

1

The Therapeutic Society & Its Discontents

> *A cultural revolution does not occur as a discernible event, or as a plurality of events, nor does it occur swiftly within a few years, as does a political revolution; only afterwards, when the revolution itself has been incorporated into the new system of controls, do such mythic condensations of cultural change occur.*
> —Philip Rieff, 1966

For close to half a century, social scientists and cultural analysts have lamented the increasing influence of psychology, the rise of therapy and counseling, and an associated preoccupation with the self and internal life. From a variety of intellectual traditions and theoretical standpoints, it has been widely argued that the ascendancy of a modern therapeutic ethos has been a pernicious development, inciting cultural decline, a narcissistic concern with the self, and leading to the rise of a so-called victim culture. Philip Rieff's influential reading of the deterioration of social and cultural life is predicated upon an interpretation of the therapeutic as remissive, that is, that it has ushered in an era of unprecedented lack of constraint and a concomitant diminishment of dignified conduct.[1] In contrast, analyses emphasizing the capitalist political economy, as well as those following Michel Foucault, advance alternative critiques of psychological knowledge and therapeutic practices as highly bound up with modern forms of social control and regulation.[2]

This chapter examines social theoretical readings of the therapeutic turn, beginning with Rieff's pioneering analysis of "faith after Freud," which has informed a diversity of standpoints. Christopher Lasch, for example, shared his moral conservatism but added a political critique, arguing that the therapeutic had incited a turn away from politics and social engagement towards a preoccupation with self-improvement and personal fulfillment. James Nolan examined its institutionalization within the apparatus of the modern state, and argued that the therapeutic is deployed as a moralizing discourse that justifies and legitimates the operations of government. More recently Frank Furedi has elaborated concerns about the ascendancy of the emotional realm and the cultivation of vulnerability, situating his analysis of the therapeutic within contemporary debates about the amplification of risk.[3]

During the four decades between Rieff's seminal treatise and Furedi's contemporary exposition, debate has shifted as the intellectual climate has changed. Rieff's analysis reflected postwar concerns, that of Lasch the cultural and economic transitions of the late 1960s and 1970s, Nolan's the therapeutic authority secured by century's end, while Furedi's account of "therapy culture" reflects the growing cultural influence of therapy and counseling in the contemporary climate of economic, political, and personal uncertainty.

From the Rieffian story of moral collapse to Marxist interpretations of capitalist control, Foucauldian analyses of disciplinary discourses, and feminist objections to therapy, there is widespread consensus that the ascendancy of the therapeutic has been deleterious to sociocultural, political, and personal life. As insightful as these approaches are, a critical analysis suggests that they have nevertheless inadequately theorized the complex and contradictory dimensions of the therapeutic society.[4] Drawing on recent directions in social theory, I propose an alternative framework for theorizing by way of a reinterpretation of the changing nexus between internalized cultural authority, the weakening of the division between the public and private spheres, and changes in family life and intimate relationships. These developments, all of which involve gendered social processes, underpin the reflexive culture of late modernity. Attention to them at the conceptual level, and exploration of their historical manifestation in the Australian context, throws light on important dimensions of the therapeutic society, especially those associated both with the struggles of ordinary people in dealing with changing social conditions, and with increased social recognition of forms of emotional suffering which had hitherto largely been hidden. To contextualize these concerns, I turn first to the theoretical accounts that have shaped understandings of the therapeutic over the last several decades.

Moral Collapse

A persistent theme in critiques of the therapeutic society is that its inherent focus on the self and internal life has fostered a pervasive moral collapse. Underpinning this line of analysis is disquiet about the displacement of traditional authority, a concern definitively elaborated in 1966 with the publication of Philip Rieff's seminal text, *The Triumph of the Therapeutic*, but foreshadowed earlier with his declaration that "the emergence of psychological man" sounded the death knell for Western culture.[5] Rather than directing the self toward communal purposes—which for Rieffian sociology is the primary function of culture itself—Rieff identified the driving impulse of the therapeutic as one of interiority.

Locating its gestation in the transition from a premodern social order, the most basic tenet of Rieff's argument is that the therapeutic emerged with changing notions of selfhood that accompanied secularization and liberal individualism. With the old order of the Christian tradition undermined, he interpreted the new organizing symbolic as scientific rather than sacred, governed not by religious authority but by psycho-affective imperatives. By contrast with the moral authority of the Christian era, he argued that the therapeutic had given rise to the birth of a society in which the "self, improved, is the ultimate concern of modern culture."[6]

Nietzsche, Durkheim, and Freud inform Rieff's pessimistic reading of cultural and personal decline. In his theorizing of the collapse of the sacred and moral orders, diminished authority and lower levels of societal repression signaled for Rieff, "the end of the historical road taken by the Western spirit."[7] According to his analysis, the collapse of communal faith and the erosion of religious authority had led to a shift in the balance of what Durkheim referred to as the system of interdicts, or as Rieff put it, "a reorganization of those dialectical expressions of *Yes* and *No* the interplay of which constitutes culture."[8] The corollary of secularization was, therefore, the emergence of a remissive therapeutic culture in which repression no longer functioned as a powerful mechanism of control and cohesion. He argued: "What is revolutionary in modern culture refers to releases from inherited doctrines of therapeutic deprivation; from a predicate of renunciatory control, enjoying releases from impulse need, our culture has shifted toward a predicate of impulse release, projecting controls unsteadily based upon an infinite variety of wants raised to the status of needs."[9]

The symbolic controls of the Christian era had, according to Rieff, provided not only the foundational elements of moral authority and social cohesion, but also the structuring principles of the personality. He was thus pessimistic about the implications of the "dissolution of a unitary system of common belief, accompanied, as it must be," he argued, "by a certain disorganization of personality."[10] According to his analysis, the subjugation of lower order wants to higher order needs, while constraining, freed the self from base instinctual desires. In the Christian era, this was most evident in the repression of sexuality, the nexus around which much of the Christian doctrine centered. The separation of procreation and sexuality, according to Rieff, served the individual and culture well. Writing in response to the social changes of the 1960s, he was troubled by the liberation of sexuality in the modern era, producing as he saw it, the liberation of the id and consequently the dominance of unruly and disruptive forces of the self.

For Rieff, the shift toward a culture of impulse release offers only an illusory freedom in that it leads to the collapse of public life, community, social responsibility, and ultimately the self. In view of his lack of interest in the experience of those marginalized by the dominant cultural order, it is unsurprising that he is cynical about the diminution of repression. His concern, rather, is that in a secular, remissive, and therapeutic culture, faith and reverence no longer function to direct individuals toward communal purpose. As he articulated the distinction as it played out in the formation of character: "Religious man was born to be saved; psychological man is born to be pleased. The difference was established long ago, when 'I believe,' the cry of the ascetic, lost precedence to 'one feels,' the caveat of the therapeutic."[11]

In Rieff's analysis, the displacement of a religious framework by a psychological worldview has resulted in diminished levels of repression that threaten the viability of both culture and the self. His preoccupation with a sacred order as essential to maintaining communal purpose reflects his debt to both Durkheim and Nietzsche. However, it is the Freudian view of the crucial role played by a strong cultural super-ego in containing the id—both at the individual and collective level—which underpins his interpretation of the threat to the moral demand system that the therapeutic ethos entails. Fundamental to his analysis is the assumption that the private domain of intimate and familial relations cannot form the basis of a moral order, which must be universal and abstract. In taking for granted the differing values of public and private life as established in Western political thought, Rieff's analysis privileges the cultural over the social.[12]

While clearly influenced by Rieff's cultural analysis, the social forms the cornerstone of James Nolan's examination of the institutionalization of the therapeutic within the political order of late twentieth century America.[13] Nolan argues that the therapeutic ethos must be understood not only in cultural symbolic terms, but also in terms of how it shapes the social landscape and the terrain of public policy. In the criminal justice system, in education, and especially in welfare, Nolan sees the therapeutic ethos as a means by which the state, facing diminishing public confidence and with weakened authority, deploys a legitimizing discourse of morality. Nolan follows Rieff in predicating his analysis on the erosion of traditional codes of moral understanding, but he draws on other theoretical traditions, notably Weber's notion of legitimation, to argue that psychological and therapeutic discourses have become a key way in which the modern state secures legitimacy.

For Nolan, a defining feature of the therapeutic state is the centrality of emotions in social and political life. Indeed, he argues that an "emotivist ethic" has supplanted traditional morality and become the touchstone for modern understandings of self and world. In such a "psychologically defined moral universe," psychologists and therapists have a particularly important role in defining reality, behavior is increasingly understood in pathological terms, and there has been a concomitant rise in a mentality of victimhood.[14]

Implicit in his analysis is a view of the moral barrenness of the therapeutic and he speculates on the ramifications, for both society and the self, of the state taking on the role of the therapist. In a somewhat gloomy prognosis, Nolan suggests that "Weber's modern iron cage may become the postmodern padded cage."[15]

In another reading concerned with the moral implications of the therapeutic, John Carroll speculates on the viability of the emerging remissive culture and its effect on personality.[16] One of his primary concerns is that with the decline of authority, "guilt is read as a psychological and not a moral problem. It is to be eradicated by therapy." In his view: "The force within the individual that enforces morality is interpreted as psychological, deriving from the parental environment. The ethical domain is merely a helpful mask, to be delicately stripped away by the analyst once it becomes troublesome."[17] Once again, as with Rieff, the psychological and the ethical—the personal and the public—are dichotomized, and it is the latter that is more highly valued. With the decline of religious authority and the ascendancy of the therapeutic, psychological experts—"secular priests" as Maurice North called them—are seen as having taken over the function of the spiritual guide.[18] In contrast to the clergy who enforced the moral order, the therapeutic professional is regarded as an advocate of the id rather than an embodiment of the cultural super-ego.

Carroll's characterization casts the analyst's role as the facilitation of subjective wellbeing through the eradication of guilt. The role of the counselor or psychotherapist is therefore to bolster self-sufficiency by banishing the dread, guilt, and anxiety that become manifest in the individual when traditional authority has been supplanted by a preoccupation with the self. As Michael Casey puts it: "Authority, after all, is the foundational problem of therapy, the problem therapy was created to solve."[19] As the pacesetters of change, Rieff himself argued that therapists have played a crucial role in the decline of Western culture. He interpreted the "psychologizers" as a pseudo authority, a face that is "all mask and makeup" rather than carrying legitimate moral weight.[20]

The psychological expert is similarly critiqued by Martin Gross, who following Rieff argued that: "The contemporary Psychological Society is the most vulnerable culture in history. Its citizen is a new model of Western man, one who is dependent on others for guidance as to what is real or false. In the unsure state of his mind, he is even doubtful of the authenticity of his own emotions. As the Protestant ethic has weakened in Western society, the confused citizen has turned to the only alternative he knows: the psychological expert who claims there is *a new scientific standard of behavior* to replace fading tradition."[21] Though sharing the concerns of Rieff and Carroll about cultural and personal decline, the analysis Gross develops is primarily driven by a critique of psychological knowledge itself and the professions constructed upon it. The problem of moral authority as held by the therapist rather than the clergy nevertheless figures prominently, with Gross suggesting that psychiatrists and psychotherapists have become the new seers. Not only have they power to define normality, but according to Gross, they are also the new keepers of the sacred order: "By offering the seeming structure of science wedded to mystical insight, the psychological and psychiatric seer successfully masquerades as a modern oracle."[22]

A similar theme of moral indignation about the role of the helping professions emerges in Christopher Lasch's analysis of the modern therapist as principally charged with consoling the discontents of the modern age.[23] For Lasch, the reliance on psychological expertise forms part of a wider set of influences—including schools, peer groups, and the mass media—that undermine parental (but notably paternal) authority. Lasch's overarching concern with the decline of cultural authority, and in particular his anxiety about the absent father, shares something of the conservatism of the Rieffian tradition, especially in relation to the shaping of personality. Reflecting the more Marxist inspired critical reading of the Frankfurt School, however, his concern about the implications of a weakened super-ego is couched in terms of the impact of capitalism on working life and familial relations. I will return to Lasch's sociopolitical critique below and conclude the present discussion of his work by noting his formulation of the "psychic repercussions" of cultural change.

While Rieff articulated the consequences of declining authority in Durkheimian terms of the shifting balance of interdicts and remissions, Lasch elaborates this theme in his theory of cultural narcissism. Rejecting the association of narcissism with selfishness, he sees the "narcissistic personality of our time" as a self under threat of disintegration, an empty self that adopts behaviors that may at the surface appear to be selfish, but in reality are indicative of the self struggling to survive against a barrage of forces that threaten psychic annihilation.[24]

As with Rieff's anxiety about the disorganization of the personality and Lasch's alarm at the rise of narcissism, there has been widespread concern that the ascendancy of the therapeutic has not only involved cultural impoverishment, but also personal decline. Extending earlier analyses, and drawing on Nolan's delineation of the emotivist ethic and escalating claims of victimization in the contemporary era, Furedi argues that the therapeutic ethos fosters a pervasive emotional vulnerability. Indeed he contends that the self in therapeutic culture is "defined by its vulnerability."[25] In contrast to Rieff and Carroll's emphasis on the importance of the sacred order, he follows Lasch in framing his moral analysis within a political critique of modern society. The experience of powerlessness that threatens the contemporary individual is understood, by Furedi, as a consequence of the cultural symbolic. In his view, people "make sense of their experiences through reflecting on their specific circumstances and in line with the expectations transmitted through prevailing cultural norms."[26]

While Furedi's critique traverses aspects of the cultural order and political economy, it lacks the theoretical depth of Rieff and Lasch. His analysis of the self rests largely on descriptions of cultural motifs of vulnerability and representations of a weak, psychologically and emotionally at risk individual, in all a "diminished self." Following Lasch, he identifies transformations in private life as particularly deleterious for the modern self, arguing that the disorganization of the private sphere is not only "the main accomplishment of therapeutic culture," but also that it represents a destructive trend of devaluing private life.[27] As he argues: "The casual dismissal of the private sphere represents a disturbingly cavalier attitude towards one of the most important sites of human experience. The separation of the public and private spheres has been essential for the emergence of the modern individual."[28]

While apparently less preoccupied than others with the decline of paternal authority, Furedi explicitly articulates what is often merely implicit in the conservative moral critique—the importance of a clear separation between an instrumental public rationality and a private domain of intimacy and emotions. Indeed, much of the intellectual outrage directed toward the therapeutic derives from its association with the weakening of the boundaries between the public and private spheres. In a lament reminiscent of Rieff, Furedi regards the ascendancy of the emotional realm, and the reduced levels of repression that it entails, as threatening the viability of public life. As Rieff wrote deprecatingly of the turn away from formalized authority: "Where public and family festivals of recognition were, there let private, even intimate, resolutions of transference relations be."[29]

While this line of argument captures widely held views about the delicacy of private life and of the necessity of repression for public life, it neglects the individual and social costs of repression and the question of whether these costs are equally distributed. Such an analysis also overlooks the possibility that the foundation of a moral order and indeed the viability of culture itself may not rest on the internalization of traditional forms of paternal and cultural authority. Nevertheless, concerns about the decline of public life associated with the perceived shift toward interiority have been widespread.

In his account of cultural narcissism, Lasch links the collapse of a common life to the development of an impoverished private one. The therapeutic is regarded as a key factor in the waning of communal bonds and civic responsibility due to its increased emphasis on personal autonomy and individual freedom, and its preoccupation with lifestyle and with the self. This strong communitarian theme is further developed in *Habits of the Heart*, in the view that the therapeutic imperative arouses and fosters individualism. Robert Bellah and his colleagues share Rieff's view of the therapeutic as remissive and deleterious to social life, arguing that the therapeutic attitude "begins with the self, rather than with a set of external obligations."[30] They implicate the rise of a therapeutic ethos in the decline of civic membership, noting that almost the only community organizations to experience growth since the 1970s have been support groups and twelve step programs. These groups, they argue, do not share a communal interest but rather encourage individuals to focus on themselves, albeit in the company of others.

Ironically, however, in spite of the stated communitarian concerns, the assumptions underlying these analyses can also be seen as predicated upon an individualist notion of the self. For the question that these accounts do not broach is whether, in spite of all its deficiencies, the therapeutic has fostered new forms of care, not only for the self but also for others. Certainly therapy and the broader therapeutic culture may promote self-absorption, but there are other dimensions that have as yet been under-theorized—for example, how a therapeutic ethos legitimates the domains of empathy, trust, and care, as well as experiences of suffering and injustice. I return to this point later in the chapter. First, however, I will examine other interpretations of the therapeutic, analyses that focus less on weakening authority and moral decline, than on social control and problems of depoliticization.

Social Control & Psychological Consolation

In accounts that emphasize the political economy rather than the cultural symbolic, historical transformations associated with the development of capitalist market economies are seen as central to the formation of a therapeutic ethos.[31] Though some, most notably Lasch, develop approaches that integrate the social and cultural with an analysis of the political economy, the major point of divergence lies in what is seen as the distinguishing feature of the therapeutic. While Rieff read the therapeutic as remissive, the political economy critique views it rather as a potent mechanism of depoliticization and social control. Grounded in historical materialism, this line of interpretation makes changes in the production and consumption systems of the capitalist economy central to analyses of the therapeutic society.

The extent to which the advent of consumer capitalism and the ascendancy of the therapeutic were mutually reinforcing has been widely noted.[32] According to T.J. Jackson Lears, the shift from a Protestant ethos of self-denial to a therapeutic culture of self-gratification provided fertile ground for the expansion of consumer capitalism. Advertisers, he notes, "began speaking to many of the same preoccupations addressed by liberal ministers, psychologists, and other therapeutic ideologues. A dialectic developed between Americans' new emotional needs and advertisers' strategies; each continually reshaped and intensified the other."[33] As Stuart Ewen has shown, psychology provided advertisers with insights into "human instinct" that stimulated the desire for consumption in mass audiences.[34] A critical dimension of this involved creating a level of unease and dissatisfaction that consumer culture then promised to ameliorate. With the promise of self-improvement through consumption, Philip Cushman argues that advertising became—like psychotherapy itself—a therapeutic activity.[35]

In displacing the ethic of salvation, the emerging ethos of self-realization provided, Lears argues, a "new and secular basis for capitalist cultural hegemony."[36] He suggests that shifting patterns of consumption were intimately connected to changing experiences of selfhood in the late nineteenth century. The corrosive effects of capitalism and technological change were intensified by the secularization of Protestantism. These factors coalesced, he argues, to undermine the solid sense of selfhood that had been maintained by Victorian moral boundaries and religious authority. There was, according to Lears, an increasing sense of anxiety amongst the educated bourgeoisie that was generated by urbanization, technological development, and greater levels of affluence: a phenomenon he refers to as "the feeling of unreality."[37]

The observation that the political and economic structures of capitalist modernity gave rise to changing experiences of selfhood is widespread.[38] Lears' evocative depiction of the "sense of unreality" experienced during the late Victorian era resonates with David Riesman's account of post-WWII shifts in culture and personality. Riesman argued that selfhood lost coherence in the rapidly changing social circumstances associated with transformations in organizational life and new forms of mass communication. In his view, corporate culture, bureaucratization, and closer to home, permissive parenting, brought about changes in social character; the "inner-directed" individual guided by internalized values, conscience and guilt, gave way to the "other-directed" conformist individual who sought cues from others. By contrast to feelings of guilt that govern the inner-directed person, Riesman argued that the "prime psychological lever of the other-directed person is a diffuse *anxiety*."[39]

Tackling similar themes several years later, Lasch extended Riesman's account of American culture and personality in his analysis of narcissism. In the *Minimal Self*, in particular, he developed the idea that changes in personality under advanced capitalism involved a hollowing out or emptying of the self as a strategy of "psychic survival in troubled times." Lasch grounds his analysis of minimal selfhood in the context of the expansion of the state and corporate bureaucracies, the rise of managerialism, shifts in cultural authority, and the decline of the family, arguing that social conditions under advanced capitalism are increasingly warlike—not only in the public sphere, but also in personal life. In his analysis, the family is no longer a "haven in a heartless world" and the private sphere "has become as anarchical, as warlike, and as full of stress as the marketplace itself."[40] The retreat inward and the growth of ideals of self-improvement for Lasch are thus understood as a direct consequence of major social change: "The growth of bureaucracy, the cult of consumption with its immediate gratifications, but above all the severance of the sense of historical continuity have transformed the Protestant ethic while carrying the underlying principles of capitalist society to their logical conclusion. The pursuit of self-interest, formerly identified with the rational pursuit of gain and the accumulation of wealth, has become a search for pleasure and psychic survival."[41]

Entering therapy, in his view, is a means of mitigating psychic disintegration. The hope of achieving mental health represents for Lasch, "the modern equivalent of salvation," with therapists, not priests, the "principal allies in the struggle for composure."[42] More broadly, the fixation with emotional life and self-improvement reflect, in his view, a repudiation of the past and the "waning sense of historical time."[43] A preoccupation with present concerns and personal change has arisen as the sole means by which individuals can exercise control over their lives. However, these strategies of "psychic survival" have brought about, according to Lasch, an unfortunate shift from political engagement to self-examination: "Having displaced religion as the organizing framework of American culture, the therapeutic outlook threatens to displace politics as well, the last refuge of ideology. Bureaucracy transforms collective grievances into personal problems amenable to therapeutic intervention."[44]

Lasch's view of the therapeutic as a mechanism of depoliticization constitutes one of the most salient contributions to debates about the therapeutic society. Indeed, following Lasch, the personalization of social problems has been widely read as its central impulse. Dana Cloud, for example, draws on this idea to argue that therapeutic consolation has established itself as "the prevailing strategy of crisis management."[45] In Cloud's analysis, the therapeutic is a persuasive rhetoric that displaces social and political action and stifles dissent within a discourse of individual responsibility and consolation. It is, in her view, the pervasiveness of this rhetoric that "makes the therapeutic so influential in channeling individual responses to exploitation, alienation, isolation, oppression, and other socially produced hardships."[46]

According to Cloud, "therapeutic persuasions" have pervaded the cultural landscape to such an extent that structural and systematic disadvantage is obscured by the rhetoric of therapy. Writing in the 1990s, her analysis takes account of the shift from the period of economic stability and prosperity to the "leaner and meaner" environment of the 1980s and 1990s—of downsizing, restructuring, workforce casualization, and technological change. She argues that therapeutic consolation obfuscates corporate responsibility, as workers are encouraged to take personal responsibility for structural change. Cloud is particularly critical of such strategies, which she interprets as offering merely symbolic consolation rather than material compensation. As she argues: "The most important rhetorical feature of the therapeutic is its tendency to encourage citizens to perceive political issues, conflicts, and inequalities as personal failures subject to personal amelioration. Therapy offers consolation rather than compensation, individual adaptation rather than social change, and an experience of politics that is impoverished in its isolation from structural critique and collective action."[47]

Furedi similarly critiques the systematic expansion and institutionalization of counseling services targeting the unemployed and those facing redundancy. He follows Lasch and Cloud in interpreting such trends in terms of control and consolation, but he picks up on Nolan's notion of pathologization in arguing that social problems are not only individualized, but are recast as emotional deficit. In his analysis, a distinctive feature of the contemporary therapeutic society that arose in the 1970s and intensified in the 1980s was a preoccupation with individual pathology. "Stress" and "mental health" emerged, he argues, as popular and political issues that displaced attention from the political and economic realms.[48]

Similar concerns have been leveled at particular therapeutic cultural forms, most notably, the television talk show and the self-help book. Locating the talk show within the genre of "recovery religion," Kathleen Lowney argues that explanations of individual behavior fail to acknowledge social and structural dimensions, and instead simply focus on the psychological. As she points out: "individualizing social problems becomes necessary since it is not possible to interview 'institutional racism' but it is possible to have a provocative interview with a 'skinhead.'"[49] Once the causes are individualized, Lowney argues, so are the solutions. A similar set of concerns regarding individualization and depoliticization is also directed toward therapeutic guides, psychological literature, and other "self-help fashions."[50] In a scathing critique, Wendy Kaminer's argues that "the notion of selfhood that emerges from recovery (the most vulgarized renditions of salvation by grace, positive thinking, and mind cure) is essentially more conducive to totalitarianism than democracy."[51]

These critiques resonate with Lasch's view that the therapeutic is an agent not of liberation but of capitalist enterprise and social control. In further elaborating issues also raised in Ewen's work, Aric Sigman argues that the appropriation of psychology by the media and corporate sector has led to a distortion of sound psychological principles.[52] As a psychologist, his concern is primarily with the proliferation of popular therapeutic discourses rather than psychotherapy or the growth of psychology itself. Sigman levels his critique of the misappropriation of psychological knowledge at the media and publishing, a trend he argues was established in the late 1960s as self-fulfillment, happiness, and personal growth superseded the modest aspirations of a contented life and religious notions of salvation. His concern with the diffusion of pop psychology is not only that it is often based on erroneous concepts, but that the imperatives of personal growth are in themselves counterproductive, generating a disapproval and rejection of one's self in a never-ending quest for self-improvement.

Sigman's condemnation of pop psychology reflects widespread concerns about therapeutic culture itself. Critiques of clinical practices of psychotherapy and counseling, however, have generally been more cautiously advanced. Cloud is quite typical in this regard, making clear that her concern "is not about what therapy does for us privately." Rather, her disquiet arises from the consequences of therapeutic discourses for politics, activism, and social change, as "therapeutic motifs at the level of cultural persuasion work against the formulation of a collective political project in the public sphere."[53]

In analyses such as this, therapy itself is bracketed from critical assessment whereas its wider cultural ramifications are read as pernicious. Separating therapy from its broader sociocultural impact does overcome some problems of theorizing, but it also stands as a theoretical contrivance at risk of unraveling. For therapy and the broader therapeutic culture are not so easily disentangled. Not only is therapy itself the central metaphor of therapeutic culture, but it constitutes a critical institution within the therapeutic society. Nevertheless, in recognizing personal distress and the capacity of therapy to alleviate it, Cloud's account differs from Rieff's moral objection. The opposition is grounded, rather, in objection to the wider political ramifications of the individualizing of social problems. Therapy in the private world of the individual is thus in itself not viewed as problematic, but in the public world of work and politics, therapeutic strategies and therapeutic rhetoric are to be thoroughly resisted.

Other accounts, however, do not concur with such a benign view of the clinical encounter. With the emergence of the anti-psychiatry movement in the 1960s, the subject of mental health came to the fore as a political issue. As David Ingleby notes, although the concerns of those involved varied, they were "united in seeing the scientific image of psychiatry as a smokescreen; the real questions were: whose side is the psychiatrist on, what kind of society does he serve, and do we want it?"[54] In a similarly critical view of the clinical practice of therapy under advanced capitalism, James Hillman and Michael Ventura assert that: "If therapy imagines its task to be that of helping people cope (and not protest), to adapt (and not rebel), to normalize their oddity, and to accept themselves 'and work within your situation; make it work for you' (rather than refuse the unacceptable), then therapy is collaborating with what the state wants: docile plebs. Coping simply equals compliance."[55] Hillman and Ventura argue that therapy constructs social problems as individual ones and in so doing displaces deficits of the body politic. They suggest that unless the institution of therapy can recognize the ways in which social problems are manifest in the individual patient, social change is thwarted and therapists are in effect colluding with the state to stifle dissent by assisting people to cope and function within oppressive social and political systems.

Governing & Constituting the Modern Self

While sharing concerns of political economy critics about social regulation, interpretations of the therapeutic society informed by the work of Michel Foucault have focused on the role of psychological discourses in the constitution of the modern self, and in the operation of modern systems of power.[56] Foucault's writings on madness, medicine, and psychology, and his theorization of governmentality and subjectification, have thus provided an intellectual and methodological alternative for understanding the significance of the therapeutic turn. In particular, his analysis of the historical significance of the development of the human sciences and his delineation of modes of internalized self-government through "technologies of the self" have been widely influential, especially in reading psychology and psychiatry as disciplinary discourses aimed at shaping particular forms of conduct.[57]

In his genealogies of the modern self, Foucault traced the ways in which the invention of new knowledges of the human subject enabled new forms of authority to be exercised over the conduct of citizens. A central tenet of his conceptualization of power and subjectivity is that under liberalism, social control and individual freedom became inextricably intertwined. Consequently, social regulation came to work not in opposition to individual autonomy, but indeed *through* people's capacity to choose and to act.

While Jacques Donzelot, for example, shared with Lasch a concern about the intrusion of experts into private life, he followed Foucault in arguing that new forms of knowledge about the individual subject were instrumental to the changing means by which populations were governed.[58] Taking the family as the site of analysis, Donzelot charted the ways in which government *of* the family gave way to government *through* the family. He argued that during the nineteenth and early twentieth centuries, state patriarchy effectively displaced the paternal authority embodied in the male head of the family. A critical way in which this was achieved was through the alliance that developed between women (mothers) and the moralizing agents of the state; that is, the family welfare professionals—first doctors and philanthropists, and later psychologists, psychiatrists, and social workers. While not sharing Lasch's psychoanalytic standpoint, he was nevertheless similarly concerned about the consequences of diminishing paternal authority. For as the state secured control over the family, the mother gained greater control within the household, but the father's position was increasingly undermined.

The authority of professional expertise, buttressed by knowledges of the human sciences, formed a cornerstone of Donzelot's critique. In his analysis, such expertise functions directly through clinical encounters, professional advice, and so on, but also indirectly, through the "regulation of images"—for example, of motherhood and fatherhood—which produced new norms of conduct in relation to family life. He was particularly concerned about the implications of the colonization of private life for families occupying the lower social strata. The state and the helping professions, in Donzelot's view, formed a "tutelary complex" directed toward the socialization of working class families, a process resulting in families being "stripped of all effective rights and brought into a relation of dependence *vis-à-vis* welfare and educative agents."[59] By contrast, bourgeois families who willingly seized on new educative, medical, and relational norms were able to exercise greater control over their relationships with social welfare professionals. Nevertheless, for both working and middle-class families, the "protective liberation" of children, in Donzelot's view, amounted to new forms of "supervised freedom" and resulted in diminished autonomy of the family.

Extending the scope of investigation beyond the family to links between political power, expertise, and the self more broadly, Nikolas Rose has built on Foucault's intellectual project in his analyses of "psy" as an apparatus of truth, power, and subjectification. For Rose, psy encapsulates the various "ways of thinking and acting" which have been brought into existence by psychology, psychiatry, and their cognate disciplines.[60] As he argues: "The dependence of government upon knowledge ... enables us to appreciate the role that psychology, psychiatry, and the other 'psy' sciences have played within the systems of power in which human subjects have become caught up. The conceptual systems devised within the 'human' sciences, the languages of analysis and explanation that they invented, the ways of speaking about human conduct that they constituted, have provided the means whereby human subjectivity and intersubjectivity could enter the calculations of the authorities."[61]

Rose underscores the centrality of psy knowledges and psy professionals in the government of subjectivity in the current era. In his account, there are essentially two means by which psychological "knowledge and know how" is disseminated. The first is via the organizational practices of those involved in the helping professions, for example in social work and nursing, but also more broadly through the work of those charged with authority over others, like teachers and managers. The second route operates through what he refers to as "psychotherapies of normality"—that is, ways of relating to oneself and others, including the development of techniques for dealing with problems, planning for the future, and devising ways of achieving happiness. For Rose, the interpretation of experience through a psychological or psychodynamic lens underwrites the vast array of therapeutic technologies, including "self-inspection, self-problematization, self-monitoring and self-transformation."[62] With the rise of psychological knowledges and the diffusion of psychotherapeutic techniques, Rose argues that "a new culture of the self has taken shape. Confession has moved beyond the consulting room" and everyday life has become subject to a kind of "clinical reason."[63]

This so-called clinical reason is evident not only in processes of self-analysis and the analysis of others, but the concomitant role of talk in the therapeutic society. Foucault's genealogy of confession is useful here. He traced the history of confessional practices, particularly those associated with sexual prohibition, from the religious realm—where confession was associated with renunciation—to the medical arena where "the obtaining of the confession and its effects were recodified as therapeutic operations."[64] For Foucault, confession is a "technology of the self," a means by which the self is constituted. In the Christian tradition, such verbalization was linked to renunciation of sin; however, with the influence of the human sciences, Foucault argues that verbalization became important in its own right: "From the eighteenth century to the present, the techniques of verbalization have been reinserted in a different context by the so-called human sciences in order to use them without renunciation of the self but to constitute, positively, a new self. To use these techniques without renouncing oneself constitutes a decisive break."[65]

As through confession, constituting the self "positively" in the therapeutic society is also enacted through consumption. Rose connects what he terms technologies of consumption with psychological technologies, arguing that the two are interlinked; consumption is stimulated through advertising and market research which utilizes psychological knowledge and techniques, while psychological expertise is itself disseminated by means of therapies and products to be consumed.

Other influential Foucauldian-inflected accounts have focused more explicitly on the ways in which the expansion of psychological and psychiatric knowledge in new networks of power has had uneven effects for individuals and groups in varying social strata. In *The Rise of the Therapeutic State,* Andrew Polsky employs a Foucauldian analysis, informed also by Thomas Szasz as well as the concerns of anti-psychiatry, in arguing that the therapeutic becomes a mechanism of normalization of marginal populations. He argues that both public and private therapeutic intervention generally operate as a means of support for the middle classes who are able to choose when to begin and when to end treatment: "By contrast, public therapeutic intervention aimed at marginal citizens proceeds from the assumption that they cannot govern their own lives. The state therefore seeks to 'normalize' them… Lower class clients do not seem to require merely a bit of support, like their middle-class counterparts, but instead wholesale personal and family reconstruction."[66]

Foucauldian analyses have provided important insights into the critical role of psy knowledges in the operation of power, notably through techniques and practices directed towards "the shaping of conduct."[67] As a framework for theorizing the therapeutic, however, a governmentality approach is not without its problems—at least insofar as it has been deployed to date. As Anthony Elliott has forcefully argued, studies of governmentality inspired by Foucault have tended "to offer a dark, oftentimes a sinister, account of social processes."[68] Not only does an inherent distrust of the routines of social life often emerge, but the model of personhood upon which such theorization hinges constitutes a fundamental weakness; it is highly individualistic, provides little attention to the workings of emotional life, and only a limited understanding the self in its relation with others. Moreover, as Elliott points out, both in Foucault's work and in Rose's extension of it, there is "no adequate account of human agency, since the self simply appears as the decentred effect of an analytics of governmentality ... In short, inadequate attention is given to the active, creative struggles of individuals as they engage with their own social and historical conditions."[69]

The notion of selfhood that emerges from Foucauldian theory is thus deeply problematic. As Lois McNay argues, the "lack of a rounded theory of subjectivity or agency conflicts with a fundamental aim of the feminist project: to rediscover and re-evaluate the experiences of women."[70] An associated problem concerns the inadequacy of Foucault's explication of the complex relation between "care for the self" and "care for others," which neglects the ways in which "care" has been socially assigned to women and construed as "feminine" and domestic.[71] This raises particular problems for interpreting critical dimensions of the therapeutic society, particularly the ways in which gender and the therapeutic terrain intersect. As feminist theorizing of the ethics of care reminds us, human dependency is a central dimension of existence and there are moral values involved in caring for another, physically, psychologically, and emotionally.[72] In spite of its limitations, the Foucauldian reading of the nexus of knowledge and power, especially as imbued in psychological and psychiatric knowledge, therapy and other therapeutic cultural forms, has provided a valuable critique of power and the regulation of disadvantaged social groups, including women. It has thus also informed some feminist approaches in theorizing the regulation of women in therapeutic culture.

The Myth of Women's Empowerment

While relations of power and control have informed many analyses of the therapeutic, the theoretical traditions so far considered have not explored the ways in which the social and cultural diffusion of psychological knowledges may register differently for men and women. In bringing the experiences of women to the centre of analysis, feminist critiques provide another lens through which to examine this pervasive cultural turn. The points of overlap and departure from other perspectives already discussed are particularly salient. For example, while Donzelot, suggested that women secured a degree of benefit from their acquiescence to and embrace of the psychological, feminists have largely interpreted psychological knowledge and practices as yet another means by which women have been controlled and disempowered. In Dana Cloud's view: "too great an emphasis on personal life—on consciousness, identity, and lifestyle—has hindered progress toward women's liberation ... 'The personal is political' may not be a revolutionary challenge to the status quo but rather an unwitting collaboration with the forces of stability in contemporary capitalist culture."[73]

The practices of psychiatry, psychotherapy, and counseling have been subject to strong feminist critique. Psychiatry in particular has provoked much disquiet, interpreted as an especially pernicious agent of social control. Indeed, the construction of the psychologically unstable woman has been interpreted as a key way in which oppressive gender relations have been maintained under patriarchy through the male authority of the medical professions.[74] In her classic text, *Women and Madness,* Phyllis Chesler contends that psychiatry is much like marriage, an institution that controls women through dependency and the reinforcement of ideals of femininity. Challenges to existing power relations are marginalized, discredited, or undermined, she argues, in the labeling of women as psychologically unstable. In Australia, Jill Matthews elaborated a similar thesis in her classic study of twentieth century femininity, *Good and Mad Women,* while Judith Allen revealed how psychological and psychoanalytic theory has historically been marshaled in the criminal justice system, often in defense of sex offenders and to the detriment of their victims.[75] More recently, there has also been widespread disquiet about the medicalization of women's unhappiness, as evidenced by diagnoses of depressive disorders and the use of anti-depressants: women are twice as likely to be diagnosed with a depressive disorder and twice as likely to be prescribed psychotropic drugs.[76]

Rather than focusing on broader questions of cultural change, a key element of feminist accounts of the therapeutic has thus been a critique of the psy professions and associated clinical practices. Reflecting similar concerns to the critiques of therapy outlined above, Celia Kitzinger, for example, argues that while many women may be helped by therapy, it nevertheless personalizes the political by concentrating on the emotional realm and the inner life of women.[77] Similarly, critiques of therapeutic cultural forms, notably self-help literature, strike a particularly strong chord in feminist accounts. As with therapy, they have been interpreted as a panacea for alienation and an impediment to social action.

According to American journalist Susan Faludi, popular psychology was instrumental in the anti-feminist "backlash" of the 1980s. In her view, the strategies of popular psychologists with prominent media profiles reinforced female isolation and pain, rather than helped to relieve it. The rhetoric espoused by self-help authors constituted, she argues, a discourse couched in the language of women's liberation, but constructed around various interpretations of the masochistic female psyche: "To the vast female readership of self-help manuals, the advice experts delivered a one-two punch. First they knocked down the liberated woman, commanding that she surrender her 'excessive' independence ... Then, having brought the 'victim' of feminism to her feminine knees, the advice writers reaped the benefits—by nursing the backlash victim. In the first half of the 1980s the advice experts told women they suffered from bloated egos and a 'fear of intimacy'; in the second half, they informed women that atrophied egos and 'co-dependency' were now their problems."[78]

Other analyses of self-help advance similar concerns, especially in terms of its focus on introspection and healing rather than social action, and in the view that engagement with therapeutic texts offer only illusory cures for what are essentially social ills.[79] Concerns have also been raised about the ways in which other therapeutic cultural forms construct notions of the feminine, and in particular, female distress. The self-disclosure typical of the television talk show, according to Franny Nudelman, "has confirmed and elaborated a certain construction of female subjectivity." In her view, we have come to believe that women "are prone to psychic pain."[80] Embodying significant attributes of the therapeutic, television talk shows and self-help literature are important cultural artifacts to consider when assessing its impact, especially for women and for gender relations.[81] For just as women have significantly higher utilization rates of therapy than men, it is also women at whom television talk shows and self-help books are primarily targeted.

Offering a broader approach that integrates an analysis of various dimensions of the therapeutic society with an examination of the institutions of psychotherapy and psychology, Dana Becker engages more directly with debates about the therapeutic itself. Critical of the gender-blind assumptions in cultural analyses like those of Rieff and Lasch, she notes: "American cultural critics, worriedly cautioning their compatriots about a falling away from the values and virtues of a communal past, never suggested that men and women had not experienced that past identically; they never looked beyond the construction of psychological man to ask: 'Who is psychological woman?'"[82]

"Psychological woman," according to Becker, "is by and large not an activist, nor is her therapist—nor are the media experts that counsel her."[83] She has been depoliticized and duped, shaped by the discourses of science and individualism, her problems are constructed as psychological, rather than recognized as social. While therapeutic culture promises her empowerment, it keeps her in her place by reinforcing dominant stereotypical feminine attributes and it offers her only a compensatory form of power. For Becker, the promise that knowledge is power is the straw man of the therapeutic society. She argues that self-knowledge and self-esteem are too readily conflated with ideals of personal empowerment. While the therapeutic promises women control over their lives, she argues that "the repackaging of the psychological as power reproduces what has long been the cultural norm for women: the colonization of both the interior world of the psyche and the small world of intimate relationships."[84]

That the helping professions—as the institutional embodiment of the therapeutic—are themselves patriarchal is also regarded as problematic. As Becker elaborates: "The story of how psychotherapy emerged as a profession ... is a story about how men developed those 'technologies of the self' ... and about how those technologies came to be broadly employed and adopted."[85] Foucault's influence is evident, but she also draws out more explicitly themes of depoliticization that are more reminiscent of Lasch. Becker thus provides an important feminist reading of the therapeutic society. In bringing women into the analysis, she reveals many limitations of earlier accounts. As a cultural ethos, and in its institutional form through professional practice, the therapeutic is experienced differently by women than it is by men.

In other respects, however, Becker's account does not move substantially beyond the existing framework. For while she questions the masculinist assumptions of theorists like Lasch and suggests, furthermore, that the therapeutic itself may be patriarchal, she nevertheless reaches similar conclusions in her assessment of its disabling effects. While her account provides a welcome complement to cultural analyses that overlook the centrality of gender, the implicit argument that women are duped by therapeutic culture is nevertheless problematic. Without recognition of the myriad ways in which women not only embrace the therapeutic, but also resist it and use it for their own ends, the complex and contradictory dimensions of the therapeutic society remain only partially understood.[86]

The alignment of therapy and feminism serves as a useful counterpoint to the therapeutic as oppressive argument. During the 1970s there was spirited debate about whether psychology and therapy were part of women's oppression or vehicles of liberation. Consciousness raising became a significant feminist mobilization strategy, offering an avowedly political context for therapeutic interactions. Radical and feminist therapy grew out of these debates, constituting as Cloud notes, "a middle ground between social movement activism and an insular therapeutic practice."[87] Rather than replicating unequal social relations, feminist therapy seeks to empower women by establishing an egalitarian relationship between therapist and client. Moreover, it is highly critical of the society in which it is practiced.[88]

In considering the question of whether psychology has been oppressive or liberating for women, Ellen Herman captures its ambivalent legacy, arguing that "it was neither and it was both." According to Herman: "Feminism's dual identity as a public campaign for formal equality and a cultural revolution in the subjective experience of gender demonstrates very clearly how much the direction of postwar political activism depended upon the hallmarks of psychological expertise during this period: the merging of public and private, the political and the psychological."[89] Psychology not only elaborated certain models of feminine subjectivity, but psychological ideas allowed feminism to challenge the patriarchal authority of experts and was also instrumental in the construction of the feminist. As Eva Illouz also notes: "Despite the patriarchal and misogynist views of psychologists ... from the start the categories of psychological discourse entertained affinities with feminist thought."[90]

Following Herman and Illouz, then, trying to determine whether psychology, and indeed the therapeutic society more broadly, have been liberating or oppressive to some extent misses the point. The pressing question is in what ways, how, when, and for whom. Moreover, as feminist analyses have been largely concerned with identifying the therapeutic as an agent of women's oppression—rather than focusing on the larger issue of cultural change—an adequate account of the gendered character of the therapeutic itself, including the shifts in masculinity that it entails, has yet to be elaborated.

Assessing the Therapeutic: Ways Forward

As the foregoing discussion establishes, social theoretical literature of the past half-century provides a wide-ranging analysis of major dimensions of the therapeutic turn. What distinguishes these varying interpretations from those emanating from within the therapeutic itself, exemplified by the promise of the human potential movement and the industry of self-help that it spawned, is a broad consensus that the therapeutic is inimical to sociopolitical, cultural, and personal life. That this dominant narrative is shared by divergent intellectual traditions—from the conservatism of Rieffian cultural sociology to radical feminism, the materialism of neo-Marxism, and Foucauldian analyses of power—suggests that it is a compelling critique. Nevertheless, there remain issues that have yet to be addressed.

The heightened concern with private problems and the ascendancy of a culture of emotionalism have to date been interpreted predominantly in a negative light. Yet much unease about the therapeutic has gendered undertones.[91] Moreover, the composite picture that emerges from existing cultural analyses still reflects traditional Freudian notions of authority, and is premised upon an unproblematic reading of the dichotomy of the public and private spheres. Through a preoccupation with attempts to theorize the destabilization of the self, there has, furthermore, been a failure to identify and draw out the implications of changes in the personal realm and shifts in the gender order. In short, there has been little analysis informed by feminist theory and, where it exists, it is limited by conceptualizations of gender relations as male dominance over women.[92] As Joan Williams argues, such a model oversimplifies the complexity of gender: "What women face is not a foot on their neck but the trivial minipolitics of everyday life, which are gendered in many institutions in the sense that they operate differently for women than for men."[93] For Williams, a more helpful model is to understand gender as a "force field" that that pulls men and women in different ways.

Utilizing a framework of gender as a system of power relations allows for a more complex conceptualization, one that can, in turn, provide the basis for an alternative reading in which therapeutic culture is more positively implicated in the destabilization of a set of traditional gendered arrangements governing public and private life. Raewyn Connell's account of gender as a social structure, a historically shifting system of power relations is particularly instructive.[94] Both Williams' notion of gender as a "force field" and Connell's conceptualization of the "gender order"—which describes the gendered patterns of social relationships—provide a way of moving beyond categories of men and women which obscure differences among men and between women.

Underpinning the analysis that I develop in subsequent chapters is the rudiment of an alternative framework from which to consider the implications of the rise of the therapeutic society.[95] The major theoretical strands in my analysis concern: the significance of cultural authority, power, and agency; the shifting relationship between the public and private spheres; and, changes in personal life. Recognition of the salience of the gendered structuring of emotions throws new light on the cultural and personal processes associated with the therapeutic society. The remainder of the chapter presents an outline of the framework I am using as the basis for my account of the rise of the therapeutic in Australia. Beginning with the question of authority, however, it also suggests alternative directions for theorizing that might be fruitfully pursued.

A belief in the necessity of authoritative controls for social order permeates many accounts of the therapeutic, as does a concomitant view of socialization that idealizes the patriarchal family.[96] The concern with diminishing authority, apparent in the interpretations of Rieff and Lasch especially, hinges upon on a Freudian model of personality development in which the father—both actual and symbolic—plays a critical role. The internalization of authority through the resolution of the Oedipus complex is regarded as critical to the development of the autonomous individual. The concern with weakening authority, or "the decline of Oedipal Man," as Jessica Benjamin puts it, thus reflects fears that the Oedipus complex "was the fundament for the autonomous, rational individual, and today's unstable families with their less authoritarian fathers no longer foster the Oedipus complex as Freud described it."[97]

In Freud's account of the Oedipal drama, it is the intervention of the father that breaks the intensity of the mother-child bond and thus makes possible both an individuated personality and social life more broadly. The "problem" of weakening paternal authority—so troubling to both Rieff and Lasch—is premised upon a reading which posits that the internalization of a powerful super-ego is critical to normal development. Yet feminist theorists have forcefully criticized this position. They have drawn on other psychoanalytic traditions, notably object-relations, to question the salience of the Freudian account of infant psychosexual development that underwrites the cultural critique. They have emphasized especially the relative neglect of the role of the mother and of the pre-Oedipal stage.[98] This work not only challenges theories of development that privilege patriarchal authority, it also calls into question key assumptions of foundational critiques of the therapeutic, assumptions that are often, perhaps unwittingly, reinscribed in more contemporary accounts.

The main alternative standpoint to the Freudian informed cultural critique of the therapeutic society is that available in the works of Foucault and his followers. Such readings have proved fruitful in understanding its regulatory dimensions and the ways in which therapeutic discourses are implicated in contemporary forms of self-government. Yet, as I have already noted, there are problems too with the implicit model of subjectivity that emerges from Foucauldian theory. The theory of selfhood in Foucault's work, according to McNay, "leads to a conception of the individual as an isolated entity, rather than explaining how the self is constructed in the context of social interaction."[99] As Elliott has also argued: "Foucault's obsessively self-mastering individual is intrinsically monadic, closed in on itself and shut off from emotional intimacy and communal bonds."[100] His critique of the Foucauldian subject goes further, as he notes that "Foucault nowhere confronts the possibility that self-realization is itself embedded within realms of mutuality, trust, intimacy and affection."[101] Examining the underlying assumptions regarding the self that underpin dominant critiques of the therapeutic society renders these readings problematic, but it also suggests a possible way forward.

Following the influential work of Nancy Chodorow, the concept of the relational self provides an alternative basis from which to understand personality development and thus also an alternative standpoint from which to consider the implications of weakening cultural/paternal/traditional authority.[102] Jessica Benjamin's critique of the Oedipal repudiation of dependency (on mother/woman) and her appraisal of the ideal of (male) autonomy advanced in her theory of intersubjectivity also illuminates important facets of past theorizing. As Chodorow and Benjamin have both elaborated in theorizing self-other relationships, the Freudian view of development bound up with the ideals of autonomy and separation is a highly masculinist one.

In contrast to the Freudian privileging of the father's authority and the Foucauldian obliteration of connectedness, both Benjamin and Chodorow emphasize the relational dimensions of psychosocial development. In their accounts, it is the balancing of separation and connectedness that is critical, and they show how the dynamics of this process plays out differently for males and females. Whilst the complexities of their accounts of gendered personality development cannot be explored here, it is possible to utilize some basic insights from feminist object-relations theory to challenge the presumed gender-neutral self of Freudian and Foucauldian theory that have buttressed theorization of the therapeutic. A different account of personality development can thus provide the basis for an alternative sociocultural critique, one that includes women, and indeed recognizes gendered social processes more broadly, especially those associated with the division between the public and private spheres.

Though Lasch, for example, mounted his case against advanced capitalism, Eli Zaretsky establishes that capitalism itself gave rise to the particular form of family life premised on the patriarchal family, the very form that Lasch was trying to defend.[103] "Defenders of the private sphere" (to borrow Benjamin's term) thus accept not only as inevitable but also as desirable the implicitly gendered dichotomization between a public rationality and a private realm of emotions.[104] The major problem with this position is that it does not adequately consider relations of domination and subordination that have been associated with this split, namely women's exclusion—both physically and symbolically—from the public sphere, as well as the unequal and exploitative social relations between men and women, and indeed children, in the home.[105] Thus the destabilization of the public/private split, lamented by Lasch and more recently by Furedi, becomes more complex in light of feminist and other social theory that interrogates assumptions about the sanctity of the domestic realm.

For as with the supposedly gender-neutral accounts of personality development which underpin many analyses of the therapeutic, a related set of suppositions about the public and private spheres takes for granted the historical emergence of a gendered division between the private world of home and family and the public world of politics, work, and civil society. As feminist theory has long recognized, the public has historically been constructed as the real world of politics, law, culture, and morality. In opposition, the private has been regarded as the world of sexual relationships, women, children, and virtue.

Zaretsky has shown too that the way in which the public/private dichotomy emerged with industrial capitalism was itself highly gendered. As work moved outside the home and the sexual division of labor became culturally entrenched, "society divided and the family became the realm of 'private life.'"[106] Zaretsky provides a lead not only in understanding the gendered division of the public and private, but also in theorizing the relationship between the two spheres as historically shifting. The shift from household production to that of the market economy not only intensified the gendered character of public and private life, it entailed a devaluation of the private and the elevation of the public. The private thus became not only the realm of women and children, but also the site of emotions, which were increasingly excluded from the public sphere. Rationality thus came to characterize the domain of men and public life, as dependency and emotions were devalued and rejected as feminine.

In light of the historical dichotomization of the public and private spheres—in which masculinity was equated with a (public) rationality that suppressed femininity and associated it with (private) emotions—the unleashing of the emotional and the "private" into the public realm represents a decisive shift, one which has not surprisingly aroused significant disquiet. The rise of a therapeutic ethos in public life thus may be read, at least in part, as a feminization of the public sphere, a development that has disrupted the gendered organization of both private and public life. Rather than proceeding, then, from the assumption that the proper place for the expression of emotion and discussion of "private issues" is the domestic realm—critical and historical perspectives problematize the idealization of the public/private split advanced by cultural critics.

What is still largely missing in existing accounts is acknowledgment of the emancipatory potential of the change in the relationship between public and private life, and how "speaking out" about personal problems, or matters historically deemed to be private, has opened up new discursive spaces in which it is not only the powerful that can have a public voice.[107] Rather than signaling moral collapse and cultural decline, the diminution of traditional forms of authority, changing gender relations, and shifts in the private sphere can equally be read as part of broader democratic currents characteristic of the contemporary era. In considering this issue, Anthony Giddens' analysis of late modernity, particularly his theorization of self-identity, intimacy, and processes of democratization, is particularly instructive.

Giddens suggests that while transformations in the personal sphere have generated new dilemmas they have also given rise to new possibilities of intimacy and self-expression. In contrast to readings of moral and social decline, for Giddens, "the transformation of intimacy" has opened up new opportunities for the democratization of the personal order, both in the sexual arena and in family life. As with the work of John Scanzoni, who has labeled changes in the family life as part of a "continuing revolution in personal life" in which women and children have gained greater power, Giddens' work suggests a less pessimistic reading of declining paternal authority.[108]

In his view: "There is only one story to tell about the family today, and that is of democracy ... Democratization in the context of the family implies equality, mutual respect, autonomy, decision-making through communication and freedom from violence. Much the same characteristics also supply a model of parent-child relationships. Parents of course will still claim authority over children, and rightly so; but these will be more negotiated and open than before."[109] Giddens' assessment of changes in the family and intimate relations has been questioned as overly optimistic and as failing to recognize the extent to which familial relations remain structured by differing power arrangements.[110] Yet Giddens himself does not imply that these changes have resulted in the disappearance of authority altogether. Rather, his work points to the ways in which communication and negotiation have become key aspirations in the conduct of family life.[111]

Linked to broader sociocultural trends of democratization, transitions in the private sphere have nonetheless generated anxiety. According to Giddens, the modern self "has to be explored and constructed as part of a reflexive process of connecting personal and social change."[112] In his analysis, therapy itself is highly bound up with the reflexivity of modernity and self-identity. Again, his interpretation offers a more ambivalent reading of cultural change: "Therapy is not simply a means of coping with novel anxieties, but an expression of the reflexivity of the self—a phenomenon which, on the level of the individual, like the broader institutions of modernity, balances opportunity and potential catastrophe in equal measure."[113]

Another alternative to overly negative assessments is similarly elaborated in Elliott's work. As with Giddens, he views therapy as deeply connected to late modernity, arguing that "psychological expertise offers reassurance against the insecurities of living."[114] Yet there is another important dimension that emerges in Elliott's work, namely his recognition of the imaginary capacity of self-representation and self-construction characteristic of the modern era. Elliott cautiously suggests that the therapeutic may be an emancipatory response to late modernity. As he explains: "In terms of the opening out of the personal sphere, psychoanalytic theory and therapy can be said to offer individuals a radical purchase on the dilemmas of living in the modern epoch."[115]

In contrast to dominant stories of cultural decline and social regulation, both Elliott and Giddens therefore point to an alternative assessment of the therapeutic turn. While recognizing that the therapeutic can foster narcissism and self-indulgence, Elliott is also open to its promise: "By constructing narratives of the self with which they feel relatively comfortable, the work of therapy ideally leads individuals to a greater emotional openness in the choosing of identities."[116] Their readings, moreover, pave the way for a different set of moral and ethical questions to be posed from those associated with the traditional social order. Before turning to this, however, it is important to note that, in developing a more complex account of cultural change, it is necessary to consider the historical factors that give rise to practices of therapy, and indeed to the ascendancy of therapeutic culture more broadly.

Again, Zaretsky is helpful. His analysis of psychoanalysis as a theory and practice of personal life demonstrates that it has both repressive and liberatory aspects.[117] Thus for Zaretsky, the legacy of psychoanalysis has been an ambivalent one, connected in very significant ways to the emancipatory projects of the twentieth century—notably the establishment of the welfare state, and the feminist and gay liberation movements of the 1970s. Yet simultaneously psychoanalysis "became a font of antipolitical, antifeminist, and homophobic prejudice."[118] He notes that in the areas of autonomy, the emancipation of women, and in personal life, psychoanalysis has produced contradictory effects. In the case of sexuality, "analysis advanced cultural understandings of female sexuality and homosexuality even as it became at times a vicious and effective enemy of feminists and homosexuals."[119] Similarly in personal life, he shows how it both undermined traditional authority and gave rise to new forms of control. Zaretsky's delineation of the ambivalent legacy of psychoanalysis holds true for the therapeutic society more broadly, especially in terms of how it has been thoroughly interconnected with shifts in the private sphere.

In many accounts of the therapeutic, such changes are often posited in terms of moral decline, uncertainty, and diminished selfhood. Yet, the transformations in intimate life that took place over the course of the twentieth century may equally be understood in terms of democratization, a process that, furthermore, has generated new kinds of moral and ethical values. Of particular importance here is the work of Jeffrey Weeks, who offers a more optimistic reading of changes in personal life.[120] As he argues, while the transformations occurring in the sexual domain and in private life may be "often muddled and confusing, marked by the uncertainty which governs public and private life today ... they also contain within them evidence of care, mutuality, responsibility and love which make it possible to be hopeful about our human future."[121]

In this context then, the weakening of traditional forms of authority, while disturbing to conservative cultural analysts, may be understood differently. Indeed, a more complex picture emerges when the weakening of cultural authority is understood as part of a reconfiguration of the cultural-symbolic logic of gender. This reconfiguration opens up a potentially emancipatory and transformative space for women and other marginalized groups, and indeed also for many men, for whom traditional ideals of manhood are experienced as oppressive.

Therapeutic culture, especially the confessional mode, has brought the personal and the private into the public sphere in distinct ways, and has also been central to the legitimizing of the emotional realm and the speaking of the hitherto unspeakable. Elliott and Lemert's recent work on the role of confessional practices is instructive here. While they paint a somewhat gloomy picture of "the new individualism," the ambivalence that characterizes Elliott's earlier work is evident, as they argue: "Confessional culture, to be sure, can promote a narrowing of the arts of public political life; but it needn't. The public confession of private sentiments can, in fact, work the other way ... and involve an opening out of the self to an increasingly interconnected world."[122] Yet it is not simply that confessional culture may promote interconnectedness, as important as that may be. For as personal pain has assumed legitimacy in the public domain, greater accountability for and recognition of distress has also emerged. Framing this as a gendered issue, we might say that the increasing legitimacy accorded to psychological and emotional life, as well as the public articulation of personal inadequacy and suffering, has disrupted a set of gendered arrangements governing public life, and challenged a particular kind of hegemonic masculinity.

This masculine ideal, perhaps best exemplified in the film genre of the American Western was, as Connell points out, constructed around a "self-conscious cult of inarticulate masculine heroism."[123] Similarly, in the Australian context, masculine ideals traditionally have been predicated on a repressive, anti-emotional expression of manhood. As Connell puts it: "the hegemonic construction of masculinity in contemporary Australian culture is outward-turned and plays down all private emotion."[124] Yet the therapeutic increasingly challenges this notion of repressive masculinity, and in doing so, is playing a pivotal role in disrupting the dichotomy between rationality and emotion, split as it has historically been into the two spheres of the public and private, or in terms of subject positions, the masculine and feminine. The extent that the therapeutic is implicated in shifts in the gender order raises important questions that accounts of cultural decline and social regulation have largely failed to consider. As Connell establishes, gender ideologies, identities, and relations are heterogeneous and subject to ongoing transformation and contestation. A key task, then, is to try to ascertain the extent to which the therapeutic is implicated in social and cultural changes that have given rise to a shift towards more equitable gender relations.

Yet there is also another dimension, that of the perceived amorality of the therapeutic society. While casting their arguments in slightly different ways, Rieff, Lasch, and Furedi all regard the therapeutic self as essentially amoral—caught on a treadmill of meaningless self-improvement in an ultimately fruitless quest for subjective wellbeing. Yet such a picture is inevitably only partial. To view therapeutic culture as amoral is to fail to recognize its multidimensionality, taking, for example, the preoccupation with self-gratification, pleasure, and happiness as its only facet. Without dismissing the potential for narcissistic self-absorption, it is important to acknowledge that valuing the self also entails recognition of suffering which has a thoroughly moral dimension. This also raises the question of power, and the ways in which a therapeutic imperative, underpinned by a confessional culture, has made possible challenges to traditional authority—particularly to forms of authority that have been abusive or unjust. From this standpoint, the sanctity of the self in therapeutic culture cannot be understood merely as hedonistic and amoral. For the therapeutic has its own moral logic, one in which the authority of the self can be marshaled to speak against oppression. To the extent that therapeutic culture encourages and legitimizes the claims of damage inflicted upon the individual (often in the private sphere), the argument of amorality becomes a problematic one.

To conclude, it is important to recognize the legitimacy of concerns about the therapeutic in relation to the issues outlined above. However, without resorting to an overly optimistic position, it is possible to challenge excessively pessimistic interpretations by working toward an alternative reading that pays greater heed to the gendered and contradictory dimensions of the therapeutic society. In moving forward, it is important to look carefully at the historical processes that give rise to the contradictions, with an eye both to the potential for social control and hollow individualism—in short, the negative strands—but also to be open to the therapeutic promise: the potential for increasing caring relations and remedying forms of social injustice.

For as well as at times a self-indulgent preoccupation with personal fulfillment, therapeutic culture has facilitated the assertion of individual rights to bodily autonomy, emotional wellbeing, and personal safety. In particular, I suggest that most existing accounts do not adequately grapple with the problem of suffering.[125] Reading the therapeutic predominantly in terms of new desires for self-fulfillment and happiness obscures an equally plausible explanation, that it is not about the desire for happiness, but a shifting orientation to suffering. Through the opening up of the private, the legitimizing of the emotional realm, and the speaking of the hitherto unspeakable, therapeutic culture has engendered more complex consequences—particularly for women and other marginalized groups—than dominant accounts have thus far suggested.

In the following chapters, I trace the ascendancy of therapeutic culture in Australia. Beginning in the late nineteenth century in the context of social, cultural, and personal change, the popularization of "nervousness" and changing ideas about mental health reflected growing concerns about the "stresses and strains of modern life." Indeed longstanding social theoretical concerns about the personal consequences of modernity, about opportunity and risk, are evident in medical and popular discourses of that time. Concerns that provided, I argue, the context for the rise of the therapeutic society.

2

Modernity, Medicine & the Problem of "Nerves"

Modern civilization with its stress and strain seems to have accentuated if not created endless phobias and remarkable behaviour patterns and the taunt "thou cannot minister to a mind diseased" leaves the physician feeling hopeless and depressed. The psycho-analyst like the ancient soothsayer or the still more ancient exorciser of demons now steps into the breach.
— *Medical Journal of Australia*, 1924

In late nineteenth century Australia, percipient observers were both optimistic and concerned about the promises of modernity. Economic prosperity and modernization generated considerable excitement, but the fast pace of social change elicited widespread consternation. In the economic sphere, new forms of capitalist production, industrial reform, and working-class mobilization, as well as the 1890s depression, contributed to a period of significant social upheaval. In the private sphere, the "woman question" arose as gender relations were threatened by the emergence of the suffrage movement, debates over contraception, and a declining birth rate.[1] Within this context of ferment, physicians and ordinary people were agonizing over the impact of modernity on the private self, and questioning the social and personal costs of progress. This disquiet is captured in the aphorism, the "stress and strain of modern life," an adage that gained considerable currency during the late nineteenth and early twentieth centuries, and one that reflected widespread concern that modern life was hazardous to individual health.

This chapter traces key dimensions of a nascent therapeutic ethos through an analysis of the discourse of "nerves" and shifting views of mental distress. Although often overlooked, notions of nervousness warrant further attention in analyses of the therapeutic society, just as in histories of medicine, psychiatry, and social life in the late Victorian era. The construction of nervous conditions captures quintessential concerns of the time. It also throws light on the ways in which capitalist modernity brought about a reconfiguration of understandings of the self and mental distress on the one hand, and the hope for cure on the other. A historically grounded analysis of the therapeutic turn suggests the discourse of nerves was cultivating a therapeutic terrain long before therapy or even psychology had any significant cultural impact.[2]

Constructions of nervousness formed a critical juncture of medical knowledge and cultural discourses, one in which complex dimensions of gender, class, and consumerism intersected in an emerging therapeutic ethos. Primarily through advertising, the press carried messages about nervous decline that both proffered solutions and stimulated new markets, while developments in medicine and ideas linking modernity with nervous strain fostered new understandings of the individual that challenged gendered constructions of the self and emotional distress. The problem of nerves as it arose in the late nineteenth century was emblematic of anxieties about modern life and, in particular, modern manhood. Medical and popular discourses of nervousness generated new understandings of the self that both destabilized hegemonic masculinity and engendered a greater concern with personal distress.

The starting point for my analysis is the popularization of the diagnostic category of neurasthenia. Within the context of historically gendered discourses and different diagnostic patterns of mental illness, the invention of neurasthenia provided a relatively respectable—some have argued distinguished—label for "nervous men." While neurasthenia was an affliction that could strike men and women alike, my analysis focuses predominantly on what Janet Oppenheim has called "manly nerves," for it was the construction of male vulnerability far more than female weakness that was to have the most far-reaching cultural consequences.[3]

Though neurasthenia was largely an acceptable diagnosis, other categories of nervous disorder more potently symbolized the modern threat to masculinity. Sexual dysfunction arising from nervous exhaustion, especially when thought to be caused by masturbation, was among a range of afflictions that caused widespread disquiet. While the integrity of the male self was already under threat, World War I and shell shock further challenged the masculine ideal. At the cultural level, the discourse of nerves was popularized and new markets were created for tonics and other remedies. A key facet of the early therapeutic period was the increasingly widespread view that modern life was to blame for the various problems of selfhood that were being identified. Yet there was also hope, for while modernity may have brought forth these problems, it also promised new—therapeutic—solutions.

Neurasthenia & Nervous Exhaustion

In October 1881, James Smith, prominent colonial journalist and litterateur, delivered a lecture to around 400 people in Melbourne for the Australian Health Society. He began with the declaration: "There are physical disorders resulting from our unnatural and disordered lives which may deservedly engage our serious attention." Smith argued that popularizing knowledge of health was an important weapon in combating disease, and introducing the topic of his lecture, "The Nervous System: Its Use and Abuse," he suggested that this held true especially in cases of nervous disorder, which was a cause of "exquisite suffering" for many. Smith shared with the audience an anecdote about "an old lady who innocently remarked that she wished she had lived before nerves were invented." In expounding the story, he explained that the "corporeal machinery" is highly complex and in an ideal state of health one is happily unaware of its functioning. "The discovery of nerves by any one of us is, therefore, a misfortune," he continued, "because it implies nervous disorder; and, consequently, the old woman's wish was by no means as absurd as, at first sight, it might appear to have been."[4]

Smith's lecture, published in the respected monthly periodical, the *Victorian Review*, and reprinted as a pamphlet for the Australian Health Society, addressed a subject of widespread concern—one that occupied the pages of learned medical journals and the popular press alike—the increasing prevalence of nervous disorder. Promulgating theories developed by American neurologist George Beard, who popularized the diagnostic category "neurasthenia," Smith argued that "the liability to nervous disorders increases, *pari passu*, with the growth of civilization, and with the development of mankind." Following Beard, he cited the unnatural speed of modern life and concomitant increased mental activity as especially deleterious, and recommended exercise, sleep, good food, pure air, and abstinence from stimulants as essential for the maintenance of nervous health.[5] Smith advanced two further prescriptions, which for the purposes of the present discussion are especially relevant. He expounded the importance of "freedom from worry" and invoked the ancient dictum to "know thyself."[6] In championing self-knowledge, Smith used the Delphic precept to underscore the value of scientific study of the nervous system in understanding the individual of the modern era.

Beard's analysis of "nervousness" as an unfortunate side effect of modern life resonated in the colonies of Australia and found a number of enthusiastic supporters, like James Smith. According to David Walker, Smith first encountered Beard's writings on neurasthenia early in 1881.[7] Beard had, however, been developing his thesis on nervous exhaustion for some time. A decade earlier, he had published an influential article in the *Boston Medical and Surgical Journal* in which he used the term neurasthenia—literally meaning nerve weakness—to describe what he believed to be a new and debilitating condition of modern civilization.[8]

Neurasthenia epitomized fin-de-siècle anxieties about the "stresses and strains of modern life." Characterized by chronic fatigue and a dazzling array of physical and mental complaints that appeared to have no organic basis, it was a diagnosis that encompassed a complex of symptoms suffered by Beard's predominantly urban, educated middle-class and upper-class patients—from headache, insomnia, and chills, to feelings of helplessness, and fear of responsibility. Beard's assertion that complex modern life itself could induce disease was premised upon the view that the nervous system was being overwrought in new ways. In his view, steam power, the periodical press, the telegraph, the sciences, and "the mental activity of women" had radically transformed civilization. Consequently, he argued that "when civilization, plus these five factors, invades any nation, it must carry nervousness and nervous diseases along with it."[9]

For Beard, neurasthenia was not only a distinctively modern affliction, it was also a respectable one. In his history of neurasthenia in America, Francis Gosling notes that nervous Americans fell between the extremes of the mentally healthy and the "subclass of unfortunates who suffered the torments of insanity."[10] In Beard's conceptualization, neurasthenia was qualitatively different from its kindred maladies—hysteria, melancholia, and hypochondria—which, as Gosling notes, all had "undesirable connotations: hysteria was confined mostly to women and usually involved functional disabilities such as paralysis or loss of feeling; hypochondria entailed imaginary complaints coupled with a desire not to get well; and melancholia implied the presence of delusions."[11] Neurasthenia, in comparison, was not marked by such associations, indeed some have argued that it enjoyed a degree of prestige. According to Beard, it was predominantly a malady of the middle and upper classes, particularly affecting, as Roy Porter has noted, "those intellectuals, professionals and businessmen who took up most intensively the challenge of modern urban life."[12]

Neurasthenia certainly boasted some celebrated sufferers, including William James, Max Weber, Charlotte Perkins Gilman, and Virginia Woolf.[13] In an early and notable sociological analysis, Emile Durkheim suggested that "neurasthenia is rather considered a mark of distinction than a weakness. In our refined societies, enamored of things intellectual, nervous members constitute almost a nobility."[14] While Durkheim's analysis is illuminating, it tends to elide the extent to which neurasthenia crossed class lines. Empirical evidence suggests that it was diagnosed among both the working and the upper classes, just as it was among men and women.[15] Yet neurasthenia did carry, as Oppenheim has argued, "a certain cachet that could hardly have failed to appeal to many people experiencing the agonies of depression."[16] Indeed, it was in many ways constructed as a fashionable disease to which members of the cultural elite were especially vulnerable.[17] The delicate constitution of the upper-class female put her at risk of developing the affliction, while for men, overwork, worry, and sexual excesses could induce nervous exhaustion.

While Beard initially postulated neurasthenia as an American affliction, the diagnostic category soon gained international currency.[18] Though life in the Australian colonies differed significantly from the urbanity of fin-de-siècle Europe and America, excitement and anxiety about the possibilities and consequences of modernity were similarly felt. The increasing prevalence and recognition of nervous disorder in Australia, as elsewhere, fed into new conceptualizations of the individual, especially through the belief that the fast pace of modern life was damaging to individual health.

The case of neurasthenia in the Antipodes has unfortunately received scant attention, save for the work of David Walker.[19] It is difficult to ascertain whether neurasthenia was as fashionable in the colonies of Australia as it was during its heyday in North America and continental Europe. Given the colonial reliance on British medical texts of the late nineteenth century, it is probable that the Australian reception reflected the view of British physicians, among whom there were some enthusiastic supporters, but for others it was viewed as a case of "old wine in new bottles."[20] Neurasthenia, nevertheless, held significant appeal. The attraction, as Oppenheim notes, was that it provided benefits to both doctors and patients. Patients were given a distinguished title for their malady, while for doctors, neurasthenia provided a classification for an array of physical and mental complaints that had hitherto created diagnostic dilemmas.[21]

In his 1881 treatise, *American Nervousness,* Beard identified more then seventy distinct neurasthenic symptoms. Dysfunction of the nervous system was primary, but the range of problems this could in turn generate was potentially limitless. As Beard himself noted: "An absolutely exhaustive catalogue of the manifestation of the nervously exhausted state cannot be prepared, since every case differs somewhat from every other case."[22] Contemporary Australian medical journals suggest that Beard's view on the complex and vast array of symptoms typical of neurasthenia was broadly adopted by Australian physicians. An 1890 article, for example, described neurasthenia as an affliction characterized by "a high degree of irritable weakness of the nervous system which progresses with the most varied disturbances of function in every possible region."²³ Central to Beard's theory, and accepted by physicians of the day in Australia, was the notion that the modern "brain worker" was especially vulnerable. The problem of "brain fag," as it became colloquially known, is described in a case study of male neurasthenia:

> A gentleman having great mental work to perform on account of his many responsible and varied duties ... he was sleepless, and his sexual power was somewhat impaired. Having to do any mental work he would feel quite unfit for it. A heaviness about his head rendered his ideas confused and his power of concentration gone. Had lost all energy, and felt as if it did not matter to him how things went.²⁴

Excessive mental stimulation clearly placed some sectors of the population at higher risk—notably middle-class men. Yet Beard's causative theory posited that simply the conditions of modern life itself could induce nervous strain. At a time in which there was growing unease about the costs of a rapidly changing social landscape, neurasthenia supported that suspicion that modern civilization was responsible for new manifestations of disease. As Walker has argued, Beard's theory was thus of signal importance, for in effect, it "democratized nervous disorders, making them an inevitable consequence of modernity." As he argues: "The shift in emphasis was important. According to the old rules, exhaustion of the brain tended to occur only after severe intellectual labour, whereas after Beard modern society itself, its pressures, its excitements and manifold anxieties, caused nervous exhaustion. Being modern, had become a medically recognized type of exhaustion."²⁵

It followed, then, that men and women from all strata of society were potentially prone to nervous exhaustion, a school of thought that appears to have met with general acceptance. Prominent British physician Sir Thomas Clifford Allbutt's view on the gender distribution of neurasthenia, published in the *Medical Journal of Australia* in 1912, was that the malady was common to both sexes, but that female neurasthenics exhibited more acute symptoms.²⁶ This, however, is a difficult area, both in relation to the historical record and a lack of consensus on the subject by historians in recent years.[27] Yet the important point for the present analysis is not so much whether men and women were diagnosed in equal number, but rather that men were diagnosed in significant numbers at all.

Certainly, neurasthenia was constructed differently for men and women. For women, the long association between femininity and weakness was a key factor in explaining nervous exhaustion. For men, overwork and sexual excesses were commonly implicated. Anxieties over male sexuality are considered below, and as I outline, the problem of sexually induced nervous exhaustion was certainly not a diagnosis to be welcomed. Neurasthenia arising from overwork, on the other hand, entailed a certain respectability, albeit one that at once also implied weakness and thus a failure of masculinity.

In terms of treatment too, there were significant gender differences. For men, the benefit of stimulating the nervous system was advanced and curative regimes included adventure holidays and the therapeutic application of electricity. For women, the rest cure was generally the preferred therapy. Choice of treatment, of course, also had an economic dimension, for just as one had to have the means to consult a reputable physician, only those of sufficient wealth could lie idle for many weeks in a salubrious location. As Michael Neve notes, rest cures were for the affluent, not the poor.[28] For those who could not afford such expensive treatments, tonics and patent medicines provided an alternative means by which the nervous system could be fortified and nervous health restored.

That neurasthenia provided a somatic explanation of mental distress—through the identification of the nervous system and the brain as the locus of the pathology—was important to the uncoupling of nervous distress and femininity. For the medical fraternity, neurasthenia captured widely accepted, albeit rather nebulous, ideas about the nervous system and subacute mental dysfunction, most notably depression. And just as prevailing views on masculinity and mental health were challenged by the attribution of the "strain of modern life" as causal, so too was the doctrine of heredity and organic origin. This facilitated recognition of a much broader range of symptoms and paved the way for more complex understandings of mental illness. The creation of categories of neurosis that could be applied to anxious, depressed, and "neurotic" men without the stigma attached to a diagnosis of hysteria, for example, is especially important. For as conditions like neurasthenia were increasingly identified, and to some extent normalized, bifurcated and gendered constructions of madness and sanity were problematized.

The array of symptoms that could be classified as neurasthenic, however, meant that it was never an unproblematic diagnosis. For the same reasons it appealed to physicians—its adaptability and breadth—neurasthenia was by the 1930s dismissed as impractical, as new diagnostic categories offered greater precision.[29] Moreover, debate as to whether modern life had indeed induced new forms of disease, or whether modern science had merely rendered timeless human conditions identifiable, further undermined its diagnostic integrity. In 1912, for example, Dr J. Montgomery Mosher questioned whether neurasthenia was just a new name for an old problem:

> It is possible that complex modern life has introduced conditions leading to new manifestations of disease. Whether this be so, or whether closer clinical study has brought to notice certain symptoms and their causes hitherto overlooked, a group of mental cases does exist, acute in character, requiring early and appropriate treatment, for whom restoration of health is to be sought and reasonably expected.[30]

Mosher's observation not only illustrates debate over the modern-civilization-as causal theory, it illuminates a dramatic shift in the understanding of mental disease, as the possibility of treatment and the hope of cure gained credence. For the medical fraternity, psychological knowledge began to undermine, or at least complement, the emphasis on nervous health, but for the general populations the problem of nerves had greater longevity. As Neve has argued: "Neurasthenia was the people's illness, however precise the medical attempts to isolate, define or discard it. A genuine example of Freud's 'ordinary unhappiness' but experienced by a far larger community than could afford to seek his particular, lengthy and expensive solutions."[31]

In the context of a general unsettling of gender and class relations during the late Victorian era, problems of nervous disorder captured quintessential anxieties of the time. While the suffrage movement had aroused general disquiet over "the woman question," there were also concerns about the decline of the male self, especially in the sexual domain. Loss of virility was part of the cluster of neurasthenia symptoms. The delicate problem of impaired sexual function nevertheless remained marginal in medical texts until the 1920s, by which time Freudian theory and the sexual element of neurosis was more widely debated in scholarly journals.[32] At the popular level, however, problems of impotence ("nervous debility") and fears about masturbation ("self abuse") were evident in a bourgeoning market for alternative remedies. Advertisements in the popular press not only reflect these anxieties but they also reveal how the emergent consumer culture proffered solutions that addressed apparent problems of male decline.

"Nervous Debility" & "Self-Abuse"

For late nineteenth century Australian men, popular concern about nervous disorder found particular expression in the area of sexuality.[33] Victorian beliefs that linked mental and physical health to appropriate sexual conduct meant that just as mental strain was a threat to one's health, so too was the inability to control sexual desire. The regulation of sexuality was promoted on moral and religious grounds, but it was also underpinned by contemporary medical orthodoxy about the functioning of the nervous system.

The belief that semen was "nervous energy in concentrated form" provided the basis of the idea that any emission was potentially hazardous.[34] According to some theories of the day, unnecessary ejaculation could cause despair and illness and the consequences of "seminal loss" was a common theme among public speakers.[35] Single men were advised to abstain from intercourse, while married men were cautioned to moderation. But it was masturbation, commonly perceived as the most pernicious of all habits, that elicited widespread concern. "Self-abuse," as it was commonly termed, was thought to be both a cause and symptom of insanity, neurasthenia, and spermatorrhoea.[36] A case study of a male neurasthenic patient published by Dr V. Marano, for example, noted that "he had freely masturbated in years past, and this was the foundation stone of his troubles."[37]

As Walker notes, problems of male sexuality generated considerable unease in the late nineteenth century.[38] The medical literature of this period, however, was still largely reticent on such matters. Marano's account is typical, insofar as concern is limited primarily to the perceived origin of the patient's disturbance. Progressive Melbourne physician John Springthorpe, however, was a notable exception. With an interest in psychology, he was one of the few reputable doctors who urged a greater interest in the sexual domain. In a lecture entitled, "On the Psychological Aspects of Sexual Appetite," delivered to the Australian Branch of the British Medical Association in 1884, Springthorpe argued that:

> In masturbation ... it is the quantity and not the method that is injurious, and though the chief immediate danger lies in the fact that it is an indulgence that speedily exceeds the bounds of moderation, the psychological results are often even more deplorable. Not only may the whole nervous system, in an extreme case, remain at the fatigue point from the excessive drain upon it, but the victim of the habit ... may, especially if he be of a neurotic tendency, gradually sink into sexual hypochondria and mental aberration of a very distressing kind.[39]

As with broader anxieties about the stimulation of modern life, there was a comparable concern about sexualization, or as Springthorpe himself noted, "the sexual atmosphere of the rising population."[40] In addressing this issue he supported the prevailing moral view of abstinence until marriage, a common enough position to take. But in a more daring move, he urged his fellow doctors to engage in open and frank discussion of sexual matters. It was Springthorpe's view that physicians needed to appreciate both the sex instinct and psychic factors as well as more adequately understand the psychological costs of sexual deviance. As for the growing problem of unfettered "indulgence," the cause was laid squarely on the stimulation of modern urban life and the problems it generated. In his address, Springthorpe went on to say that, "civilization has undoubtedly delayed the natural gratification of marriage ... [whilst] modern civilization has increased the sensibility of the nervous system to stimuli of all kinds, amongst which sexual stimuli naturally take their predominant place."[41]

While concerns about sexuality, particularly male sexuality, were not limited to Australia, the gender imbalance and class structure of the colonies exacerbated local anxieties. Though the sex disparity of the early colonial period had significantly diminished, men still outnumbered women by the turn of the twentieth century.[42] For a large number of men throughout the nineteenth century this meant that marriage was never an option. The management of male sexuality in Australia was therefore fraught from the outset, and by the late nineteenth century, in the context of the popularization of nervousness, it assumed another dimension. Though masturbation had long been regarded a cause of insanity, there was growing suspicion that it was also to blame for other types of mental disturbance. In the case of neurasthenia, sexual potency was thought to diminish in view of the general weakening of the nervous system. The "urogenital" form, or "sexual neurasthenia," however, was diagnosed in cases of sexual dysfunction believed to be the result of excessive masturbation. It was a condition doctors were loath to treat, as Allbutt's account suggests:

> There is, perhaps, no more unwelcome visitant in the physician's waiting room than the sexual neurasthenic; and the least welcome are those who, by slackness or caprice of moral fibre, have dabbled in dirty ideas until mind and body have fallen into common frailty.[43]

Concerns about sexual dysfunction nevertheless presented a commercial opportunity, one that was seized upon by quacks and patent medicine manufacturers, as well as some reputable doctors. Consequently, the subject occupied a prominent place in the classified pages of the popular press. Pamphlets, books, and home cures for "nervous debility" were widely, albeit euphemistically, advertised, as alternative practitioners and orthodox physicians alike promised the "simple restoration of manhood." Typical copy of the late nineteenth and early twentieth century featured testimonials from "cured" patients. The "celebrated Danish herbalist," Herr Rassmussen, commonly published such declarations. Others, legitimized by medical credentials, promised cures for all types of nervous conditions. Dr Patterson, for example, appealed to men young and old to invest two shillings and six pence for a copy of *Male Generative Function in Health and Illness*, or his other book, *Nervous Debility*.

Both orthodox medical specialists, and less reputable ones who preyed upon men concerned about sexual function, utilized modern electrotherapies in the belief that it would restore vigor. Appliances were also available for use outside the consulting room

Large advertisements for credentialed physicians and quack doctors alike were carried in the popular press. This advertisement for Dr Perry's Pamphlet on Nervous Diseases appeared in the Bulletin, 6 February 1892.

and advertisements for electric belts were commonly carried in the popular press. The German Electric Appliance Agency, for example, purported to cure nervous weakness with a belt that was said to emit a steady, soothing current felt through all the weak parts of the body.

The marketing of pills and tonics, well established by the 1880s, also tapped into contemporary anxieties about male decline. Mumford's Medicated Nervine Pills, emblematic of this kind of advertisement, promised to cure all nervous weakness arising from

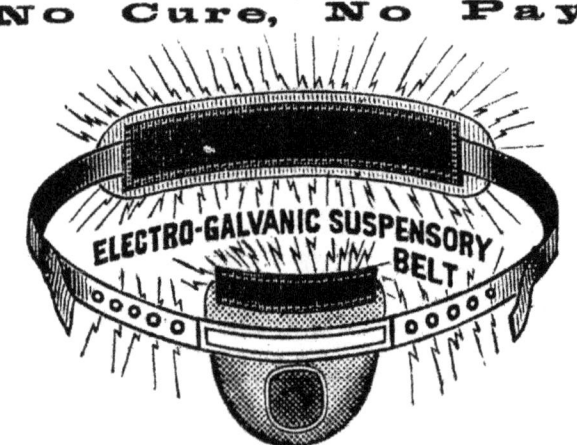

Electric belts were commonly marketed as a reliable cure for nervousness. This advertisement appeared in the Bulletin, 11 January 1896.

"errors in youth," neurasthenia, and spermatorrhoea. The threat to mental and physical health that nervous complaints posed was commonly emphasized, as were the perils of leaving such conditions untreated. Readers were advised that if ignored, these ailments could lead to consumption, insanity, and suicide.

Yet alongside the dismal message was an optimistic one, which stressed the futility of suffering and promoted an ethos of care for the self. The widely promoted idea of "self-cure" promised the empowered consumer relief from suffering without the need for expert consultation. Respondents to advertisements for pills and tonics, or books and pamphlets, could describe in writing their affliction and have merchandise shipped to them in non-identifying plain post. If Allbutt's views on the so-called sexual neurasthenic were typical of those of his fellow physicians, it is unsurprising that the alternative medicine market prospered. For the merchant, peddling self-cure options was extremely lucrative. For the patient, the appeal was no doubt affordability as much as it was anonymity as patent medicines of the late nineteenth century averaged about one tenth the cost of a visit to a physician.[44]

It was not only "problems of manhood" that tonics and other remedies promised to cure, but a range of afflictions, including neurasthenia other nervous complaints, as well as an assortment of physical aliments. In the context of ongoing concerns about ner-

WHY WILL YOU SUFFER from NERVOUS WASTING and DEBILITATING DISEASES which destroy the VITAL FORCES of MANHOOD? You may now cure yourselves without CONSULTING a DOCTOR. Send Six Penny Stamps for the new MEDICAL BROCHURE, containing the French method of QUICK, PERMANENT SELF-CURE.

Address: **Parisian Agency Co., Box 766, Sydney.**

The Parisian Agency Co. cure for "nervous wasting" pictured above appeared in the Bulletin, 5 March 1892.

vousness, the marketing of tonics continued well into the twentieth century. I return to the subject of popular cures below, where I discuss discursive shifts that saw nerves increasingly understood as a problem of women. First, however, I turn to another manifestation of nervousness in the male population. Although anxieties about male sexuality began to decline in the first decade of the twentieth century, an even more disturbing threat to men's nervous health was on the horizon. As Australians entered the "Great War," a new problem emerged. It was couched in the language of nerves, but was undeniably psychological in nature, and was to have profound and long-lasting consequences.

"Shattered Nerves"

Despite certain diagnostic limitations, neurasthenia had provided a category for nervousness in men that avoided the connotations of other maladies, particularly hysteria.[45] With its intractable association with femininity, hysteria was an insult tantamount to emasculation.[46] Soon after the outbreak of the First World War, however, issues of diagnosis and treatment of neurasthenia and hysteria took on an urgent and unprecedented significance as the horrors of modern warfare were brought into stark relief. The undeniable psychological cost of combat meant that the excitement of rallying for the Empire in a global conflict was to be short-lived. On an unprecedented scale, soldiers returned from combat with symptoms that confounded medical authorities: from cases of blindness, deafness, muteness, and stammering, to uncontrollable fits, and chronic shaking, men were presenting with a range of symptoms that appeared to have no apparent organic cause.[47] The inadequacies of existing diagnostic categories were acutely felt, as what were soon recognized to be hysterical symptoms emerged in a most unexpected population—the bravest and toughest of men. The problem of psychological trauma became impossible to ignore, and in the context of heated debate about Australia's part in the Great War, and fears of escalating cases of malingering, diagnoses of mental disturbance also took on a new political significance.

The case of Gunner Perry

In February 1915, less than six months after he had enlisted for active duty, Gunner William Walter Perry of West Melbourne returned from the Middle East. His early repatriation resulted from an injury sustained to his spine after being kicked by a horse shortly after arriving in Egypt. Following the incident, Perry was examined by the eminent Dr Springthorpe, diagnosed with spinal neurasthenia, and sent home. Upon his return to Melbourne, however, attending physicians found no physical evidence of a functional nervous disorder, and they suspected he was malingering. To determine whether or not he was indeed "shamming," the superintendent of the St Kilda Base Hospital, Dr F.G. Meade, subjected Perry to a series of crude physical tests, including kicking him, and applying electricity to his tongue. With the aid of these "experiments," Meade was convinced that there was nothing wrong with his patient. Perry was subsequently charged and court-martialed. Unsurprisingly, he cried foul and complained that he had been tortured.

Fortunately for Gunner Perry—ironically an electrician by trade—the court-martial was eventually dropped. The exoneration did not, however, resolve his predicament. For according to his account of events, upon his return to the Base hospital after the court-martial hearing Meade came to him, "livid in the face, and white with passion, denouncing the gentlemen of the court-martial as a set of blockheads."[48] Meade's cruelty intensified, Perry claimed, and when it became unbearable, he "escaped" with the help of some friends. However, in leaving the hospital in this manner, he had effectively discharged himself, and his war pension was immediately withdrawn. It was at that point that he sought assistance from the Trades Hall Council and his local Member of Parliament, the widely respected Australian Labor Party (ALP) member, Dr William Maloney.

Maloney secured an assurance from the Minister for Defense that Perry would not be arrested following his unauthorized discharge. However, despite the Minister's guarantee, Perry was forcibly removed from his home at eleven o'clock one evening. It was in the wake of these events that the matter was bought before Parliament and widely reported in the Australian press. Perry maintained that from his first acquaintance with the army physician,

Meade had called him "a malingerer, a schemer, an imposter, and a crawler."[49] He also claimed that he had been threatened with committal in a lunatic asylum.[50] Meade did not deny that he had kicked Perry during the examination. Nor was the fact that he had intentionally inflicted pain with the use of electricity in dispute. The issue was whether this amounted to cruelty.[51]

It is not surprising in the political climate of the time that all charges of cruelty made against Meade were dismissed by the Magistrate eventually appointed to investigate Perry's claims. The incident, however, was enough to provoke disquiet amongst the medical fraternity. The *Medical Journal of Australia (MJA)* ran an editorial in December 1915 congratulating Meade on the outcome of the inquiry, and stating that the use of electric current to determine cases of malingering "is so common that, were this held to constitute legal cruelty, medical practitioners would be in frequent danger of being subjected to charges of this kind."[52]

The editorial overlooked the minor detail of Perry's exoneration. Indeed, the tone reflected a persistent suspicion of malingering. With Maloney's support and a magisterial investigation, the matter was eventually resolved and Perry received his pension, but not before the late evening abduction—which according to the military version, was for Perry to be taken before the military medical board for further examination—and not before the army inflicted one last blow: a diagnosis of hysteria.

The odds were stacked against the electrician from West Melbourne. Even though physicians suspected that many men suffered from hysteria during the First World War, it was a diagnosis that Australian doctors, like their international counterparts, made only reluctantly, due to a "certain degree of obloquy attached to the word."[53] The intersection of the political and the psychological—just one instance of which was Gunner Perry's case—was apparent from the outset of the First World War. Perry's case illustrates some of the tensions at home. Further afield, the problems that emerged for Australian soldiers in the first year of battle were of such magnitude, however, it was soon recognized that a significant cost of war would be paid with the mental life of soldiers.

Throughout the years of conflict, editorial comments in the *MJA* focused on the difficulties enlisted physicians faced on the front line. Problems of inadequate supplies and working under extremely difficult conditions was one dimension; another was the nature of the injuries themselves, as this *MJA* editorial makes clear:

> Men are apt to be silent after they have tasted the bitter bread of battle. The horrors shatter the nerves of many, rob not a few of reason for a time or permanently, and create in all a sense of revulsion and an instinct of desperation, which is difficult to describe and wholly impossible to measure with anything approaching accuracy. In Flanders, many men have become amnesic, aphasic, and deaf; many have shown a variety of symptoms of mental disturbance and other nervous lesions. In the Gallipoli Peninsula, these brain and nerve effects have not been wanting, and yet it is unlikely that the full accounts of the fearful effects of shell and shrapnel have been described by anyone.[54]

Army doctors soon knew that the scars of modern battle were quite unlike anything seen previously. While battle trauma was not unheard of prior to 1914, what was exceptional was the magnitude and particular type of debility that the First World War invoked, a condition that soon became known as "shell shock."[55] A bewildering affliction, shell shock was initially thought to be caused by minute brain lesions resulting from exploding shells. However, it soon became apparent that many soldiers displaying psychological trauma, "the classic symptoms of anxiety, neurasthenia or hysteria," had not been exposed to exploding shells, and some had not even been close to the front line.[56] This 1917 report reveals attempts to come to terms with the baffling condition by moving towards greater diagnostic precision, and shows too, how problems of esteem, dignity, and stigma were of central importance:

> The functional neuroses comprise a most interesting group of patients, commonly said to be suffering from "shell shock"… Distinction must be made between those cases that are the direct result of an actual shell exploding near by, and, those the outcome of the continued stress and strain of the firing zone. The former are considered by the War Office

to be a battle casualty, and are evacuated as shell-shock (W.), whilst the other group may be labelled shell-shock (S.), and are considered as sick, not wounded. Hence the former have the privilege of wearing a gold arm stripe, and appear on the casualty lists ... The non-battle group of cases may be labelled as above, or not infrequently as neurosis, neurasthenia, or even debility ... The condition can best be described as nervous exhaustion.[57]

The diagnostic dilemmas posed by shell shock were clearly evident. In the same year that the above account appeared in the *MJA*, one physician described shell shock as "another 'scrap heap' where all the so-called functional diseases of the nervous system are put."[58] Nevertheless, the term continued to be used even after the war—albeit with recognition of its imprecision—by even the most esteemed physicians. In 1919 Dr A. Jefferis Turner conceded that the term shell shock was "charitably stretched to cover a number of very different afflictions and where it could not be used, that is to say, in the case of men who had never been to the front, some other euphemism was adopted, such as 'neurasthenia.'" In Turner's opinion, some of those cases were "frank-hysteria" and he recounted the observation of an English physician who had reportedly "seen more cases of hysteria in soldiers during one year of war than in men, women, and children during ten preceding years of peace."[59]

Yet doctors were, by and large, exceedingly reluctant to make diagnoses of hysteria. Springthorpe favored alternative terminology, arguing that hysteria should be more accurately termed "neuromimetic." Under the rubric of "war neurosis," he developed a classification of five conditions: neurasthenic (physical strain); psychasthenic (psychical strain); neuromimetic (dominant ideas); traumatic (concussion); and "shell shock" (caused by explosives).[60] Contributions in the medical literature from Australian physicians, however, suggests that although the term shell shock was subject to refinement, its use continued, either alongside or under the broader category of war neuroses. The persistent appeal of the term was perhaps, as Stephen Garton suggests, that "it rendered a literal and vivid image of the 'cause' of these troubling conditions."[61]

Modernity, Medicine & the Problem of "Nerves"   69

As a concept, shell shock captured not only the public imagination but also that of the medical fraternity, and just as neurasthenia had prized open a new category of dysfunction, so too did shell shock pave the way for new understandings of trauma. As Berthold Gersons and Ingrid Carlier have observed: "There was no way after World War I for society to ignore shell-shock. People became aware that neuroses could develop on a large scale and that society had to pay a high price."[62]

Social recognition of shell shock played an important role in the engendering of a greater concern with mental health more broadly. The ongoing psychological trauma experienced by many returned soldiers had a significant impact on families and the wider community, rendering accepted British patterns of stoicism in the face of emotional suffering more difficult to sustain. It also prompted major shifts in medical theory and practice, shifts that involved the search for causal factors on the one hand, and the development of new approaches to treatment on the other.

Mending the Mind

The experiences of medical officers in the treatment of traumatized soldiers during the First World War radically challenged existing medical orthodoxy. Prior to the war, the psychological dimension of mental disturbance had been subordinate to psychiatry's reliance on organic explanations. Even neurasthenia, though it departed somewhat from endogenous accounts, was still understood primarily in physical terms. War neuroses, however, forced a re-evaluation of existing knowledge and it was in attempts to find causal explanations and develop suitable methods of treatment that psychological and psychoanalytic approaches were to prove useful.

The medical fraternity had become familiar with Freudian concepts prior to the outbreak of war in 1914. It was not until the problem of traumatized soldiers exposed the inadequacies of existing knowledge and treatment methods, however, that doctors began to seriously consider the utility of psychoanalytic approaches. In the absence of cogent alternatives, Freudian theory provided a conceptual framework from which to make sense of war neuroses. The theory of neurosis as a defense mechanism appealed to physicians of the day, and the key concepts of repression, the unconscious, and sublimation also found favor. The idea of internal conflict also resonated, not as postulated by Freud in developmental terms, but in the idea that war created in the soldier a conflict between the obligation to fight and the desire to survive.[63]

Freud's theories were nevertheless taken up selectively. Explanations of how war could weaken mental defenses by putting the mechanisms of repression and sublimation under pressure were clearly owed to Freud, but military doctors never accepted the role of sexuality as a cause of neurosis. Neither did the analytic method find widespread support. Although there was limited experimentation with dream interpretation and the "talking cure," psychoanalysis remained subordinate to psychological techniques of hypnosis and suggestion. Suggestion was certainly endorsed by Springthorpe, who became the pre-eminent expert on war neuroses in Australia.[64]

While psychoanalytic therapy was not widely adopted, the psychological procedures that proved useful in treating war neuroses nevertheless drew on theories of the unconscious, and related concepts such as "mental conflict." A case study published in the *MJA* in 1919, for example, describes the plight of a 26 year-old soldier suffering from shell shock. The soldier's three brothers had been killed in battle and during the journey home to Australia he was often dazed, he experienced tremors, and suffered from insomnia. As the ship neared his homeland, his condition worsened. While he was able to talk about his battlefield experiences with fellow soldiers and doctors, he experienced tremendous dread at the prospect of discussing details of the war with his parents. In presenting the case, Dr A.C. Fraser provides a typical account of how doctors understood mental conflict and the psychological techniques they commonly employed to treat it:

> Treatment was commenced by making an analysis of his lack of mental decision clear to the patient. It was insisted on repeatedly that he must not shrink from the thought of meeting his parents. He must face it and come to a decision as to what he would say to them and what he would refrain from telling of battlefield details. This was gone over in full detail until the patient got a clear idea of the line he

would take. In other words, he was persuaded to come to a solution of the mental conflict that was troubling him. During the interview his tremor markedly increased, so that he could hardly sit on a chair. He was then hypnotized and suggestion given that he would now be able to settle his mental difficulties and that thereafter his tremor would disappear.[65]

The marginalization of the analytic method was not only a question of efficiency—its time consuming nature was a significant obstacle—but also, importantly, it did not fit with the prevailing orthodoxy about appropriate methods of treatment for men. Prior to the war, neurasthenia and nervous debility had already unsettled the ideal of the powerful and autonomous male self. The prevalence of war neuroses—or as many doctors suspected, male hysteria—threatened to undermine it further. Just as hysteria reflected pathological femininity, shell shock was akin to a failure of masculinity. There were, therefore, also broader issues in the cultural construction of gender at stake. According to Garton, military doctors preferred suggestion and persuasion because they more closely accorded with male rationality; that is, they were more "manly."[66]

These views also reflected British skepticism towards "fashionable American and Continental extremes and extreme remedies," like psychoanalysis.[67] During the early years of the war, Australian physicians were rather scathing about psychoanalytic methods, as evidenced by reviews in professional journals.[68] In contrast, texts with outlines of psychiatric treatment that accorded with the established view of psychoanalysis as a dubious practice were more favorably reviewed. For example, Joseph Rogues de Fursac's 1916 *Manual of Psychiatry* was approvingly regarded for it only briefly mentioned "the far-fetched and fantastic theories of the psychoanalysts."[69]

There were of course exceptions. Springthorpe, for instance, advocated psychoanalysis as indispensable to the armory of treatment for war neuroses. And in what was clearly a direct challenge to the general position taken by Australian doctors of the time, he remarked in a 1919 lecture that it is "true that everyone who has made extensive use of psychology in his treatment, has been acting on psycho-analytical lines, without, in most cases, finding it necessary to resort to its official formulae and, indeed, gaining satisfactory results more speedily." Neither was he uncritical of Freud though, stating in the same lecture that, "it is not too much to say that the war neuroses have completely shattered the original perverted notion of a sexual basis and driven such Freudism to oblivion."[70] Springthorpe was clearly ahead of his time but others soon followed. In just a few years the *MJA* went from describing psychoanalysis as "far-fetched and fantastic" to acknowledgement that it "may thus readily be of service to the medical practitioner in his daily duty towards so many unhappy human beings who turn to him for help."[71]

In the years that followed the First World War, the influence of Freudian theory was becoming more apparent. In the early 1920s, Dr M.C. Lidwill of The Royal Prince Alfred Hospital in Sydney was describing a typical neurasthenic patient as a businessman with financial trouble, experiencing vague symptoms "such as insomnia, a feeling of ill-being and a floating feeling of anxiety which tends to attach itself to every thought." The affliction, he stated, "may be produced in anyone when there is a condition of worry, mental conflict or when a profound emotion is prolonged."[72] The nineteenth century notion of nervous energy was still present—Lidwill noted that neurasthenia arises in such persons when the expenditure of energy exceeds the intake—but the condition was by this time understood to also have a more overt psychological dimension. Similarly, Lidwill's description of hysteria, that it "is the result of a repression of profound emotion consequent upon mental conflict in a patient whose nervous system is not strong enough to bear the strain," reflects the shift in medical thought.[73]

At a theoretical level, explanations of war neurosis proffered an amalgam of Freudian concepts with theories of hereditary predisposition and individual differences, as support grew for the idea that some "types" were more prone to neurosis than others. At the institutional and practical level, the ongoing problem of managing the psychological disturbance of sufferers remained. Dealing with the psychological fallout of the war meant that the medical profession had to address a new problem: the increasing prevalence of mental and nervous breakdown. This provided the context not only for an acceptance of psychoanalytic ideas, but for the legitimation of psychological knowledge more broadly.

The value of psychology was, shortly after the end of the war, being lauded by Australian physicians in lectures and in the pages of their professional journal. Dr J.V. McAree opened his lecture to the 1920 Meeting of the South Australian Branch of the British Medical Association by asserting:

> Till recently psychology has been neglected by the medical profession. The older form, based on introspection, was barren of practical results, whilst the newer was left severely alone, because the methods were considered unorthodox, such as hypnotism and psycho-analysis. However, if we study the history of our science we find that there has usually been resistance to our greatest discoveries.[74]

McAree went on to argue that "it is just as important for a medical practitioner to known something of applied psychology as it is for him to be acquainted with physiology."[75]

In the immediate postwar years, papers concerned with psychology and psychoanalysis were more frequently delivered at Branch Meetings of the Medical Association, and related topics were increasingly appearing in its journal. In an article published in June 1922 on the topic of psychology and its application, Springthorpe declared: "After an unpardonable delay psycho-therapy is coming to its own."[76] Having promoted its value since the 1880s, he must have been well pleased that psychology was finally gaining acceptance. By the early 1920s, as "psycho-therapeutics" gained greater legitimacy, physicians debated the most appropriate techniques. Medical discourse by this time reflected an increasing acceptance of ideas of the conscious and unconscious mind, and to varying degrees doctors subscribed to psychological methods, primarily hypnosis and suggestion. Freudian terminology was adopted, albeit selectively, and psychological idioms became part of the medical lexicon.

The legitimation of psychology and associated developments in psychiatry were, however, to signal the beginning of a decline in concepts of nervousness, at least in the medical arena. While the problem of nerves was to have a more enduring life at the cultural level, medical discourse of the interwar years reveals the progressive adoption of more explicitly psychological understandings of mental disorder. Having exposed the horrifying reality of human weakness and indeed of male vulnerability, the unraveling of the soldier's psyche brought about a greater depth of understanding of the complexity of psychological and emotional life. Indeed shell shock was to signal the end of an unproblematic distinction between mental health and illness—the seeds of which had been sown earlier with the invention of categories of nervous disorder such as neurasthenia.

The treatment of soldiers with war-related neuroses thus provided not only the impetus for new theoretical models of mental disturbance, but also paved the way for professional, institutional, and legal reform. The demise of "madness" and "lunacy" was finally enshrined in legislation in most Australian states by the 1960s with the introduction of Mental Health Acts. The eventual repeal of nineteenth century Lunacy Acts is symbolic of the changes that occurred throughout the first half of the twentieth century. While the details of Australian mental health reforms are too complex to canvass here, it is important nevertheless to acknowledge the significance of these developments for the evolution of the therapeutic society.

Along with the disruption of the bifurcated categories of madness and sanity, there was growing acceptance of the value of psychiatric treatment and the possibility of cure. Again, World War I was important, for it provided further impetus to earlier calls from asylum doctors who had been lobbying for the expansion of mental health services. As Garton notes, by the early twentieth century, doctors were asserting "their claim to expertise in the treatment of lunacy more vigorously and demanded the right to treat the ill rather than just the incarcerated."[77] In 1908, for example, Dr Andrew Davidson, Medical Superintendent of the Callan Park Hospital for the Insane in Sydney, called for the establishment of outpatient clinics, arguing that "the management of the early stage of mental disease is one of the greatest public importance."[78] It was not just physicians, however, who were agitating for change. The Returned Soldiers Association was instrumental in the establishment of special facilities so that ex-servicemen could be treated without the stigma usually attached to mental illness.[79]

The expansion of mental health care during this period extended beyond the provision of extra services for returned soldiers, and involved major developments in the field of psychiatric medicine more broadly. During the 1920s psychiatry made significant professional advances, with the expansion of private practice, the opening of outpatient clinics in hospitals, the establishment of the first Chair in Psychiatry in Australia, and a growing recognition that mental illness could be effectively treated. While resistance to increased funding and services for mental health came from some quarters, from others there was significant support. The Minister for Health in Western Australia, for example, reflected the progressive view with a declaration to parliament in 1927 in which he stated: "It is now observed that a mental or nervous disease is merely an illness like other disorders ... a mind diseased can be treated as well as a body."[80] The shift from models of madness to a much broader understanding of mental health represented not only a reconfiguration of medical knowledge, but fostered new understandings of the troubled psyche amongst the general population.

There was, however, another important consequence of the broadening conceptualization of mental disturbance. Garton notes that a new polarization emerged with the expansion of psychiatry during the 1930s, not between the sane and insane as had existed before, but between the established population of the insane (and incurable), and the new class of patients with less serious conditions who were ideally suited to therapeutic intervention.[81] This development was critical to the expansion of therapeutic understandings of the self. Conceptualizations of mild to moderate mental disorder meant that a much broader range of psychological and emotional states could be understood under the rubric of nervous, mental, or psychological distress, and moreover, that such conditions could be treated.

In the wake of legislative reform, mental health care moved from a model of control and containment to one of individualized treatment.[82] Changing conceptualizations of mental health, however, brought about a range of contradictory effects. As the psychiatric profession expanded and new diagnostic categories were created, emotional and psychological difficulties came under the medical gaze in new ways. While these processes lend themselves to an interpretation of the expansion of "disciplinary discourses," it is important not to lose sight of the fact that the increased power of the psychiatric profession was generated in the context of societal need. Certainly, these developments benefited the professional status of psychiatrists. Yet they also provided new treatment possibilities for individuals seeking relief from psychological distress.

Popular Cures for a Nervous Nation

Emergent understandings of the self and mental distress not only influenced professional theory and medical practice; they also shaped the broader culture. As illustrated earlier in my discussion of nervous debility, commercial interests capitalized on prevailing anxieties about individual decline and in the process disseminated popularized forms of medical knowledge. Before stress, anxiety, and depression entered the popular vocabulary, nerves was the rubric under which a variety of symptoms of mental distress were widely understood. Neurasthenia and other acute nervous disorders were at one end of the spectrum; at the other was a variety of less serious physical and psychological afflictions.

The ascendancy of nerves as a common malady in the late nineteenth century was both buttressed by advances in medical knowledge, and driven by a blossoming consumer culture as well as an already well established advertising industry that promoted products to restore health and vigor. Underpinned by prevailing medical orthodoxy that stressed the value of strengthening the brain and the nervous system, and amid anxieties about the increasing prevalence of nervous disorder, there developed "a growing demand for therapies that would revitalize exhausted brains and worn nerves."[83]

For an increasing number of "nervous moderns," the march of progress may have engendered new forms of disease, but scientific knowledge also promised solutions. Nerve tonics were widely advertised and routinely prescribed, and electricity was applied with reportedly remarkable results by quack doctors and credentialed physicians alike. In addition to seeking help from alternative practitioners, the idea of self-cure was also promoted, especially through advertisements for "private complaints." The assortment of afflictions falling into the category of nervous disorder made it an especially appealing commercial opportunity for patent medicine manufacturers. The promotion of an array of medicines to fortify the self was made possible by the fact that symptoms attributed to nerves could encompass almost anything, from physical weakness and headaches to weeping attacks and melancholy.

Commercialization itself was not new. The growth of advertising throughout the nineteenth century reflected capitalist expansion more broadly. But what is important for the present discussion is the role of advertising in the dissemination of ideas about nervous distress on the one hand, and relief from suffering on the other. Importantly, the concept of "needless suffering" emerged as a central motif. As an advertisement for Kruschen Salts in the *Bulletin* advised its readers in 1917, "to suffer with fortitude is heroic, but to suffer needlessly is idiotic."[84] The diffusion of such ideas became possibly as important to the process of democratization of nervous distress as Beard's theory was in attributing the strain of modern life as causal. Just as neurasthenia prompted a new social acceptance of mild to moderate psychological disorder, advertising was critical to the cultural construction of nerves as an insidious problem of modernity—albeit a problem that could be treated with the right product. Consequently, as Walker has noted, Australians consumed nerve tonics in high volume in the belief "that to be modern was to be exhausted."[85]

The dreaded "brain fag," as mental fatigue was colloquially known, was subject to an extraordinary range of popular cures. It was one of a number of neurasthenic conditions that tonics like Cassell's Tablets, Mother Seigel's Curative Syrup, and Hean's Nerve Nuts purported to cure. In an analysis of gender, class, and nerves in late nineteenth century America, Dona Davis examined the impact of Beard's theory of nervousness on the marketing of Lydia Pinkham's Vegetable Compound, a popular home remedy for "female complaints."[86] She notes that the origin of nerves as an affliction of the upper class was used to appeal to a much broader market, as the emotional vulnerability of women became an increasingly widespread motif. In her analysis, Vegetable Compound ads were as concerned with "legitimizing nervous complaints, as with curing them."[87]

Cassell's Tablets were widely advertised throughout the 1920s and 1930s to strengthen nerves, cure sleeplessness, and treat digestive problems. This advertisement appeared in the Argus, 25 August 1930.

Cigarettes were commonly advertised as a means of calming the nerves. This advertisement appeared in the Mercury, 8 July 1936.

Whisky is admirably suited to the man in his prime.

Medically speaking, its composition is particularly pure, aiding the digestion instead of taxing it.

The quantity needed for health stimulation is small. The secret, as in so many things, is moderation, plus insistence on sound quality.

The best Australian brands are excellent in flavour and purity, and have been brought to a high level of excellence by ageing for over 5 years.

The capacity of alcohol to relieve stress was frequently conveyed though advertising. This advertisement appeared in the Argus, 24 July 1946.

You'll get new pleasure out of life and the children when you take Fishaphos Nerve Tablets. This modern formula gives prompt and lasting relief from nervous tension and disorders, such as emotional excitement, depression, mental strain, sleeplessness and run-down conditions generally. Get a box of 30 tablets (5/6) from your chemist to-day, and start taking them straight away. You will feel the benefit from the very first dose. INSIST ON FISHAPHOS NERVE TABLETS.
NERVE TABLETS—Safe to take—not habit-forming.
FISHER AND CO., 554 GEORGE ST., SYDNEY.   NT1

By the 1950s, advertisements were including depression as one of the ailments that could be relieved with nerve tonics. This advertisement appeared in the Sydney Morning Herald, 13 May 1957.

Similarly, in Australia, advertising and the popular press played a pivotal role in the normalization of nervousness. And it was not only the lay public that was subject to marketing campaigns in which psychological distress was recognized as a commercial opportunity. An advertisement for Berger's paint, for example, published in the *Medical Journal of Australia Advertiser*, appealed to physicians and hospital administrators to recognize the benefits of color therapy. Headlined "Shell Shock Color Cure," it informed readers of experiments undertaken in military hospitals that had revealed therapeutic effects of color in the treatment of neurasthenia.[88]

By the interwar years, the popular construction of nerves was shifting. Less anchored in the physical, nervousness was increasingly framed in psychological terms and, moreover, increasingly presented as a problem of women.[89] From the arrival of nerves to their demise, the affliction could strike men and women, but the emphasis, at least in terms of the public concern and the proffering of solutions, certainly reveals that the trajectory of the discourse of nerves shifted significantly from a problem of male vitality to one of feminine weakness. Albeit finding different expression—for men often sexual inadequacies, for women problems of the emotion—the spectrum of nervous complaints was important not only as an early expression of psychological dysfunction, but also in the making public of "private" issues.

As advertising became increasingly sophisticated and widespread, a larger range of products were marketed for their capacity to soothe emotional and psychological states. Throughout the 1930s and 1940s alcohol was marketed to men in particular for its relaxing properties to assist with the alleviation of stress following a long day at work. Readers of the *Sydney Morning Herald*, for example, were told in 1947 that "Tintara Port 3 times a day, brings restful sleep and spirits gay." Tobacco was also promoted for its beneficial effect on "jumpy" nerves, as were other products, like chewing gum. Wrigley's, for example, claimed in a 1930 advertisement in the *Brisbane Courier* that "the act of chewing soothes and relaxes the whole nervous system." Like medicines and tonics, alcohol, cigarettes, and a range of other products promised to help the weary combatant withstand the pressures of modern life. Increasingly, advertising suggested that such products would not only fortify the physical self—especially the nerves, the blood, and the brain—but also claimed mood-altering properties.

The shift towards a greater concern with the emotional and psychological, however, did not diminish the prevailing belief about nervousness and modern life. Indeed, the link between mental states and exhausted nerves, as Beard had discussed it in the 1880s, was a recurrent theme of popular discourse throughout the first half of the twentieth century. Soothing the nerves and keeping calm continued to be depicted in the popular press as an ongoing challenge of modernity. The widely advertised Sanatogen nerve tonic alerted readers across Australia in the 1940s that "feeling tired, run-down, 'nervy' and depressed" is evidence that the body is "unable to cope with the stress and strain of modern life." In the 1950s, newspaper advertisements for Fishaphos Nerve Tablets claimed that "the modern formula gives prompt and lasting relief from nervous tension and disorders, such as emotional excitement, depression, mental strain, sleeplessness and run-down conditions generally." A decade later the same company was promoting its products in a campaign that promised their tonic could assist in coping with problems of everyday life: "Everyone has worries, anxieties, mental stress and physical strain. However, so long as the nervous system is fortified by the therapeutic properties of Fisher's Phospherine, it's easy to cope with those everyday problems."

The various complaints that could be alleviated with such remedies were, by the middle decades of the twentieth century, increasingly linked not only with psychological wellbeing, but also with enjoyment and happiness. Dr Morse's Indian Root Pills were guaranteed to "make you feel brighter" and Vincent's powders gave one "confidence," while Dr McKenzie's Menthoids promised to "turn a life of failure and depression into one of achievement and happiness." Notions of the futility of suffering in the face of simple, affordable cures for nervousness continued to be promoted by advertisers throughout the 1960s. The marketing campaign for Sanatogen nerve tonic, for example, informed readers that: "It isn't *right* to feel 'nervy' and tense. And it isn't necessary. For with the help of Sanatogen, you can be the happy contented person you once were."

84 The Rise of the Therapeutic Society

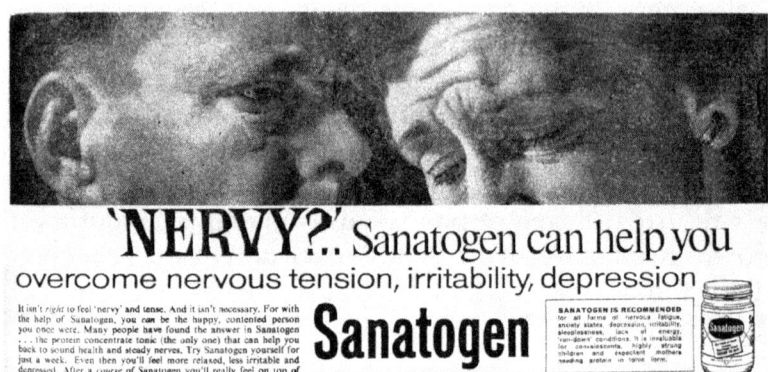

Changing understandings of mental health and wellbeing were reflected in advertising, just as the quest for happiness was increasingly promoted. This advertisement appeared in The Sun-Herald, 16 September 1962.

Popular ideas about nerves were inextricably bound up with the advertising of remedies that promulgated ideas about stress, depression, and mental wellbeing. The marketing of products that promised to fortify the self reinforced the belief that physical health was linked to mental health, and in the process contributed to lay understandings of nervous conditions. Through conceptualizations of nervousness, advertising was a significant carrier of therapeutic culture throughout the first half of the twentieth century. In addition to the ways in which the popularization of nervous disorder destabilized gendered patterns of psychological distress, it helped generate a new public concern with suffering, if one driven largely by commercial interests.

Discourses of nervousness in the late nineteenth and early to mid-twentieth century suggest that the "triumph of the therapeutic" has involved more than the emergence of psychotherapy and the popularization of psychological knowledges, as important as this has been. Before the rapid growth of psychology, and the major advances of psychiatry following the First World War, discourses of nervousness were already fostering therapeutic understandings of the self. Deeply embedded in these processes were changes in the gendered understanding of mental distress. For as men were subject to diagnoses of anxiety and depression in new ways, not only were established views on gender and mental health challenged, but prevailing views about gender more broadly were also disrupted. Medical and popular constructions of nervousness were also instrumental to the cultivation of new cultural and societal expectations about relief from suffering. On the borderlands not only of mind and body, but also of madness and sanity, the terrain of nervousness provided fertile ground for the blossoming of a therapeutic ethos, one that rapidly flourished with the establishment and growth of the discipline of psychology.

3

The Legitimation of Psychological Expertise

To me it seems not only likely, but inevitable, that increasing attention will be paid to mental science. The child, drawn out of himself by the sights and sounds which solicit the senses, acquires a knowledge of surrounding objects and persons before he gains a distinct idea of himself; and so the human mind, enriched by its triumphs in physics, in chemistry, and in biology, must return upon itself, feeling that the circle of its knowledge is incomplete till the secrets of the mind as well as of the material universe have been thoroughly explored.
—Henry Laurie, 1893

In the context of continuing anxiety over social change and increased pressures from modernization, rationalization, and bureaucratization, psychological knowledge secured institutional legitimacy in Australia. In doing so, it laid the foundation for a new understanding of the self, one that cast the individual as knowable and calculable, indeed as comprehensible, through scientific knowledge. Theories of individual differences, in particular, provided a basis upon which populations could be managed within an increasingly complex social milieu. Psychologists promoted their own professional interests, but within broader social developments, especially the expansion of state education systems and massive transformations of commerce and industry. Throughout the first half of the twentieth century, psychological discourse in Australia was largely characterized by an instrumental rationality, and psychologists were not "therapists," as they were later to be popularly perceived, but "technicians of the self" who administered and interpreted psychometric tests.

The scientific discourse of the self that characterized the nascent psychology accorded with the traditional ideal of the rational autonomous subject. Yet it also destabilized it in important ways, as psychological knowledge brought to light problems of selfhood. As a more therapeutic strand of psychological knowledge emerged—in which the self came to be understood more in relational and psychodynamic terms—psychology provided a discursive scaffolding for the articulation of therapeutic concerns. While the cultural diffusion of this more complex articulation of the self during the second half of the twentieth century has been the focus of most theoretical debate, the emergence of a rational-scientific discourse of the self was a critical step in allowing this to develop.

This chapter considers the development and institutionalization of psychology as the professional foundation of the therapeutic society, exploring the ways in which—with support of the state and industry—it became embedded in institutional structures in the public sphere. Just as psychology's conceptualization of the self was compatible with the notion of the liberal subject as rational and controllable, the public sphere was constructed as a domain that could be improved by psychometrics and workplace testing. Through attention to two important institutional sites, those of education and the workplace, the emergence of a psychological discourse of "normality" can be traced, one which had significant consequences for public life. While psychological knowledge was also applied in other domains, notably in the health, criminal justice, and welfare sectors, the rationalized construction of students and workers is of particular interest. Rather than how comparable knowledges of the "sick" or "deviant" were generated and deployed, my analysis reveals how the application of psychological knowledge to "normal" populations in everyday life became embedded in the social and institutional framework of modern Australia.

Yet examining institutional sites in which psychological knowledge and practices developed illuminates more than the processes of legitimation that were at work. For what also comes to light is how new understandings of the individual in turn generated new questions. Both in education and industry, psychology's claim to make the individual knowable through a scientific and instrumental rationality gave way to another modality. While enormous effort was directed towards developing knowledge of self, the rationalizing tendency itself gave rise to a more therapeutic orientation, one that in many ways contradicted its premises. In the face of criticisms that there was an excessive focus on measurement, attention shifted to more complex dimensions of personality and its social context, and to the ways in which psychology could be applied to a broader range of personal problems. In education, new individualized approaches were developed to assist children with special needs, and in the workplace humanistic psychology to some extent challenged principles of scientific management. Shifts in the application of psychological knowledge in the workplace provide a particularly striking example of the way in which reflexivity came to complement technical rationality, as "therapy"—in the broadest sense of the term—was institutionalized from the 1960s.

The application of psychology in education and the workplace was crucial to the spread of psychotherapeutic ideas and practices to normal populations. In tracing these developments, it becomes evident that psychology provided a discursive frame for concerns that were at first largely confined to the public sphere and wedded to an explicitly technical rationality, but later became increasingly therapeutic and oriented to personal life. These developments were made possible by the institutional base of psychology, established during the 1920s, and its professionalizing focus that was to mark the discipline in the years that followed.

From Mental Science to Psychology

In Australia, as in Britain, the discipline of psychology grew out of philosophy. Mental science—as the nascent psychology was termed—was introduced into university departments in the late nineteenth century, and by the turn of the twentieth century the universities of Melbourne, Sydney, and Adelaide had each appointed Chairs in mental philosophy. From the outset, Australian psychology was marked by a scientific approach and a utilitarian ethic; the discipline advanced largely through empirical work, rather than through theoretical developments in understanding the mind and behavior.[1] The enduring influence of British empiricism and American psychology, according to Peter Sheehan, has shaped Australian psychology as "deterministic, quantitative, inductive, relatively mechanistic, and not overly theoretical."[2]

The emphasis on the practical application of psychological knowledge, and the importance attached to the conceiving of psychology as a science, manifested quite early in two important ways. One was the promotion of experimental psychology and psychometrics by the early "philosopher-psychologists." The other was in the alignment of psychology with education. The Australasian Association for the Advancement of Science (AAAS) was a nexus for both these concerns. In 1893, just a few years after its inauguration, the AAAS added Section J, "Mental Science and Education" to its organization, providing "the first public Australian platform of education and psychology."[3] Henry Laurie, Professor of Mental and Moral Philosophy at the University of Melbourne, was appointed President of the chapter, and in his inaugural address noted that education and mental science were "very closely allied."[4]

Despite its association within the academy, the promotion of mental science as distinct from philosophy was critical to the establishment of psychology as a discipline. The marriage of mental science and education helped achieve this, and the AAAS became an important vehicle for the dissemination of psychological knowledge. In his 1893 presidential address, Laurie emphasized this point, arguing that the establishment of Section J affirmed that: "Psychology is now separated from philosophy, and is based, like other natural sciences, on a survey of positive facts." Laurie went on to assert that it is the task of psychology to deal with mental facts, and that those facts—like facts observed in the natural sciences—should be investigated and classified. Of the place of philosophy in the new psychology, Laurie left no doubt about his views, noting that while "the modern psychologist has, doubtless, his philosophical creed ... he acts wisely when he tries to keep the questions of philosophy out of the way.[5]

At the first meeting of Section J, a committee was established to consider how psychophysical and psychometrical investigation might best be progressed.[6] Taking note of the advances psychology had made internationally, committee members sought advice from their colleagues in America and England. Their report, furnished the following year, promoted experimental psychology and defended psychometrics against what was regarded as the "debased meaning which has been attached to this word by some writers.[7] However, they reported with regret that the recommendations made by their esteemed international colleagues—including the establishment of an endowed Chair, a library, and a laboratory—could not be immediately implemented due to the limited infrastructure and resources of the Australasian universities. Still, the promotion of experimental psychology and psychometrics could be furthered through the alliance with education. The report noted that: "It has been the special aim of the committee to devise a scheme of statistical inquiries, of theoretical and practical value, in connection with the State school systems of the Australian colonies."[8]

In the broader social context, psychology's alliance with education coincided with an increasing concern with the scientific management of populations—especially children.[9] In the first decades of the twentieth century, school medical services were established, new importance was accorded to both physical and mental measurement, and theories of child development became orthodoxy in both the health and education sectors. During this period the child became an object of scientific study and assessments of "mental fitness" were routinely made.[10] Child Study Associations were established and universities began teaching child study in mental philosophy courses.[11]

It took some time, however, for academic psychology to fully establish itself in Australian universities. In the 1920s, psychology began to secure disciplinary independence as it became progressively separated from philosophy, and increasingly influenced by the needs of the medical profession and the education sector. Applied psychology developed steadily during the 1930s and 1940s, but it was not until the postwar period that psychology attained the legitimacy of a core academic discipline in Australia.[12] The seemingly slow development of academic psychology to some extent belies its influence during these formative years, for psychological ideas were also fermenting in other disciplines. Alison Turtle notes that during the interwar years, it was common "for the same author to publish in two or more categories of the psychological, philosophical, political, educational, economic, medical, and anthropological literature."[13] Even as early as the 1880s, the prominent physician John Springthorpe, for example, had published scholarly articles that drew on psychological theory, and through the first decades of the twentieth century he continued to strongly advocate the value of psychology for medical practice.[14]

Despite achieving greater academic independence, limited infrastructure meant that psychology remained in what might be termed a marriage of convenience with philosophy throughout the interwar years. Though the alliance was never an easy one, it provided a platform for the dissemination of psychological research beyond the AAAS congresses, as well as opportunities for collegial fellowship. The formation of a professional association and the subsequent publication of the first psychology journal in Australia is testament to the efficacy of this alliance. The Australasian Association of Psychology and Philosophy (AAPP) was formed in 1923 and remained the primary professional association for psychologists until the formation in 1944 of the Overseas Branch of the British Psychological Society (BPS). The editorial introduction to the inaugural *Australasian Journal of Psychology and Philosophy* (*AJPP*) made clear the difficulty of such an alliance, but also recognized its niche at a time in which psychology was still embryonic:

> In England and America, the technical and the humanistic or universal interests are represented by many different types of scientific and philosophical Journals. In Australia and New Zealand, until specialisation shall have increased with greater differentiation of studies, and until increase in population shall have brought with it a greater body of cultured opinion, interested in things of the spirit, one Journal must attempt the double task. In doing so, it runs, as we have said, a double risk. It may be too general to satisfy the few. It may be too technical to interest the many. But unless it undertook the twofold task, it would not survive the year.[15]

The diversity of subjects covered by *AJPP* articles included an eclectic mix of philosophical and psychological inquiries. During the 1920s the influence of Freud is evident in the numerous articles on psychoanalysis, but for the two decades that psychologists were part of the organization, the focus ranged from psychometrics, individual differences, and mental development, to industrial psychology and education. Though the interests of psychologists were increasingly diverse, it was not until the post-WWII period that academic psychology was to expand significantly, directly driven by the momentum of the war. University enrollments under the Commonwealth Reconstruction Training Scheme (CRTS) saw a large number of ex-servicemen enroll in psychology courses. The popularity of psychology as a subject of choice was regarded, at least by some, as a result of exposure to psychological science during military service. Donald McElwain, based at the University of Melbourne in the late 1940s and early 1950s, noted that: "Virtually all full-time CRTS trainees had been psychologically examined, and so had been acquainted, in however small a measure, with psychological practice."[16]

By the late 1950s, prominent psychologists were declaring that academic psychology in Australia had "come of age."[17] Tremendous growth occurred within the context of the popularization of the new social sciences, Commonwealth funding of Australian universities, and the increase in demand for tertiary education generally. Student enrollments in psychology more than trebled in the period of the mid-1940s to the mid-1960s at the University of Sydney. This pattern was replicated in psychology departments across Australian universities, creating, as Simon Cooke has noted, both a demand for academic psychologists and a growing number of psychology graduates.[18] With newly available Commonwealth Government funding, psychological research also increased.[19] Within this context, doctoral level study became available and in some universities psychology moved into science departments, imbuing it with greater scientific status and academic legitimacy.

The postwar growth in academic appointments accelerated during the 1960s to such an extent that between 1960 and 1965 the number of academic psychologists in Australia almost doubled.[20] By the 1970s sixteen of the eighteen universities were teaching psychology courses.[21] The pattern of growth within the academy has steadily continued, buoyed not only by demand for psychology majors, but equally by the inclusion of psychology as an ancillary subject in a range of tertiary courses.[22] The latter, in particular, propelled further the reach of the discipline so that psychological knowledge has increasingly been disseminated to students in the female-dominated fields of primary health care, counseling, social work, teaching, and child-care. Most significantly, though, it also has reached the more masculine domains of the commercial world through human resource management, economics, and business. The great expansion of psychology during the postwar years reflected not only new opportunities in a rapidly changing society, but also an extremely effective project of professionalization.

The Making of a Profession

The professionalization of psychological workers occurred within the broader context of the rise of the professions in Western societies during the second half of the twentieth century, and for a number of occupational groups, a concomitant securing of increasing levels of occupational control.[23] While psychologists had enjoyed the benefits of professional association since the early 1920s, the Australasian Association of Psychology and Philosophy was an alliance that reflected psychology's past, rather than its future. The formation of the Overseas Branch of the British Psychological Society (BPS) in 1944, however, marked the beginning of a new era.[24] The establishment of an Australian Branch provided a platform from which psychology could mobilize its occupational power and professional interests. Within five years, psychology had established an important degree of control over disciplinary and professional knowledge with the launch of the first dedicated psychological periodical in Australia, the *Australian Journal of Psychology*.

By 1966, the Overseas Branch had become the Australian Psychological Society (APS), and a second journal, *Australian Psychologist*, was also in production. The desire for professional identity had gained some strength during the interwar years, but it was state control over the labor force during the Second World War—under the auspices of the Directorate of Manpower—that provided the catalyst for stronger moves towards professionalization. During the war, psychologists were recruited from the field of industrial psychology, primarily to assist with the administration of psychometric tests for selection and placement. As the war proceeded, the need for intelligence and other psychological tests diminished and experts adept at dealing with neurosis and psychosis were in greater demand. The Second World War thus provided a vehicle for the expansion of psychological principles and techniques, offering a harbinger of later developments—as the preoccupation with measurement yielded to more therapeutic strategies for dealing with an ever broadening range of social and personal problems.

However, while a therapeutic orientation characterized some strands of psychological work from the outset, professional status was largely secured through scientific inquiry far removed from the clinic. In 1943, the Directorate of Manpower convened several advisory committees to survey the numbers of scientists available to assist with the war effort. Appeals were made through the media and professional associations, calling for particular occupational groups to register with the Directorate—among them, engineers, chemists, pharmacists, and psychologists.[25] The inclusion of psychologists as a key occupational group to assist the state during wartime is evidence of the extent to which, by the 1940s, psychology had already secured significant legitimacy. The fact that the British military had also decided to procure the assistance of industrial psychologists was clearly also a factor.[26] All people with two or more years of training in psychology and undertaking "psychological work" were required to make themselves known to the Directorate. A surprisingly large number of registrations resulted—almost 1,500—although only around 150 satisfied the training and occupational criteria deemed adequate.[27]

From the point of view of professional status, the results of the Manpower survey caused some professional alarm, insofar as there were large numbers of people practicing as "psychologists" or working in the psychological workforce who had at most very limited formal training. The need for a greater degree of professional organization was thus apparent to those with a vested interest in the regulation of psychology. According to Bill O'Neil, one of the men involved in setting up the Overseas Branch of the BPS, what they wanted was "an association confined to technically qualified psychologists committed to observational methods."[28] According to his recollection of events: "Proponents wanted an association of psychologists with a basic qualification in terms of knowledge and skills which would confer some professional status, and which would enable Australian psychologists through periodical national and regional meetings, and perhaps even a journal, to exchange technical knowledge, observational findings and conclusions based on them."[29] What they possibly also wanted was an association reflecting the gender hierarchy already well established within psychology. For despite the high number of qualified female psychologists—more than fifty percent according to the Manpower survey—no women were present at the meeting that set in motion the formation of the Australian Branch.[30]

Women did soon assume a significant organizational presence—at least in terms of numbers if not power—and by 1965 comprised almost one third of the membership base.[31] Nevertheless, the Society remained male dominated. During the period of its affiliation with the BPS, only one of the twenty-one Chairpersons was female. Since the gaining of independence with the formation of the APS in 1966, only four of the 36 presidents have to date been women.[32] In terms of membership, the Association has never reflected the gender distribution of psychology graduates. As Cooke notes, even by the mid-1990s when three quarters of graduates were women, the female membership base of the APS remained at only 58 percent.[33]

The historical association of women with the less occupationally powerful social welfare sector may explain the incongruity, at least in the early years. The early female psychologists were primarily located in the area of child welfare, with no women appointed to full-time university lectureships until after the Second World War. As Turtle explains, the predominance of women in this field "was part of the general pattern in the emergence of the 'helping professions' with their programmes of intervention in family life. Continuing with their research into new techniques of mental measurement for the youthful population at large, the male academics left it for the most part to women to concern themselves with the application of these techniques to the retarded child population."[34] Not surprisingly, the professionalization of psychology was not advanced through child welfare work, but rather was driven predominantly by men in academia.[35]

A key measure of the success of the professional project has been its capacity to secure regulation over psychological work. From the early 1940s, psychologists sought to safeguard their interests—and those of the public—through demands for state registration.[36] Legislation limiting the practice of psychology and the use of the term psychologist was first enacted in Victoria in 1965, and similar laws were progressively passed in all states and territories of Australia. State regulation marks psychology's distinction from its kindred occupations of social work, counseling, and psychotherapy. Importantly, registration not only confers status and rights for psychologists, but it also entails responsibilities. The conduct of psychologists is subject to intense scrutiny, with such controls functioning at least in part to ensure that they take seriously the welfare of those to whom they have a duty of care.

While securing control over professional practice constituted one of psychology's most important strategies, another has involved a seemingly contrary process: the broad diffusion of psychological knowledge. The considerable influence psychology came to assert during the twentieth century resulted not from the restrictions enforced by regulation—although this clearly increases the esteem of the discipline and the profession—but rather as a result of the ways in which it became a complement to other professional knowledges and practices, in education, health care, social welfare, and in the workplace. As Nikolas Rose wryly put it: "Unlike many other professionals, psychologists in general and psychotherapists in particular, are incredibly generous. They give their knowledge away, they give their language away, they give their techniques away."[37]

Equally important, though, the production of psychological knowledge has itself been shaped by psychology's colonization of key social institutions, for example in education and in the workplace. Developments in these domains not only illustrate how psychology came to be regarded as useful in different institutional contexts, it sheds light on the complexity of the therapeutic society and the critical role psychology has played in its evolution.

The institutionalization of psychological knowledge both in education and in the workplace involved processes whereby forms of technical rationality ironically gave rise to the emergence of a therapeutic outlook. Importantly, psychologists' concern with their own occupational growth and the securing of legitimacy has gone hand in hand with the "giving away" of their knowledge, language, and techniques. It was the promotion of psychology as a science and the capacity to embed itself in important institutions that signaled its success, with education involving the earliest and most significant development of psychological-based knowledge under the auspices of the state.

Education & Applied Psychology

As the early philosopher-psychologists predicted, experimental psychology and psychometrics proved the key to psychology's future, and in no area more so than education. The late nineteenth and early twentieth century demands of modernizing Australia again provided the genesis of these developments. During this period, a shifting understanding of the individual intersected with national, and racially-inflected, concerns about industrial and civic progress and the need for the expansion of state-provided education. By the late nineteenth century, it was widely recognized that the educational system of the time was inadequate for the needs of a modern industrial society, the kind of society Australia imagined itself to be.[38]

Criticisms of state education culminated in Victoria, for example, with a Royal Commission into Technical Education (1899-1901). While the brief of the Commission was to inquire into the deficiencies of the technical sector, David McCallum notes that it also revealed the gross inadequacies of state schooling generally and "became a sounding board for information about developments in post-primary education abroad."[39] What followed was the slow but steady expansion of state-provided post-primary schooling. The growth of secondary education—which was to gain real momentum following the Second World War—was driven by changing social and economic imperatives, not the least being the demand for an increasingly skilled and educated workforce. Psychological theory played an important role in this development. As McCallum observes: "The move of the state into secondary education in Australia was accompanied by an important shift in the direction of educational theory, away from a more generalized philosophy of education which had characterized the study of pedagogy in the

The Legitimation of Psychological Expertise 99

nineteenth century, and towards a concern with individual differences and the question of 'fitness' for secondary education."[40]

Especially during psychology's early years of expansion in the 1920s and 1930s, the cross-fertilization of educational philosophy and applied psychology shaped the direction of both. With its concern with the individual child, the New Education movement played an important role in the expansion of experimental psychology.[41] There was, however, skepticism from some progressive educationalists about the extent to which psychological principles should be embraced. In 1909, for example, the Director of Education in New South Wales, Peter Board, called for a broad educational system that prepared the individual for the complex demands of modern life, but cautioned educators and bureaucrats about the degree to which this should be underwritten by psychological knowledge. In his view: "Education work that is controlled entirely by the principles of educational psychology is individualistic and leaves out account of the community."[42]

Nevertheless, despite some debate over the degree to which it should inform educational theory and practice, the conceptual and institutional foothold of psychology had been firmly established. That the first experimental psychology laboratory was set up at the Melbourne Teachers' College in 1903—long before observational or experimental psychology gained traction in universities—reveals the extent to which educationalists were instrumental in promoting the emerging psychological science. As O'Neil notes, the use of psychology in the classroom was recognized as one of the first sites to which psychological knowledge could be usefully applied. The value to educators of understanding the mechanisms of learning, motivation and adjustment, thinking and memory, as well as the principles of individual differences, was readily apparent.[43] But the early psychologists also recognized the important part that educators themselves could play in the development of knowledge about the individual child. As early as 1893 Henry Laurie acknowledged the benefits of a symbiotic development of mental science and a more scientific approach to education:

> A science which proposes to throw light on mental facts, and which includes, therefore, the consideration of atten-

tion, habit, memory, imagination, reasoning, and the emotions and desires, has an intimate bearing on the question of the best methods of educing the powers and capacities of the human mind; and the teacher who from month to month and year to year has had ample opportunities of watching the development of the young, or of imparting special knowledge, may in turn contribute important facts and generalizations to psychology.[44]

While these ideas were already in circulation, the use of intelligence tests in state education systems during the first decade of the twentieth century constituted the first major step in the application of psychological knowledge—and thus to the institutionalization of psychology in Australia. While a variety of interests came under the joint purview of education and psychology, it was the mental testing of children—buttressed by theories of individual differences—that was the most significant. The use of intelligence tests in Australia followed quickly the publication of Binet's first scale of intelligence in France in 1905, and by 1913, an Australian modification of Binet's revised 1911 scale was in use.[45] With the spread of very limited state-provided secondary education during the interwar years, psychological assessments offered a rational-scientific means of selection.[46]

During the 1920s and 1930s the alliance of psychology and education was further advanced with the establishment of school psychology services. The appointment of psychologists in state education departments not only enabled the expansion of mental testing, it provided teachers and school principals with a new avenue of referral for suspected "subnormal" and "problem" children. Accordingly, the work of early educational psychologists was largely concerned with the classification and placement of children, primarily those identified as "different" but also, though less frequently, children deemed to be delinquent or of extremely high intelligence.[47] Mental testing found widespread support amongst educationalists and many endorsed the value of expanding the practice beyond the elementary level. As John Smyth, Professor of Education at the University of Melbourne, observed in 1926, intelligence tests "are now used to separate sub-normal and normal children, and to determine whether a boy or girl of average or super-average intelligence is placed in the right class in school. The question at once arises: Cannot similar tests be applied in the selection of pupils for a secondary school course, and further in the selection of students for Colleges and Universities."[48]

According to Turtle, the First World War interrupted what might have otherwise been "an explosion of mental testing activities."[49] Nevertheless, calls for its expansion reflected the degree to which the movement—particularly strong in the United States—was influencing Australian practices. In the broader context of educational expansion, and anxieties about "mental hygiene," the interwar years saw the extension of mental testing to so-called normal children. As Kerreen Reiger's analysis reveals, this marked a significant shift from a concern with abnormality and mental deficiency to an interest in normal psychological development.[50]

In 1930, mental testing secured significant and enduring institutional support with the establishment of the Australian Council for Educational Research (ACER).[51] Founded with the aid of a bequest from the Carnegie Corporation of New York, ACER cemented the alliance between psychology and education by bringing together theoreticians and practitioners within the organization. The production of Australian psychometric tests was central to the Council's work, and ACER developed test instruments for use in schools and in vocational guidance, and later, tests for use in the military and among civilian adult populations.

Throughout much of the Second World War, the Council's work centered on war related activities, predominantly, the devising of psychological tests. Its founding director, K.S. Cunningham, promoted ACER's expertise by writing directly to the Prime Minister. For Cunningham, the use psychological expertise—particularly psychometric testing—constituted a critical strategy in minimizing the "number of misfits and wasted effort" that could be avoided if "appropriate tests and properly trained psychologists" were employed for the war effort.[52] While his offer of expertise was not initially taken up, ACER eventually became the main test constructor for the army, providing 150,000 copies of its tests in the period 1944-1945 alone. During these final years of the war, the regular educational activities of the organization were suspended as the full complement of ACER's psychological workforce was applied to the "selection and allocation of manpower."⁵³ The focus on testing during the war strengthened ACER's activities in this area and in 1945 a separate test division was established to formalize what had been perhaps the most important function of the organization since its inception. According to O'Neil, the establishment of the test division, which was responsible for the production, adaptation, and administration of psychological tests was "of great importance to the post-war burgeoning teaching programmes and services activities in clinical, counselling and vocational psychology."⁵⁴

While the development of test instruments continued to constitute a major part of the work of ACER, by the 1950s there was growing criticism of psychometrics on the grounds that such tests "were too limited and failed to cope with accelerating social and technological change."⁵⁵ The whole-child approach had brought to light—for both psychologists and educationists—the many limitations of intelligence quotients and psychometric measurement, and by the 1960s, psychologists themselves were increasingly questioning the validity of applying normative data to individual children.⁵⁶

The rationale which had provided the basis for psychometrics since the early decades of the century—the selection and streaming of children for post-primary schooling—had also passed into obsolescence to some extent by this time, with mass secondary education curtailing the need for mental testing as a basis for classification. There were also concerns about the misuse of tests and questions about value of testing more broadly, concerns which intensified during the 1960s and 1970s.⁵⁷ Such qualms reflected international debate, in terms of concern about test validity, the sorts of assumptions of normality that underpinned testing, and disquiet about gender and cultural biases.⁵⁸ At the popular level too, intelligence testing met with resistance and skepticism from a public that was becoming increasingly knowledgeable about psychology. Although measurements of IQ remained a significant area for educational psychologists, by the late 1950s, testing increasingly came to be used as a basis upon which individual differences could be identified for the purpose of providing remedial support to students.⁵⁹

McCallum argues that it was through the adoption of theories of individual differences by educationalists that psychology had its most significant and enduring institutional impact. In his analysis, it was the application of these theories—applied to children by teachers in the classroom—that underpinned the development in Australia of "a differentiated and socially hierarchical secondary education system."[60] The capacity to measure intelligence legitimized theories of individual differences and significant consequences followed from the application of those theories to both "normal" and "sub-normal" children. For the "normal" but disadvantaged, McCallum argues that psychological theory legitimated and reinforced differences in educational outcomes stemming from the disadvantages of social class. According to his analysis, new forms of classification made possible new forms of discrimination.

Yet the stress on psychology's role in the creation of ever expanding categories of debility obscures the complexity of these processes, and indeed the ways in which such categories have also worked in the interests of disadvantaged children. The recollections of former Principal Psychologist and Guidance Officer in Victoria, John Hall, suggest a more complex reading, particularly for children identified as having "special needs." In his view, the acceptance by educators of the concept of individual differences resulted in a shift in which "children who didn't cope began to be seen as different rather than perverse."[61] The major consequence of this shift was the development of educational alternatives; first special schools and classes for children identified as different, and later, with separate education facilities falling out of favor, a range of educational support services for children in integrated classrooms.

According to Hall, the role of the school psychologist also underwent a marked transformation between the 1950s and the 1970s, from that of "mental tester of children who did not meet the school's intellectual or behavioural demands" to assisting teachers "assume real and continuing responsibility for the rehabilitation of troubled children within their own school setting."[62] As with the blurring of the boundaries between "madness" and "sanity" discussed in the previous chapter, in the move away from conceptualizations of perversion, psychological constructions of difference paved the way for the introduction of a range of student support services and therapeutic interventions. While the imperative of managing so-called difficult students may have been a factor, so too was a genuine concern with finding ways of assisting young people who had problems or were experiencing educational disadvantage.

An important development in this area was the introduction of clinical services for children both within and outside of the state schooling system. While psychologists had been employed in education departments since the 1920s, and many had undertaken clinical work, a new institution emerged in the 1930s: the child guidance clinic. Staffed by multidisciplinary clinical teams comprising psychiatrist, psychologist, and social worker, these clinics provided treatment for emotional, psychological, and behavioral problems in their early stages. In Sydney, child guidance clinics were established under the auspices of the New South Wales school medical service. They were also set up in a number of cities across Australia in connection with hospitals and children's courts.

Based on a model of preventative psychiatry, the establishment of child guidance clinics constituted part of a broader preventative mental health strategy in which clinical intervention was applied in order to circumvent social and psychological maladjustment. The duties of a psychologist appointed to such clinics generally involved the administration of an intelligence test, while the psychiatrist would interview and examine the child.[63] These clinics provided an early model for the provision of clinical services more generally, for, as David Ivison notes, it was in child guidance clinics that "many, if not most, of the pioneering clinical psychologists got their start."[64]

The appointment of psychologists in education departments in the 1920s, and the establishment of child guidance clinics and educational and vocational guidance services soon after, both shaped psychology's professional project and broadened its cultural impact. Although a dominant technical rationality governed psychological practice in education through mental testing, it is important to note that an alternative psychological discourse also existed. In child guidance clinics, a range of approaches shaped the management of the so-called difficult or problem child. And even before psychometrics fell out of favor, other schools of psychological thought also shaped educational thought.

During the 1920s, Freudian theory had some impact. In 1923, for example, when the Principal of the Teachers' Training College of Hobart, J.A. Johnson delivered his Presidential address to Section J at the annual AAAS meeting, he extolled the virtues of psychology for its capacity to offer insights into the working of both the conscious and unconscious mind. He saw this as essential to meeting the massive demands of a compulsory, secular system of state education, one in which "the masters are the masses, and the problems of education are concerned with the base rather than the pinnacle of society."[65] However, this more egalitarian vision remained in contrast to the dominant psychological knowledge, with its hierarchies based on the educational testing of individual capacities.

Nevertheless, theories of individual differences and indeed mental testing had contradictory consequences. For while they emerged from within a conceptual framework of technical rationality, the result was a new recognition of difference that gave rise to therapeutic responses to personal problems and individual "deficiencies." These contradictions between the rationalizing and humanizing dimensions of psychology—or testing and counseling—came into sharper relief in the context of the rise of mass secondary schooling by the 1960s. During this time too, with the popularization of humanistic psychology, emphasis on emotional and relational dimensions—rather than simply the measurement of intelligence—gained greater impetus. This trend also took an institutional form somewhat earlier, with the development of counseling within the framework of educational and vocational guidance.

Educational & Vocational Guidance

Changes in the economic sphere and the limited availability of state-provided secondary education during the interwar years set the context for the introduction of educational and vocational guidance. A number of factors, including concerns about national efficiency, the growing prominence of psychology, and the influence of international educational practices, drove the establishment of guidance services in and outside of the state schooling system. More mobile populations and diminished communal ties to local employers provided other precipitating factors. In attempts to rationalize processes for the classification and placement of young people, both in secondary schooling and in work, forms of educational and vocational guidance were institutionalized.

The wider context for these developments involved a new national importance accorded to the educational enterprise and a shift in educational philosophy to a focus on the individual child. According to G.R. Giles, Victoria's Vocational Guidance Officer in the early 1930s: "The post-war period in the Commonwealth has witnessed an increase in the realisation of the national responsibility for the future citizens of this great island continent. In no direction has the change been more marked than in the consideration of educational matters. Schools once 'certificate-centred' are now 'child-centred.'"[66] Giles could well have described the new child-centered model as classification-centered, given the overarching aim of matching the right boys and girls with the right jobs.

Educational success, it was believed, depended upon the placement of young people into appropriate educational settings as preparation for their future working lives. The successful classification of children was thus the lynchpin of the differentiated educational system that existed in Australia prior to the advent of mass secondary schooling, and it was in this context that psychological knowledge was primarily utilized. Theories of individual differences provided the rationale, and psychometrics the means, of determining differential levels of ability and aptitude.[67] Both in determinations of educational placement and in formalizing vocational guidance, psychological approaches were enthusiastically embraced.

In his Presidential Address to Section J of the AAAS Congress in 1924, the Superintendent of New South Wales Technical Education, James Nangle, devoted much of his presentation to delineating the techniques he had devised to assist in ascertaining the most suitable vocational choice for boys entering trades. While he defended his established approach with evidence of a large number of successful cases, it was nevertheless his view that the future of vocational guidance lay in the adoption of a scientific method underpinned by psychological theory. As he said: "During recent years the problem of reducing to a scientific basis the matter of testing for vocational aptitude has had attention in many parts of the world. Necessarily, it has been approached largely from the psychological point of view."[68]

As Nangle's account illustrates, guidance in many ways represented the formalization and evolution of longstanding practices of teachers and others offering assistance, advice, and counsel to young people in relation to their academic life and future careers. Australian educators were anxious to emulate the best British and American models, and guidance was seen as an important part of that aim. A number of men who held prominent positions in Australian education traveled abroad in the 1920s and 1930s to come back enthused, primarily by vocational guidance, but also educational and psychological guidance. Vocational guidance promised to be an effective means of steering young people towards suitable careers, and educational guidance an efficient and effective way of managing post-primary selection and placement.

Not surprisingly, there was significant support from those involved in technical education. Nangle, for example, strongly advocated the value of formalized vocational guidance, arguing that "it is impossible for any citizen to be either happy or efficient if forced to live a life of work in a calling for which he is fitted neither by taste nor aptitude."[69] Nangle was particularly concerned about the drift of boys leaving school at age fourteen and finding themselves unemployed soon after. A similar position was advanced by the New South Wales Minister for Education, Thomas Mutch. Like Nangle, he regarded the work of vocational guidance as a preventative measure against a problem which he noted had become all too apparent—the drifting of boys into dead-end occupations. It was his view that the establishment of a bureau to place the boys passing through Junior Technical Schools into apprenticeships was a step in the right direction, but he wanted this idea developed further so that all children finishing school could be assisted to become self-supporting and self-reliant citizens. To this end, he committed £2,000 for the establishment of a vocational guidance bureau within the Education Department of New South Wales.[70]

The bureau commenced operation on a limited basis in 1926. That this occurred in New South Wales is not surprising given psychologists in that State already had a relatively strong occupational presence. Certainly, they had significant influence within the Education Department, as it was in New South Wales that the most explicitly psychological approach to vocational guidance was taken. Initially, the bureau was primarily concerned with placement, but with the appointment of a psychologist in 1928 its work became directed more towards mental testing and increasingly psychological approaches to analyzing skills and aptitudes were utilized.

By the 1930s most states, at least to some degree, had formalized educational and vocational guidance services. Though using varying approaches, the guiding imperative differed little across the country. It was the successful placement of the child into a suitable vocation that marked, as Giles put it in 1932, "the climax of the education drama."[71] The commonalities and divergences, however, indicate the various ways in which the rational view of the self was being articulated by education departments of the time.

In New South Wales, the system entailed a comprehensive analysis of the child, informed by progress reports from school teachers, a series of psychological tests, and the counseling of the child. Counseling in this context largely consisted of advice and guidance based on demonstrated intelligence and aptitude. But it was not uncommon that in the course of such interviews personal problems would come to light. At the Australian Institute of Industrial Psychology (AIIP) in Sydney, which also provided vocational guidance to secondary school pupils, this aspect of service delivery was referred to as the "worry clinic."[72] A psychologist counseled young people with minor personal problems considered an impediment to vocational success, while those with apparently serious problems were referred to a psychiatrist.

The analysis presented by Giles on the state of vocational guidance in the early 1930s reveals, though, a varying degree of acceptance of the extent to which psychology could inform educational and vocational services. In presenting the Victorian case, he contrasted that State's more "holistic" approach to the provision of services:

> Vocational guidance in Victoria is regarded from a wider point of view than that which presupposes the application of a battery of psychological tests or the arrangement of a series of interviews as the main planks in the platform of the movement. It is considered that helping boys and girls to make the best use of the school facilities so that they may be fully equipped to make their contribution to society is an integral part of the scheme. Individual vocational service

based on an appreciation of the privileges and responsibilities of citizenship in a democratic community epitomises the philosophy of the movement.⁷³

The first part of the Victorian scheme was to establish the most appropriate avenue of education for the individual. Depending on aptitude and ability, young people were streamed in academic courses, or directed towards pre-vocational education that would prepare them for professional or commercial occupations on the one hand, or towards technical education tailored to rural and industrial callings on the other. For girls, there were also avenues for careers in home management. Directions in other states in the establishment of such services reflected varying interests. South Australia, for example, not only recognized the importance of scholastic and psychological inclination but accorded greater significance to moral and social aspects. Queensland at the time was engaged in measuring the effectiveness of a medical model that emphasized physical and psychological examinations.⁷⁴

Though educational and vocational guidance services expanded during the 1930s and 1940s, this did not occur without resistance, either from the public or from those working in education. In 1937, one principal in New South Wales remarked to the press that "intelligence tests at school are of little value" and vocational guidance is "an anaesthetic to lull the people into thinking that something was being done for the unemployed youth."⁷⁵ There was also opposition from some teachers' unions, partly on the basis of concerns about teacher workload, but also from a more philosophical standpoint about the purposes of schooling. In 1930, for example, members of the Victorian Teachers' Union argued that vocational guidance and placement was not an issue that schools should be concerned with. They rejected the idea that the primary purpose of schooling was preparation for work, and instead argued for the importance of teaching young people how to spend their leisure hours wisely. As J.H. Dewsnap forcefully argued: "Attention should be given to the question of sending boys from the primary schools to schools where they would receive a cultural training to prepare them against industry and not for industry.⁷⁶

The guidance officer also met with resistance from the public, especially when utilizing psychological techniques. According to Bill O'Neil, a general suspicion of psychology at times made difficult the task of the guidance officer in trying to counsel a young person about "his" future. It was his view that: "As psychology is unfortunately associated in the public mind with various mystic cults and fortune-telling procedures, there is a tendency for many persons to yield a minimum of information about themselves. They take it that the business of the counsellor is to tell them all about themselves."[77] Nevertheless, despite some resistance, educational counseling and vocational guidance became increasingly important to the educational landscape. The growth of these fields was also critical to the development of applied psychology more broadly, employing the bulk of practicing psychologists up to the 1950s.[78]

By the postwar years, the growth of psychology in education reflected not only a degree of faith in vocational and educational guidance, but also a greater concern with emotional and behavioral problems in children. The expansion of school psychology services in turn brought increasing numbers of children into contact with psychologists and guidance officers. By the late 1950s, the Assistant to the Director-General of Education in New South Wales noted that the School Counseling Service in his State, "instituted originally as a means of giving guidance at the transitional stage, and of preparing for vocational guidance has become a service of general practitioners in educational, vocational and all kinds of psychological guidance."[79]

Psychological measurement, predicated on theories of individual differences, had brought to light a range of emotional, psychological, and behavioral problems that in turn demanded a new focus of attention to individual need. One consequence of this development was that the needs of children with intellectual and physical disabilities came to be recognized in new ways. Rather than assigning these children to institutional care settings that were essentially minding places, educational psychologists began providing remedial assistance with the aim of fostering greater social participation and "self-dependence."[80] From its genesis in a scientific model of the self underpinned by test-based diagnostics, throughout the middle decades of the twentieth century guidance services gradually moved towards a more therapeutic orientation as attention to individual differences brought to light not only differing aptitudes and abilities, but also personal and emotional difficulties. [81]

The diminishing focus on psychometrics, however, did not lead to reduced state support of educational psychology. On the contrary, psychology experienced tremendous growth from the 1960s onwards. Indeed throughout the 1970s, the public education system remained "one of the largest fields of psychological practice in Australia."[82] During the last decades of the twentieth century, state support of psychology strengthened. In 1948, there were approximately 40 psychologists working in education services in Australia; by 2007, the number exceeded 2,000.[83] Psychology thus remains deeply embedded in the bureaucracy of the state.

The role of psychology in schools illuminates broader trends in the development of a therapeutic ethos. As the case of psychometrics and guidance reveals, the application of psychological knowledge has brought about contradictory consequences. On the one hand, as McCallum argues, it was drawn upon to legitimize differences in educational outcome along class lines. However, theories of individual differences and psychometrics also threw light on scholastic difficulties, personal problems, and experiences of suffering to which psychologists and others sought to respond. Similar tensions and contradictions are evident elsewhere. As in educational settings, the application of psychology in industry grew out of a technical rationality but shifted in the second half of the twentieth century as therapeutic strategies were increasingly embraced.

Psychology at Work

New knowledge of the individual promulgated during the early twentieth century found similar expression in the modern workplace as it did in education. While the imperatives of modernization traversed disparate domains—from the family and sexuality to education, health, and welfare—it was in business and industry that the quest for efficiency was most strikingly manifest. In the context of industrial expansion during the interwar years, the prosperity of the postwar period, and concomitant changing economic conditions, psychological knowledge was drawn upon in attempts to rationalize the management of labor.

Psychology was applied to industry in the belief that human factors, like others in the production process, must be subject to scientific calculation in order to maximize efficiency. The capacity to measure and classify aptitude and ability was critical to the development of industrial psychology, which itself formed part of a broader approach to modernizing the workplace. Frederick Taylor's theory of scientific management provided an important conceptual foundation.[84] Indeed, Taylorism was central to the cultural and organizational shifts of the early twentieth century in which production—and workers—became subject to imperatives of efficiency. Incentive payments, like time and motion studies, typified the new approach to organizing labor, one whose raison d'être was to increase productivity.[85] Rationalizing the human element, however, was a complex task that required specialist knowledge. The emerging field of industrial psychology provided the necessary expertise, and thus played an important part in putting the efficiency movement into practice.[86]

The complexities, and for that matter critiques, of Taylorism are less important for this discussion than the context in which scientific management emerged, and the role of psychology in that process. As Nikolas Rose has argued, Taylorism was not simply a functional outcome of capitalism: "Rather, it was part of a wider family of political programmes that sought to use scientific knowledge to advance national efficiency through making the most productive use of material and human resources ... Taylorism was also part of a new attention to individual differences among persons, seeking to know them and managing them from the perspective of social and institutional goals and objectives."[87]

As with similar imperatives shaping education, the emerging science of psychology proved a useful complement to scientific management and psychologists were, as Kevin Blackburn has noted, "quick to follow Taylor's lead." As he agues: "By incorporating scientific management methods into industrial psychology, its early practitioners advanced the profession's value to industry, and thus increased their own status and power."[88] A key component of psychology's appeal was that it promised benefits to both the organization and the worker; not only would improvements in efficiency yield greater profits for business, but industrial fatigue would decrease, job satisfaction would rise, and ultimately higher wages would follow as a result of increased production. Not surprisingly, as psychology embraced principles of scientific management, something of a symbiotic relationship resulted. Psychological knowledge began shaping industrial practices, and in turn, industrial imperatives began to influence the development of certain strands of psychological knowledge.

The work of Bernard Muscio illustrates these interconnections, as well as the international influences that not only came to bear on Australian psychology, but also those that were exerted by Australian psychologists. Holding a position in the Philosophy Department at the University of Sydney, Muscio delivered a series of lectures on industrial psychology during 1916 and 1917, in which he argued that the placement of workers in jobs for which they were best suited benefited the organization, the individual, and indeed society at large.[89] The publication of these lectures and Muscio's subsequent appointment to the Industrial Fatigue Board in London played a pivotal role in the establishment of industrial psychology in Britain.[90] Elton Mayo was another Australian who gained international acclaim in the area of industrial psychology. At the Harvard Business School in the late 1920s, Mayo began pioneering research on the "human factors" in industry. Extending the study of scientific management into the area of "human relations," his work on the importance of job satisfaction to productivity became widely influential.[91]

There were a number of other areas in which psychology proved useful to business and industry. By the 1920s, intelligence tests were being used for the purposes of staff selection in some organizations, but commercial interests also came to encompass concerns about the health and safety of workers. Industrial hygiene, as it was then known, came under the purview of the medical fraternity, which was charged with a duty of care that at times put doctors in conflict with both management and psychologists.[92] During the 1920s, editorials appearing in the *Medical Journal of Australia* endorsed the establishment of so-called industrial clinics and the appointment of medical officers. Yet they stressed that it was specialized medical knowledge rather than psychological knowledge, that was of utmost importance to the health and welfare of workers.

An editorial in 1924, for example, declared that the psychologist was suitable only as a technician of psychometrics, whereas the medical industrial hygienist had the capacity to understand the complex interplay of physical and mental factors—including recognition of "nervous instability" and the capacity to "gauge the effect of a continuous series of events on the mind." The so-called lay psychologist, on the other hand, was "without any knowledge at all of the application of psychology to human beings in health and disease. He may understand perfectly the methods of determining intelligence quotients and so forth, but will be utterly at sea when confronted either with a malingerer or with the necessity of making a determination with regard to a person suffering from neurasthenia."[93]

The claim to authoritative knowledge in the area of nervous instability was clearly an attempt to secure professional control, but it also suggests resistance to what was conceived of as too narrow an approach, one solely informed by a science of the mind. During the interwar years—following Freud and recognition of "shell shock"—it also represented a claim to a more complex understanding of the psyche than that of the nascent psychology, which until then was dominated by principles of measurement and calculation. The medical involvement in industry was therefore also significant because it promoted a more holistic understanding of the individual, one in which both mind and body were accorded significance.

The antagonism of doctors towards psychologists did not abate with the increasing legitimacy of industrial psychology. By 1946, the Senior Medical Officer of the Australian Paper Manufacturers Limited, for example, was asserting that:

> The rise of Industrial Psychology as a profession has given an immense fillip to interest in mental fitness for particular types of employment; and, in view of the human tendency to concentrate on one craze at a time, there is a risk that modern industry will jump to the conclusion that the psychologist has all the answers needed for making an assessment of the fitness of any person for any work. The trained psychologist would be the first to repudiate such an argument; but, unfortunately, industry is not always very criti-

cal of the training of those who claim to be psychologists. The psychologist is concerned, rightly, to remind us that people have minds; and that those minds differ, one from another: therefore, if one is to place people in jobs in which they will be reasonably contented, or efficient, or both, one must have some knowledge of how their minds work. Occasionally, it is necessary for us to remind ourselves that, as well as minds, people have bodies; and that those bodies differ, one from another; therefore, to place employees really successfully, one must have some knowledge of how their bodies work, and of how differences in structure may affect ability to perform various kinds of work.[94]

Concerns about the capacity of psychologists to make determinations of "fitness" for work reflects a degree of skepticism of psychology that has gone hand in hand with its growth—in industry, as in other fields to which it has been applied. The antipathy towards psychology has not, however, diminished its sociocultural influence or its professional power.

In Australia, industrial psychology established an institutional presence and a corresponding degree of legitimacy with the founding of the Australian Institute of Industrial Psychology (AIIP) in 1927.[95] A year later, Ronald Walker, lecturer in economics at the University of Sydney, took the opportunity of the 1928 AAAS Congress to promote the AIIP. He began by informing delegates that "industrial psychology studies labor from the human viewpoint, as distinguished from the mechanical and economic viewpoints."[96] Walker outlined international developments, pointing out differences between American and British emphases. The work of the National Institute of Industrial Psychology in London differed from its American counterpart, he told delegates, in that it arose out of the Fatigue Research Board and thus had a greater concern with health and welfare. Vocational selection, by contrast, was the foremost concern of industrial psychology in the United States.

Walker saw the work of the Australian Institute as following the British lead, insofar as it would be primarily concerned with providing vocational guidance and undertaking research. Nevertheless, the economic imperatives of managing the workforce were also a high priority, as Walker's comments on vocational guidance indicate:

> The importance of vocational selection is emphasised, not only for its own value, but because it is the prerequisite of vocational guidance, for it is in selection that are perfected those methods of measuring vocational aptitudes which are essential to vocational guidance. Further, vocational selection should both improve the quality of a firm's staff and reduce labour turnover. The most important methods are psychological tests, the interview, and character ratings by close acquaintances, as well as ordinary credentials.[97]

Despite the extent to which the health and welfare of the worker was accorded significance, it was clear that the proverbial bottom line of industrial psychology from the outset was the application of psychological knowledge to improve economic efficiency. The more interesting dimension involves what Rose refers to as "the apparent discovery of a fortunate coincidence between personal contentment of the worker and maximum efficiency and profitability for the boss."[98] Even doctors by the 1920s were arguing that a happy worker was a productive one and that the key to contentment lay in the best match between mental equipment and work tasks. This was to typify the psychologically oriented approach to the problem of labor and capital during the interwar years. Articles on mental hygiene in the *Medical Journal of Australia*, for example, frequently reminded readers:

> An employee, engaged in work for which he is mentally unsuited, will not be happy, he will lag behind his fellows, he will require to make continuous effort which he will not be able to sustain, and as a result he will be miserable and discontented and his health may ultimately become affected, probably by a functional affection of the nervous system. It is also likely that an employee who is capable of mental effort of a high order, will find his work irksome and monotonous, if he is engaged on some task thought by him to be dull and mechanical. Regarded from the point of view of

the employer mental hygiene is of interest because it promotes harmony in the establishment and tends towards a larger output of work.[99]

Following the outbreak of the Second World War, it was concern about mental fortitude—rather than happiness and contentment—that dominated the work of both medical officers and industrial psychologists in assessments of "mental fitness."

In his official history of the role of science and industry in the Second World War, David Mellor noted in 1958 that the demands of wartime brought to the fore a new problem for the military—how to select the most appropriate recruits by the most expedient means.[100] Skilled in psychometrics, industrial psychologists were enlisted to assist with the recruitment and selection of "mentally suitable" men for service. In the case of the Army Psychology Service, Mellor notes that after an initial trial period in which it proved its worth, "the same weight was attached to the advice of the psychology officer concerning a recruit's mental fitness to serve, as was attached to the advice of the medical officer on his physical fitness."[101]

The capacity of psychological tests to identify mentally unstable individuals was regarded as an important tool in the management of the defense force. Wartime activities of Australian psychologists were largely restricted to the area of psychometric testing and the identification of the mentally unfit, with few doing clinical work. In this regard, Australian psychologists in the armed forces differed from their American counterparts, who according to Cooke, "were heavily involved in providing therapy, giving them a taste for clinical work and their patients a taste of analysis."[102]

Although therapeutic work undertaken by Australian psychologists in the military was limited, the war proved to be a formative time for Australian psychology. It managed to stake a small but significant claim to expertise in the area of mental health, disrupting what had hitherto largely been a medical monopoly. The exposure of very large numbers of men to psychometric and psychological examination, some 350,000 in the case of the Army Psychology Service, was clearly an important development in the securing of professional legitimacy.[103] In Mellor's view: "Perhaps the best indicator of their impact on the military side was that after the war all three

Services (army, airforce, navy) established permanent psychological organisations. The overall result was that applied psychology emerged from the war period with a greatly enhanced status in the commercial and industrial world, and in the next decade found much wider use."[104]

That imperatives of psychological work during the war differed from the economic imperatives of business offered an opportunity for industrial psychologists recruited to the military to expand their professional practice and knowledge base, particularly in the area of mental health. Concern with efficiency and with mental fitness and personality type certainly straddled the demands of both war and industry. But the literature of the immediate postwar years does not indicate that in industrial psychology, or in the emerging field of personnel management, there was an overriding concern with questions of mental health. Rather, the focus was on rationalization, with results of psychometric measurement aiding in the recruitment and selection of suitable workers. It was much later, by the end of the century amid the "depression epidemic," that the question of the economic cost of mental illness became a significant concern for industry.[105]

During the interwar and postwar years, it was not only in the management of labor, however, that business and industry turned to psychology. Another important economic dimension involved the uptake of psychological ideas in advertising and marketing. The promise of economic advantage for business and advertisers by using psychological principles and drawing on research evidence was increasingly promoted by the 1950s. Australians keenly followed international developments in applied psychology and experts were engaged to advise Australian business on successful marketing strategies.

In 1958, for example, the Australian Association of National Advertisers brought Dr Ernest Dichter of the Institute of Motivational Research to Australia. Dichter advised local commerce and industry representatives on American developments in applied psychology, and shared with Australians ways of applying psychology to the customer.[106] Recognition of the value of psychology to advertising and marketing during this period is also evidenced by its presence in business and management periodicals. As Stella

Lees and June Senyard have noted: "Every issue of Rydge's carried articles and comments showing the advantages of applied psychology—market research to establish the psyche of the consumer, public relations to soften up resistance, and advertising (referred to as its handmaiden) to induce the customer to make unforeseen purchases."[107]

During the same period, formal personnel work also became increasingly common in Australia. In the context of the postwar economic boom with the demand for labor outstripping supply, industrial relations dramatically changed. High labor turnover shifted the power dynamic between employers and employees and forced industry to examine its management practices. As Chris Wright argues: "Management could no longer rely on the threat of the 'sack' and unemployment to enforce labour discipline and efficiency."[108] These trends were evident even by the late 1940s, as personnel officers were increasingly appointed to assist industry in attracting and retaining employees. Professional journals responded with the publication of a large number of articles devoted to employee selection, labor turnover, and absenteeism. Much of the psychological research of this period focused on manual workers but, with the expansion of personnel management, white-collar workers became more and more subject to the psychological gaze.

Economics certainly was the foremost concern. However, as evident in other domains, the application of psychology in the workplace gave rise to a number of unintended consequences. Albeit in different ways, first through testing but increasingly through training and the activities of personnel departments, workers of varying social strata came into contact with a variety of psychological knowledges and practices. The institutionalization of psychology in the workplace, therefore, meant that significant numbers of people, particularly men, were exposed in the public sphere to new constructions of the self. Initially, a rational scientific conception of the individual was predominant, but by the second half of the twentieth century a more therapeutic orientation was to some extent co-opted as another efficiency technique. Yet it had wider, more contradictory implications than merely reinforcing scientific management and the control of the workforce, for these developments coincided with increased popular appeal of psychology and the growth of therapy and counseling.

Therapy at Work

While an instrumental rationality of calculation and measurement had dominated labor management processes for several decades, during the 1950s a new strand of psychological knowledge began to exert its influence on the Australian workplace. The use of psychology in staff selection and in the development of incentive schemes to aid retention continued. Yet coming to complement existing practices and related knowledges was a conceptual shift from the individual worker as simply knowable, to a conception of the self as adaptable, flexible, and changeable.

For the white-collar worker especially, the value of self-improvement—the overcoming of personal deficit in particular—as a means by which one could achieve success, gained considerable currency. Corporate training and management consultancy firms provided organizational structures from which such ideas about personal change could be widely disseminated. By the mid 1950s, the Dale Carnegie Institute was offering leadership courses in Australia that promised to help people overcome personal problems that might impinge upon goal attainment. In contrast to the prevailing ideas in circulation at the level of popular culture—in which the psychological was harnessed to understand emotions and private life—shaping the self and behavior to achieve professional advancement and success had more of a utilitarian edge. Carnegie's metaphor of self-change, that individuals, like cars, often needed overhauling, symbolized an influential rendering of the new corporate psychology. By the early 1960s, the Carnegie Institute claimed that 6,000 Australians had attended their training courses. Two decades later, that figure had increased ten-fold.[109]

During the 1950s, advertisements for Carnegie courses promised improvement in work and social life by helping people develop greater self-confidence, improve memory, minimize anxiety, and speak more effectively. Images of apparently successful women and men were accompanied with slogans such as: "These people all have problems like yours," or, "How well dressed is your personality?" Others advertisements proclaimed: "You can be better than you are, in so many ways." In the corporate sector, this new orientation to the self was institutionalized by the growth of companies specializing in human resource management. By the late

1960s, a reported 123 management consultancy firms had already been established in Sydney alone.[110]

It was not simply the language of psychology that had become embedded in business, but an analytic attitude and techniques of therapy had also been corporatized. In 1967, reporter Charles Higham described an executive training program that was more or less indistinguishable from group therapy. The training involved participants analyzing themselves and others with the assistance of a psychologist. The analysis was aided with the conceptual tool of a "Johari window," essentially an imagined box consisting of four sections that participants pictured in their mind's eye. As Higham described it: "The "free" area is what you already know about yourself and can discuss freely; the hidden area is that part of your mind which you know about but others don't; the third part is that which others can see in you but you can't; and the fourth is the really blanketed area that is unknown to you and others and only a practised psychiatrist can uncover."[111] The role of the psychologist was to facilitate the analysis of group members to the end that all present would come to "know" both themselves and each other. The purpose of the exercise was for each participant to become "something of an amateur psychologist himself," as an aid in dealing with interpersonal problems that arise in the workplace.

Clearly, the stakes were higher at the executive level and such costly investment in human resources was for the most part limited to those in management positions. While intensely analytical practices were not the mainstay of staff training programs, they do reflect the increasing objective from the 1960s onwards not only for the organization to "know" the worker but for employees also to "know" themselves. As the subjectivity of the worker came under greater purview of management, the influence of psychology was increasingly directed towards the analysis and shaping of the self, albeit still couched within a rationalized discourse wedded to scientific legitimacy.

It is difficult to ascertain with any accuracy how widespread these practices were during the 1960s and 1970s. However, what is clear is that in addition to any influence directly exerted in the workplace, psychology was also shaping ideas about work more broadly, as evidenced in the dissemination of psychological knowledge through the popular press and business journals. The *Bulletin*, for example, routinely reported on developments in industrial psychology, and in doing so exposed a wide audience to new work practices and the psychological rationales that drove them. Further, the discursive construction of self-development in the context of business became increasingly pervasive, not only promulgating ideas about self-improvement, but also the value of an analytic attitude—especially to men.

Therapeutic imperatives disseminated through business and industry constitute a significant dimension of the multifaceted popular and institutional discourses of the self that were shaping popular consciousness. While earlier decades were marked by a more mechanistic, scientific, and calculative approach to the human dimension in the workplace, by the 1960s the ethos of self-development and the benefit of self-analysis had clearly come to the fore. Psychological knowledge was, as Rose has argued, increasingly working *through* individuals rather than working upon them. This operated especially through notions that individual goals were at one with organizational success. IBM, for example, was promoting this idea to young executives during the 1960s. The message the company was attempting to instill in its employees was clear: "By all means have drive, but first and foremost let your ego be absorbed into the company's overall needs, and work with the selfless absorption of a football league player as a profit-making company man."[112]

Not only had psychodynamic notions infused business practices, but psychological measurement had evolved from the relatively crude measures of intelligence first developed half a century before, to more complex assessments of personality that became widely influential in the corporate sector. Australian business increasingly looked to aptitude and psychological tests to establish the requisite personality traits possessed by potential employees. These included keenness, drive, lack of neurosis or oddity, and the ability to get along with others. By the late 1960s it was reported that almost 300 companies in Australia were using personality tests developed by the Australian Institute of Industrial Psychology, while many others utilized American tests. Applicants were reportedly screened and rejected on such grounds as being too defensive, too compliant, or too impulsive.[113] Psychological knowledge harnessed by industry and commerce during this period, moreover, was being used in increasingly diffuse ways.

The professionalization of personnel functions within large organizations during the late 1960s and early 1970s provided another professional opportunity for psychologists and for the diffusion of psychological ideas and practices in the workplace. The selection and testing of employees had already established a role for industrial psychologists, but in the context of growing economic instability, they were able to secure greater professional control, as an expanded role of psychology in employee management promised additional improvements in productivity and a further reduction in staff turnover. As with other areas of psychology, the influence of American and British theory and research was considerable. The human relations tradition remained highly influential in management education and personnel practices, and there was increasing recognition of the social and emotional needs of employees.[114] By the 1960s and 1970s, the incentive schemes characteristic of the old industrial psychology model had all but made way for a more therapeutic imperative that was infusing workplace training and management programs.

In the following decade, the centrality of the human dimension to the organization was reflected in the rapid growth of human resource management which supplemented the emphasis of earlier personnel practices with a more strategic and integrated approach to human capital.[115] The emergence of human resource management as a profession and an academic specialty was buttressed by psychology's knowledge of the individual. During the 1980s, Chandlers Personnel Group, for example, promoted its services to organizations on the basis that it could "go beyond appearances to get to the real person." Through advertisements in the *Bulletin*, it also cautioned those seeking employment that the decision to hire or not is made, "perhaps unconsciously," within the first five minutes of an interview. By the 1990s, therapeutic practices had become well entrenched.

The changing nature of work, coupled with the new conceptualization of subjectivity, was to have a far-reaching effect on the relations of labor and capital, one arguably even more dramatic than the advent of scientific management. According to Rose's analysis, it provided a means by which managers could "stimulate the self-actualizing forces in employees." Moreover, such knowledge was harnessed in the reconfiguration of the organization itself, "so as to release the autonomous subjectivity of the worker in such a way that it aligned with the aspirations of the enterprise, now construed in terms of innovation, flexibility and competitiveness."[116] In his analysis of the "post-bureaucratic corporation," James Tucker makes a related argument, suggesting that therapeutic managerial control has replaced more hierarchical authoritarian forms of control. Tucker's conclusion is that organizational power has not diminished, but the ways in which control is exercised has significantly changed.[117]

The extent to which the application of psychological knowledge in the workplace has been adaptive is perhaps the most striking dimension of all. As "emotion" came to gain greater cultural legitimacy, psychometrics became more complex. By the 1990s, much of the earlier impetus of psychology and psychometrics found new expression in the concept of emotional intelligence (EI), popularized by psychologist and journalist, Daniel Goleman. With the advent of the emotional quotient in the workplace, "knowing thyself" and having the capacity to think, feel, and act in appropriate ways became part of the construction of the intelligent, successful worker.[118]

That the emotional realm became subject to capitalist imperatives raises a series of questions about the alignment of the interests of business and the individual. The colonization of even this dimension of subjectivity may well constitute a form of regulation. But it too has been a paradoxical development, especially insofar as it has disrupted the public/private divide. The advent of emotion in the office, as Helen Trinca and Catherine Fox have observed, unsettled the demarcation of work as a public domain that excluded the emotional realm. This separation, they approvingly note, provided a boundary between work and private life.[119] Putting to one side the question of whether such a strict demarcation between the public and the personal was ever so dramatic a feature of women's work, it is certainly the case that there has been a blurring of the boundaries between public and private life—in the workplace, as elsewhere.

The Legitimation of Psychological Expertise   125

Yet, particularly for women, the bracketing out of the personal could be a strain—with domestic and caring responsibilities ever threatening to intervene—and the greater freedom of expression in the workplace may for many have been a welcome relief. There are other issues too, which are in need of further analysis. The new emphasis on emotion was central to the opening up of a discursive space for critiques of sexual harassment and twenty-first century discourses of family friendly workplaces. Indeed, the discursive space made possible by the language of psychology and an associated embrace of therapeutic imperatives, enabled issues of workplace bullying and sexual harassment to be articulated as damaging to individuals. This has been especially important for people with less social power, especially women and those from ethnic and sexual minority groups.

It would be remiss, however, to read these developments as only portending greater equality in the workplace. Indeed, some of the most compelling critiques of the therapeutic are on the subject of the manipulation of personnel in the interests of organizations. Dana Cloud's analysis of practices of consolation, in place of compensation, is an incisive account of the pernicious use to which such strategies can too easily be directed. Certainly a sensitivity to the ways in which therapeutic discourses may be used against the interests of the worker is necessary, but so too is recognition that there have been a range of sometimes contradictory consequences that have followed.

The embrace of a therapeutic ethos at work challenged the gendered underpinnings of the public world of work as it had been constructed since industrialization. By the late twentieth century, this dissolving boundary was not only occurring in the workplace but, as I explore in the following chapter, had also come to shape public life more broadly. As part of a broader set of processes that were also occurring culturally, the diffusion of psychological knowledge—notably through the popular media—was constructing new psychological notions of a reflexive self.

4

Cultural Diffusion of the Analytic Attitude

> *In psychotherapy you take your troubles to the thoughtful and intelligent attention of a listener who, by word and manner, gives you the impression that he'd very much like to hear what's bothering you, and you tell him.*
> —*Sunday Herald*, 1950

The cultural diffusion of psychological knowledge propelled the ancient maxim to "know thyself" in an altogether new direction. By the postwar years, an analytic model of reflexive selfhood had gained considerable currency in Australia. Greater significance was being accorded to the emotional realm and matters hitherto considered "private" increasingly entered the public domain. Concerns with psychological and emotional life intensified in the wake of the period Eric Hobsbawm describes as the "age of catastrophe."[1] Two world wars and the Great Depression shaped the Australia of 1914 to 1945, and in the years that followed problems of soldier resettlement, grief, and emotional trauma, reverberated widely.[2]

Yet the period following the Second World War also brought renewed hope, as economic prosperity and the rise of the welfare state provided relief from some of the hardships of earlier years. The quest for identity and self-expression were dominant themes at the popular level, and psychoanalytic concepts and psychological terminology captured these imperatives through a model of reflexive selfhood. New expectations of personal fulfillment also emerged in the context of an idealization of domestic life promoted by government. As John Murphy argues: "Postwar ideas of the family connected conceptions of the self, and the possibilities of personal identity and expression, with the aspiration that domesticity could be the means of expressing the self."[3]

Yet for many, the idea of finding happiness in the home was at odds with the reality of postwar domestic life. In 1947, divorce rates reached an all-time high.[4] The advent of marriage guidance in this period reflected both the new hopes of personal fulfillment and a growing concern for the sanctity of marriage and the family.[5] By contrast to the application of psychological knowledge in domains like education and the workplace, at the heart of marriage guidance was a concern with private life and intimate relationships. It involved, therefore, not simply the use of psychology as a science of the self, but incorporated therapeutic techniques in which the emotional realm of ordinary middle-class women and men was subject to new forms of analysis.

While marriage guidance and the emergence of other forms of counseling carried a therapeutic ethos into the private sphere, parallel developments were also reshaping public life. The popular media was an important means by which psychological knowledge and an analytic attitude were disseminated. Psychology's professional project included marketing strategies and the active engagement of leading therapists with the media, in the interests of promoting greater psychological and emotional literacy. Yet it was the making public of private pain—and in the process the politicization of private life—that was arguably to have the most far-reaching consequences. From the Royal Commission on Human Relationships in the 1970s to recent revelations of depression by professional footballers and other public figures, the cultural reach of therapy has been propelled by the public disclosure of private experiences of emotional pain and psychological distress. These changing dispositions towards the self transformed both public and private life through the second half of the twentieth century, the basis of which was laid by constructions of psychologically reflexive selfhood that emerged during the interwar years.

Analyze Thyself

Though it would take until the last decades of the twentieth century for a therapeutic ethos to become fully embedded in the national psyche, by the interwar years psychological and psychoanalytic concepts were becoming increasingly important cultural motifs. During the 1920s, women's magazines began reflecting what Joy Damousi refers to as an "emerging Freudian preoccupation with the self and the mind," and by the following decade the language of psychology had entered common parlance.[6] In the popular media, the discourse of nerves remained an important means by which therapeutic sensibilities were disseminated. Yet with the growing legitimacy of psychology and a new emphasis on personal life generated by the popularization of Freudian theory, the discourse of nerves expanded to reflect broader concerns about the self, the emotional realm, and private life.

The popular media reflected the growing cultural significance of the analytic attitude and helped promulgate it, as it carried notions of reflexive selfhood and the therapeutic message to mass audiences. Women's magazines regularly featured psychological expertise in articles addressing matters of personal life. Therapeutic ideas were also carried in magazines with largely male target readerships, as well as through newspapers aimed at a general audience. It was, nevertheless, in women's magazines that concerns about the intimate and the domestic first arose—themes that were to become increasingly dominant in a wider range of publications, especially in the postwar period.

Advice columns provided an important means by which ideals of reflexive selfhood were promoted. Techniques of self-analysis and relationship management were conveyed within a conceptual framework that privileged the psychological and the emotional, with the emerging field of psychological research informing such expert advice. A 1940s article in the *Women's Weekly* serves as a useful example. Drawing on American research, the article provided tips on strengthening marital relations through practicing self-control. Keeping one's emotions in check and refraining from unnecessary expenditure were promoted as important attributes a woman should cultivate for a successful marriage. Lest such advice be forgotten and not integrated into marital life, it was suggested to the reader that: "You might find it profitable to file this article away and bring it out every few months for a check-up. Your behaviour may take on a new meaning if you learn to look back over it objectively in retrospect."[7] Indeed the benefit of observing and analyzing behavior, thoughts, and emotions was commonly advanced. Self-understanding was promoted as an essential dimension of successful selfhood, for it provided the basis from which self-improvement could be enacted.

For women, messages about the transformative power of self-reflection were never disconnected from the private realm of home and intimate relations on the one hand, and the shaping of the physical self on the other. Advice on strengthening one's marriage and developing better child-rearing practices was staple fare. So too were tips on improving the body and physical appearance through diet and exercise. By the 1950s, the psychological benefit of self-transformation was being lauded in stories about plastic surgery, advancing further the conceptual link between the transfiguration of the body and of the mind.

The psychology of beauty was a recurring topic of interest, and psychological research informed popular analysis of the desire for feminine attractiveness. Interestingly, shaping the body and fashioning the self were both promoted and analyzed not only in women's magazines, but also in newspapers. One such article, reviewing a new book on the "modern woman," asserted that: "The glamour girl is a neurotic and the cult of glamour is a symptom of modern woman's lack of happiness and self-confidence."[8] Readers were informed that women are driven to buy cosmetics and beautify themselves because of unconscious anxieties about being loved.

Freudian ideas found particular resonance at the cultural level, and research legitimized and popularized both psychological and psychoanalytic concepts. The unconscious in particular was frequently used to explain behavior—from the mundane to the quizzical. Women were predominantly the focus of such analysis, though the probing of men's psychical life also provided fodder for the popular press. A 1950s article in the *Sun-Herald*, for instance, cited American psychological research to "reveal" that men are equally as vain as women. While women openly take care with physical appearance, readers were informed that men do so covertly.[9]

Advice columns frequently drew on academic research to support the merits of self-examination—not only to improve relationships, but also to achieve individual happiness. For those serious about self-reinvention or seeking relief from mental distress, books and home study courses in applied psychology provided a more systematic means by which psychological knowledge and techniques could be utilized. Such material was widely advertised during the 1940s. Given the very limited availability of psychological support services at this time, this literature constituted an important vehicle for the dissemination of psychological knowledge and techniques of behavior modification. Though it is not possible to gauge the impact of the marketing of these books and courses, recurring advertisements do suggest a degree of commercial success. Indeed the very proliferation of such material is itself significant, for it reflects the increasing encroachment of the psychological in the pages of newspapers and magazines.

Yet to understand how the nascent therapy culture was also reflecting—and rendering—changes in social, cultural, and personal life, it is necessary to move beyond recognition of its increasing prevalence to also explore its dynamics and consider its potential ramifications. Representations of reflexive selfhood promoted to both women and men a model of subjectivity in which psychological and emotional life were privileged. These emergent ideas about the self, along with a new attention to the domain of personal problems, challenged the established gender divisions of public and private life and associated constructions of emotional and psychological wellbeing. This is particularly striking in the marketing of applied psychology courses, as advertisements reveal how psychological constructions of gender difference were refracted through the popular press.

In the 1940s, both the *Women's Weekly* and the *Bulletin* carried advertisements for a number of home study courses in psychology. The *Bulletin* advertisements, targeting a largely male readership, promoted the "scientific training of mind, memory, and personality." Self-confidence, willpower, social ease, and concentration could all be improved, such advertisements asserted, with "psychology applied to one practical end: the successful conduct of life." By contrast, similar advertisements in the *Women's Weekly* were marked by an emphasis on emotional and internal life, and often couched in psychoanalytic terms. One advertisement, which appeared in the 1940s for a book containing strategies to banish nerves, shyness, and social anxiety stated:

> Most of the mental and physical ills which take the joy and sparkle out of living are directly traceable to negative forces deep down in the Subconscious Mind. Inferiority Complex alone is responsible for an incalculable waste of health, happiness and personal efficiency. By showing you how to eradicate these negative forces which stunt and cripple your entire personality, the modern science of Applied Psychology literally opens the door to LIFE. If you are only half-happy, half-well, half-successful—if you are disappointed or dissatisfied with your present circumstances—then NOW is the time to change the face of the future. A world-famous Home Study Course will show you—in a few short months of fascinating study—how to overcome "nerves," depression, shyness, and lack of confidence, and become the radiant, forceful personality that Nature intended you to be.[10]

On the one hand, many advertisements reflected the established gender order: psychological discourses reinforced the gendered division of the public and private spheres by promoting an expressive form of self-reflexivity to women and a utilitarian form to men. The utilitarian form involved a calculating approach to life in which personal success—especially of the economic kind—was highly valued. By contrast, an expressive form of self-reflexivity privileged internal states and emotional life. Importantly, however, both types of advertisement identified emotional problems as an impediment to happiness. With the help of psychology, inferiority complexes and self-consciousness—in both women and men—could be overcome. That self-consciousness and feelings of inferiority were the subject of advertisements directed towards men is itself noteworthy. Clearly such marketing campaigns were driven by commercial imperatives. Yet as with the nerve cures discussed in Chapter Two, commercialization also gave rise to another dimension: the expansion of the emotional realm and a greater openness towards experiences of distress and suffering.

Cultural Diffusion of the Analytic Attitude 133

HOW TO MAKE YOUR LIFE A SUCCESS IN THE POST WAR WORLD

SUCCESSFUL BUSINESS LIFE — SOCIAL LIFE — FAMILY LIFE

Once you master your mind you can master the world. But first you must find out how your mind works . . . know where your strength lies . . . what are your weaknesses. Psychology teaches you this. The Victory School of Psychology does more. It teaches you how to develop your strong points . . . how to correct those weaknesses. Many who are to-day leaders in business, social and community life were once shy, retiring, convinced they were failures. Enrol now for

This Home Study Course in Applied
PSYCHOLOGY
SUPERVISED BY A GRADUATE OF TWO UNIVERSITIES

NEW COURSE IN APPLIED PSYCHOLOGY SHOWS YOU
How to Develop Personality
How to Develop Willpower
How to Develop Leadership
The Art of Successful Conversation
How to Train Your Memory
How to Overcome Fear,
Etc., Etc., Etc.

By devoting a few hours of your spare time weekly to this easily followed simplified course in Psychology you can obtain the benefit of years of study by a graduate of Melbourne and London Universities, holder of the degrees of M.A., Dip.Ed., who supervises your progress. This is the sound, sensible way to learn to overcome the obstacles in your path towards a glorious full life. In this inspirational course, based on sound Christian principles, everything is explained in simple, easily-understood language. Anyone who can read can follow it

INFERIORITY COMPLEX BANISHED

An inferiority complex may be of four kinds: Physical, Mental, Moral, or Social. The defect may be real or imaginary. The trouble is not in the defect, but the feeling created by the defect. The problem is to get rid of the unhappy feeling of inferiority and replace it with a sense of confidence and poise, if not of superiority. By right thinking, this can be done. Your life follows your thoughts. Every success of a Churchill or a Roosevelt or a MacArthur follows a thought-out plan and purpose. You are shown in this course how to think thoughts of health, success, power, and of faith. Through the 17 lessons sent weekly to your home by The Victory School of Psychology you are guided step by step towards complete mental efficiency. The characteristics are developed in you that distinguish the people who are liked, admired and respected by all the people who are welcome everywhere . . . the type of people who are chosen as leaders in every sphere. You are shown how to completely eradicate fear, inferiority, and nerves.

FREE BOOK! *Inspirational, vital, gripping new book about Applied Psychology Tells you how YOU can apply psychology to YOUR problems. Send 2½d postage for your copy NOW!*

Get Yours!

To the Secretary,
VICTORY SCHOOL OF PSYCHOLOGY
Box 1489, G.P.O., SYDNEY.

Please send me the free booklet, "The Key to Success Through Psychology," giving particulars of your Course. I enclose 2½d for postage. (Write name in Block Letters.)

NAME ....

ADDRESS ....

ARGUS. 23/9/44.

Advertisements for home study courses in applied psychology were widely advertised during the 1940s and 1950s. This one appeared in the Argus, 23 September 1944.

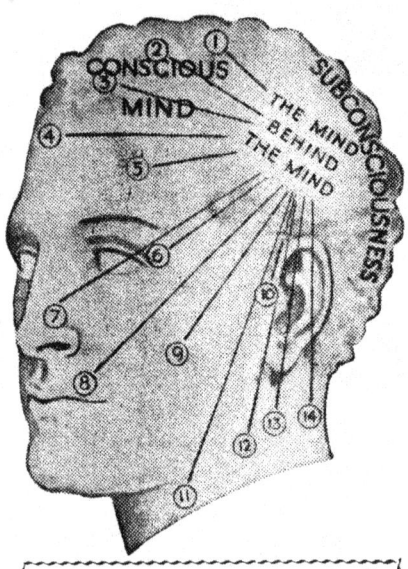

Advertisements for self-help books commonly conveyed detailed, albeit distilled, information about psychology. This one appeared in the Sun-Herald, 4 July 1954.

By the mid-twentieth century, psychological and emotional difficulties became increasingly prevalent themes in advertising as well as in general copy, and psychological experts were more commonly featured. When the English psychologist Bernard Calmus was in Australia in the early 1950s to promote his method of "Life Stream Psychology," his self-help book was advertised in the *Bulletin* as a reliable means of eradicating fears, phobias, and inferiority complexes that make life a misery.

The inferiority complex is worthy of particular attention for it achieved significant currency. Culturally, the concept had a similar function to that of nerves, articulating a moderate level of psychological dysfunction that in contemporary discourse would be understood as a problem of self-esteem. Yet in contrast to nervous conditions that were anchored in the physical, the inferiority complex was unquestionably a psychological problem, one that had a debilitating effect on social and emotional life. As with tonics and other remedies for nerves, treatments for inferiority complexes were widely advertised and became an important carrier of the analytic attitude. In transmitting the idea that the self could be worked on and improved, the British Institute of Practical Psychology advertisements of the 1950s and 1960s provided detailed information about psychological problems. Without even sending for a free copy of their book, *I Can—And I Will*, readers could learn that:

> An inferiority complex is a disturbance in the Subconscious Mind which manifests itself in self-consciousness and lack of confidence—in nervousness and "nervyness"—in causeless worry—in depression and a sense of futility—in lassitude and lack of enterprise—in nerve pains and other ailments—in weakness of will and habits—in stuttering, blushing, and nervous mannerisms—in forgetfulness and lack of concentration. These are symptoms that there is "something wrong" within your personality which you can put right—the effect of conflicting forces within yourself or the result of some emotional experience or some destructive influence during your personality development.[11]

Yet despite increasing psychological literacy, emotional and psychological problems were still addressed with a degree of reticence. That advertisements for self-help books often contained the reassuring note that material would be posted in non-identifying plain wrap is reminiscent of nineteenth century advertisements promising cures for nervous dysfunction. Indeed the promise of privacy suggests that despite the increasing popularity of psychology and self-analysis, experiences of emotional and mental distress largely remained problems of a private nature.

Nevertheless, the cultural reach of psychology had increased considerably since the 1930s. Distilled and popularized, psychological and psychoanalytic theory generated new understandings of the self, in terms of how it could be "fashioned and created," as Damousi has noted, but also in terms of dysfunction.[12] By the mid-twentieth century, the emotional and the somatic were no longer conflated under the rubric of nerves: irrational fears, phobias, and inferiority complexes were clearly represented as psychological problems. The discourse of nerves was still present—and indeed would remain until it was usurped by the psychological discourses of depression and anxiety later in the century—but nerves no longer encompassed the range of psychosomatic complaints that it had in previous decades.

There was also a shift in understanding how the "stresses and strains of modern life" could affect the self. The nineteenth century notion of the stimulation of modernity causing nervous strain had given way to a more complex conceptualization, one that delineated how key aspects of a person's intimate, social, and working life affect mental health. A feature article of the early 1950s—headlined "Checking the Crack-Up"—serves as a nice example. The story provided a taxonomy of stresses and supports that affect mental health, alerting readers that: "the crack up" results "when the stresses wear you down."[13] Fear of war, quarrels at home, sickness, troubles with friends, cost of living pressures, sexual problems, and unsatisfactory employment were listed as some of life's major stressors. On the other hand, good housing, good friends, religion, self-confidence, good relationships, good physical health, and satisfactory employment provide the kind of support necessary for mental health. Like many articles of the time addressing psychological issues, it was based on the findings of American research and cited advice from prominent American psychiatrists.

Although psychoanalysis remained marginal as a clinical technique, concepts drawn from psychoanalytic theory and its derivations reverberated widely, appreciably shaping popular understandings of the self. In addition to the promulgation of concepts like the inferiority complex—which was represented as an obvious indicator of emotional problems—the idea was advanced that careful analysis of the self could also uncover hidden psychological deficits. Thus, observing and analyzing one's behavior could give a clue to the sorts of emotional turmoil one may be experiencing unconsciously. Reporting on psychological research conducted in the 1950s, a *Sydney Morning Herald* article revealed that:

> Recently psychologists have discovered that your eating habits provide a fascinating key to the kind of person you are—and reveal more about your character and personality than you'd ever dream. Where emotional troubles are concerned, they can tell "what's eating you"... It was found that when people are feeling sorry for themselves, there is a tendency to crave the following foods: sweets (particularly chocolate), hot dogs, or nuts. Under conditions of stress or when security was threatened, cravings shifted to milk or various dairy foods. Special cravings for "grownup" foods, such as coffee, tea, alcoholic beverages, and so on, was noted among persons who sought to reassure themselves about their adult status.[14]

The article also reported that it was possible to analyze the state of one's marriage by looking at the food that adorns the family table, that in cases of guilt, people deprive themselves of food as a form of self-punishment, and that others use food as a substitute for love.

While ideas about developing greater self-reflexivity were implicitly advanced through such articles, practicing self-analysis was given greater fillip—especially in women's magazines—by the arrival of popularized psychometric assessments. This kind of analysis, explicitly promoting and fostering the reflexive self, was to be found in the quizzes and personality tests that had emerged

This image was part of an advertorial for Kellogg's All-Bran that proffered advice on how to overcome dependence on laxatives. It warned readers: "It is better to be wise now than sorry later—when you are trapped in a harsh laxative bottle," Australian Women's Weekly, 27 November 1957.

by the 1960s and became a regular feature of women's magazines. By answering a series of multiple choice questions, one could engage in quick and simple self-assessments on such varied topics as parenting style, stress and fear levels, honesty, or assess how one measured up in a crisis. Readers were thus able to determine whether their behavior or thoughts fell outside the normal range. Should their score indicate an abnormality, simple psychological advice was proffered.

Pop psychology quizzes promoted a particular ideal of normality, which in turn was reinforced by representations of abnormality. While the inferiority complex captured psychoaffective difficulties, and nerves encompassed a range of psychosomatic complaints, the problem of addiction also found expression by the late 1950s. Dependence on prescription and over-the-counter medication was a subject of particular concern. Following years of extensive advertisements for laxatives as a modern means of regulating the body, for example, the dangers of addiction to such medication was highlighted, sometimes through chilling psychological motifs. Warnings from medical and psychological experts on the overuse of "pills" began featuring in advice columns and in articles by social commentators. Margaret Sydney, writing in the *Women's Weekly* in the early 1960s observed that:

> Social historians, looking back will probably know this as the Pill Age. Never in the course of human history were so many medicines taken by so many for so few good reasons! Painkillers and vitamins, pep pills, tranquillisers, pills to calm you down and pills to stir you up again after you've been calmed, and indigestion pills to cure the pain of having so many pills rattling round inside.[15]

During the 1960s, the subject of psychiatric illness also began to appear more frequently in the popular press. From sensational tabloid articles to reports outlining concerns of mental health professionals about undiagnosed mental illness, emotional injury was increasingly linked to problems of mental health.

By the late 1960s, the affective realm was not only coupled with mental health in the popular media, but it also became contested in new ways. On the one hand, the idea that repressed emotions were damaging to psychological health emerged. "Bottled up anger," psychiatrists warned, was not only an impediment to happiness but it was also hazardous to physical and mental health.[16] However, the desirability of decreasing levels of repression was fiercely contested. Also prominent was a contrary view that unfettered emotional expression—especially by men—was a disturbing trend. Former consultant psychiatrist to the New South Wales state government, Dr John McGeorge, for instance, was troubled by the emergence of less repressive forms of masculinity. The emotional expressiveness of men on the sporting field was emblematic of declining standards of manhood, which for McGeorge, was highly regrettable. As he was quoted as saying in 1967: "Personally, I think the whole thing is rather undesirable. It may be all right on the Continent, where the men are more explosive, but here we tend to be more stoical, in the British pattern ... it's a bit revolting to see men hugging each other ... adults should learn to control their emotions better."[17]

Clearly, in the process of securing cultural legitimacy, the therapeutic has been subject to resistance. McGeorge's concern with decreasing levels of emotional repression as a disturbing trend is emblematic of a counter-therapeutic ethos that also commonly ran in the popular press. Coming from a psychiatrist with a prominent public profile, it also indicates a level of ambivalence amongst those commonly viewed as promoting the emotionally charged therapeutic ethos. Psychiatrists, like therapists and counselors, faced particular difficulties too. For even as therapy and counseling became more widespread during the 1970s and 1980s, therapists were still treated with a degree of suspicion. Critique ranged from views associated with anti-psychiatry, such as the power of the psychological professions to define reality, to more ephemeral concerns about self-centeredness and narcissism that might be encouraged by the helping professions.

A common expression of the counter-therapeutic ethos in the popular imagination has involved the reversal of the ideal of the therapist as the embodiment of wisdom to one in which the therapist is represented as "crazier" than his or her patients. Such disparagement may be a reasonable response to questionable psychotherapeutic practices and cultural imperatives, but it also reveals

Cultural Diffusion of the Analytic Attitude 141

This Harley Schwadron cartoon appeared in the Bulletin, 14 April 1982. Kindly redrawn by the artist for publication here.

deeper issues at stake in the ascendancy of an expressive therapeutic culture—notably, how it has threatened ideals of self-reliance, stoicism, and hegemonic masculinity. Indeed, when therapy is derided it is often linked to effeminate masculinity. The 1980s cartoon pictured above depicting a therapist and a man in analysis is a striking example of this, as dependency is ridiculed within a context of disrupted sexuality.

The relationship between the therapeutic and gender is a complex and sometimes contradictory one, as therapeutic motifs in some ways reinforce the traditional gender order and in other ways challenge it. Popular psychological theories of gender difference have buttressed prevailing assumptions and ideals of masculinity and femininity. Yet central dimensions of the therapeutic sensibility also destabilize these categories—through blurring the boundaries between the public and private spheres, the disruption of hegemonic masculine ideals, the normalization of a destabilized self, and through the recognition of emotional life not only as important to women but to men as well.

It is important to note, too, that representations of reflexive selfhood have not only been linked to a discourse of dysfunction. One recurring theme is that of positive thinking. The concept of positive thinking is predicated on the power of the mind to shape one's reality—particularly one's emotional and psychological health. In some ways this runs counter to the notion of a relentless self-examination and a deficit model that focuses on one's problems. By contrast, the path to happiness is to be found through optimism. Such ideas preempted concepts that would become staples of positive psychology, a school of thought that had become especially influential in various strands of self-help literature by the late twentieth century.

While the focus of my analysis thus far has been the mass media, there were of course other means by which psychological knowledge and the analytic attitude found cultural transmission, not the least of which has been the self-help genre. Widely embraced and enormously popular, self-help books have been a significant carrier of the psychotherapeutic ethos in Australia, as elsewhere. As with the growth of psychology more broadly, the popularity of self-help literature has been driven by various factors, not the least of which are commercial. Like other manifestations of the therapeutic, the genre of self-help reflects the changing emphasis of psychological ideals of reflexive selfhood. Dale Carnegie's utilitarian text of 1937, *How to Win Friends and Influence People*, to the 1970s transactional analysis classic, *I'm Okay, You're Okay*, are emblematic of twentieth century transformations of the therapeutic society. More recently, texts like John Gray's *Men are From Mars, Women are From Venus* series and Dr Phil McGraw's "get-real" therapy books have found widespread appeal.

The blossoming of the genre of the therapeutic guide in the 1970s occurred during a time in which the therapeutic ethos had gained considerable strength. In the context of significant social change, the cultural revolutions of the late 1960s and early 1970s—especially feminism—drew on and strengthened ideas about personal empowerment. Counseling was more broadly institutionalized by this time, there was a shift in which the ordinary suffering of everyday life was being recognized, and openness and communication became important cultural motifs. While the early promotion of reflexive selfhood stressed the importance of understanding oneself and shaping behavior, later trends encompassed a greater focus on the emotional realm.

Before moving to some of the more recent expressions of the therapeutic, I turn first to the movement that formalized the application of psychology to problems of intimate life. With a therapeutic terrain already cultivated in which talk of the self and problems of everyday life were circulating in the popular media, the ground had been laid for the emergence of new experts of the domestic realm. In the years immediately following the Second World War, when fertility rates were low, divorce rates high, and government was promoting the dream of domesticity, traditional religious values aligned with psychological and therapeutic ones in the advent of marriage guidance.

Specialists of Private Life

Prior to the mid-twentieth century, psychotherapeutic intervention was largely confined to the sphere of medical practice and the treatment of mental disturbance.[18] Certainly there were opportunities for the discussion of personal problems with experts, such as one's doctor, but this was limited in form and scope. So too was the pastoral counseling provided by the clergy, for it occurred within a religious framework under the spiritual and moral authority of the Christian churches. However, in the late 1940s in the context of significant social upheaval and trauma following the Second World War, a new set of problems became subject to psychological analysis and psychotherapeutic intervention: problems not of mental disturbance, but difficulties in private and intimate life.

The emergence of marriage guidance is a critical historical marker of changing attitudes towards private life in which the reflexive orientation to the self and intimate relations found institutional expression. While pastoral counseling had hitherto provided a means by which ordinary problems could be talked through with a spiritual guide, marriage guidance reflected a new approach to dealing with problems of intimate life, at a time in which relationships were under considerable strain. As John Murphy sums up the postwar situation: "Over half a million men had been in the armed forces, and some 40,000 had been killed, while the same number returned injured or ill. Legacies of loss and grief, of damaged men and the women who shared or suffered the consequences, echoed through the immediate postwar years."[19] One effect of this was the peaking of divorce rates in 1947.[20]

It was in this context that marriage guidance arose, largely as a church-based response to the relationship difficulties and threats to family life that followed the Second World War.[21] In contrast to similar developments in other areas—for example the medical imperatives affecting changes to the provision of mental health care, or the principles of efficiency driving developments in industrial and educational psychology—the threat to the institution of marriage was essentially a moral problem and the preservation of the traditional family was a philosophy shared by both the church-based and secular organizations that made up the movement. As Vice-President of the Victorian Marriage Guidance Council, Dr W.L. Carrington, pronounced in a lecture on "modern marriage" in 1949, successful marriage is not only "the foundation of happy family life" but is "vital to the well-being of society."[22] Safeguarding the family unit was the first principle of marriage guidance. The second was: "That the right foundation for this unit is permanent monogamous marriage, which alone provides satisfactory conditions for the birth and upbringing of children, for the expression of the function of sex, and for a secure relationship between man and woman."[23]

The desire to preserve the institution of marriage was a concern not only of conservative and religious groups, but also of members of the professional middle class with an interest in mental health—notably physicians, social workers, and teachers. Sexual education was one way in which those involved in the movement sought to improve marital relations. Even as early as the 1940s, public lectures on "the art of married love" included frank discussion of "foreplay and orgasm, sexual problems and issues of sexual adjustment."[24] More broadly, the educative approach was underpinned by the belief that a greater understanding of psychology provided a means by which relationships could be strengthened. A series of lectures on "education for marriage and parenthood" presented by

Carrington in 1951, for example, began with "The Modern Concept of Mental Health."[25] Carrington brought to his role in the Marriage Guidance Council established medical expertise and an interest in psychology and pastoral counseling. A strong advocate of both psychology and religion, he regarded each as playing a vital role in managing the vicissitudes of modern life and preventing and resolving problems of mental health.

The extent to which the Christian churches were at the center of the earliest developments in relationship counseling in Australia is noteworthy. In addition to volunteers from the personal service professions, counselors in the early period were comprised largely of the clergy and their wives. Women were instrumental in the establishment of marriage guidance, both as lay counselors and as the majority client base. To become a counselor, the first requirement was to be happily married; thereafter, one needed to have "life experience," common sense, and not possess any "personality handicaps."[26] In the early years, interpersonal skills and

---

WOULD YOU LIKE TO BE A COUNSELLOR?

A new training course for marriage counsellors will begin in Brisbane early in 1964. The Council would like to hear from men and women who are prepared to offer themselves for selection as candidates for training. The work of counselling is honorary, and it entails giving up several hours (day or evening) each week. Counsellors are usually selected from happily-married (or widowed) men and women between the ages of 30 and 50. Educational background is not necessarily important, but a trainee should have the ability to follow studies at a tertiary level. Since counsellors need to have a particular type of personality, candidates are asked to go before a selection committee.

If you would like to offer yourself for selection, or to know more about marriage guidance, please contact the Director, Queensland Marriage Guidance Council, 159 St. Paul's Terrace, Brisbane. Telephone 2 4301.

This advertisement appeared in Marriage, the journal of the Queensland Marriage Guidance Council, in September 1963.

the disposition of the counselor were regarded as paramount, and selection and training consisted of interviews, psychological tests, educational lectures, and simple role-plays. By the 1960s, however, training was becoming more systematic as internal tensions within the movement—between the British model of part-time voluntary workers and the American trend of credentializing—gave way to professionalizing currents.

Before the professionalization of marriage guidance, counseling was conducted largely on an ad hoc basis. According to Nancy Miller: "Counsellors counselled in very difficult environments. Some counselled in ex-army huts, borrowed church vestries, or under noisy or cramped conditions in tiny rooms. In other places the counsellor had to eject the receptionist from the single room office when clients arrived, or fall back on counseling on the back stairs of the building."[27] By the 1960s, however, the movement was becoming more formalized, having gained support from government and non-government organizations as well as the public. Legislation provided for more systematic funding of services and a waged position was established in the federal Attorney General's department to oversee marriage guidance across the country.[28]

Prevention of divorce was the primary objective upon which state support was secured. The maintenance of marriage and the upholding of the traditional family as the principal purpose of counseling was at the same time, however, challenged in the social context of the 1960s with the new emphasis on personal liberation. As Kerreen Reiger's analysis shows, this shift had its genesis in the 1950s: "While the educational work continued to promote fairly traditional images of the family, the strategies used and the changing social context of the 1950s pulled the movement in a more 'therapeutic' direction, that is to an orientation towards personal development rather than social stability."[29]

Certainly, there had been a therapeutic dimension to the counseling practices from the outset. The pastoral care work of ministers of religion had provided a model of intervention in which client-centered listening was the preferred technique. The wider cultural imperatives of personal development and happiness, however, challenged the sanctity of the marriage bond and its orthodoxy as a cornerstone of civil society. Further complicating the ideological foundation of marriage guidance during this period was increasing recognition of the ways in which personality and individual psychological make-up affect intimate relationships. In 1964, for example, the President of the Victorian Marriage Guidance Council, Allen Stoller, argued that psychological problems—especially sexual maladjustment—must be recognized as a source of marital conflict. He argued that: "Some persons, because of faulty personality development, enter marriage with considerable anxiety and guilt in relation to sex." As a result, according to Stoller, "they are likely to develop such neurotic symptoms as insomnia, depression and irritability, which radiate into other areas of the marital relationship."[30]

Reflecting the growing influence of psychological theory and professional training, notions of individual pathology increasingly entered the discourse of marriage guidance. Psychology was drawn upon not only to explain individual deficit, but marital partnerships themselves were also subject to this kind of analysis. That relationships could be neurotic, for example, was a view advanced by Brisbane psychiatrist Barry Nurcombe in 1963. In a similar vein to Stoller's position on personality deficiencies, Nurcombe argued that neurotic relationships could develop out of motivations to marriage that were immature or abnormal, such as "marriage in order to obtain a substitute parent" or marriage by a "mother-fixated man, driven to prove his masculinity."[31]

By the 1970s, theories and techniques informed by transactional analysis and gestalt therapy had become significant influences, reflecting not only the growing authority of psychology, but also that of American counseling trends. Throughout the 1960s and especially into the 1970s, individualistic models gave way to a focus on relational dimensions, a shift which also involved the move away from individual counseling towards couples counseling.[32] There was considerable debate about the merits of conjoint counseling, the details of which were largely about its effectiveness, but more important for the broader counseling trends in question here is the extent to which the new relational model gained legitimacy. Not only did it represent a shift from an individual focus, but with more men involved, it also challenged the established gender organization of the movement.

Counseling sessions were for a long period conducted only with individuals—almost exclusively with women—and it was not until the late 1960s and 1970s that working with couples became accepted practice. By this time the approach to marriage guidance was largely professional: counselors were paid specialists rather than volunteers, economic support had been provided by the federal government, and service provision was increasingly underpinned by a therapeutic ethos rather than a moral-religious ethic. In the mid-1960s, less than ten percent of counseling sessions involved both partners.[33] In the decades that followed, individual counseling sessions persisted but relationship counseling in which both partners participated became the dominant model.

Over time, technology also began to change the way in which counseling for relationship difficulties was conducted. Though less common, telephone "interviews" provided a means by which people could access support. In the early 1980s, for example, the Church of England Marriage Guidance Council alone was taking hundreds of calls per year.[34] The telephone support model, however, was not entirely new. For as with marriage guidance in the 1940s, Christian ministries of the 1950s were at the center of another innovation in counseling, one that saw the new media and communication technologies enable the expansion of the therapeutic in new ways.

In 1958, just two years after television was introduced in Australia, the Reverend Alan Walker of Sydney's Central Methodist Mission was appearing weekly on an evangelical program called, *I Challenge the Minister*. Each week, he would address a subject before taking questions from the audience. The show was enormously successful: reportedly the highest rating evangelical television program in Australia's history. Walker's foray into television and his subsequent success followed many years of radio broadcasting. Politically left but socially conservative, his evangelism clearly struck a chord. His style was very different from the kinds of religious voices that later came to dominate public discourse. According to Stephen Crittenden, presenter of ABC Radio National's *Religion Report*, "he [was] not someone who brandishes the bible at you ... or who begins the answer to every question with a quote from St Paul ... His starting point [was] people's real, everyday lives."[35]

Cultural Diffusion of the Analytic Attitude 149

Walker clearly possessed a capacity to understand people's everyday lives and appreciate, moreover, the difficulties people often faced. His appearances on television and radio prompted a number of people in crisis to telephone him directly and seek advice. So desperate were some of the pleas for assistance and such was the demand for help via the telephone that, with the support of the Central Methodist Mission in Sydney, Walker founded in 1963 the first telephone counseling service of its kind in the world: Lifeline.

Lifeline provided a new model of support for people in distress. Within days of commencing operation in Australia, the helpline had received more than 100 calls, and by 2009 was taking over 1,200 calls each day.[36] As with marriage guidance, it emerged out of Christian pastoral counseling but became more therapeutic in its orientation. The establishment of a prevention program of telephone counseling for parents of abused children was one such therapeutic initiative Lifeline spawned. Bill Crews, Director of the Crisis Centre at Sydney's Wayside Chapel, explains how their "Prevention" program arose in the 1970s:

> The whole idea came because one father came in whose wife that morning had killed their child and he said, "Where do you go? I had come in various days and the child had had a black eye or something and she would say it hit itself with a spoon or fell off its high chair. I knew there was something wrong, but where do you go, when you have doubts?[37]

The man's question—*where do you go?*—is a poignant rejoinder to vociferous critiques of the therapeutic society. As with other forms of social and psychological support, the advent of telephone counseling did not simply arise as a result of a successful professionalizing project. Nor can it be explained away as an outcome of the collapse of religious authority. On the contrary, its emergence signaled a greater responsiveness of religious authorities to suffering in the private domain. Recognition of how (and why) therapeutic practices and dispositions emerged in particular social and historical contexts suggests an alternative reading of these developments. Some anti-therapeutic critiques are all the more troubling because, in the renunciation of emotions in the public sphere, the social reality of suffering is obfuscated. Sometimes parents do kill their children, just as some women, and some men, are the victims of domestic violence.

Certainly, as theorists since Christopher Lasch have reminded us, counseling is no panacea for social ills, but neither does its growth simply reflect the collapse of the moral order. A more nuanced and historically grounded reading would recognize the emergence of these services as part of a series of responses to suffering and social crisis—responses that are, moreover, not antithetical to social justice, but in which questions of justice are thoroughly implicated, particularly those which involve attempts to prevent abuse of the less powerful in society.

Complex interests have intersected in facilitating the rise of the therapeutic—not only in the embrace of the psychological in institutional settings, as discussed in the previous chapter, but also in explicitly therapeutically oriented interventions like counseling. That the expansion of therapeutic services occurred on a number of fronts indicates that it was driven by a variety of interests. While some services that had their origins in pastoral counseling began with a moral-religious underpinning, others were established to serve more bureaucratic purposes. But even in those forms of guidance or counseling that had a more utilitarian edge, the welfare of the individual increasingly came to the fore.

Emerging from within the institutional framework of universities, counseling services for tertiary students were established in Australia in the 1950s. Extending the earlier work of vocational guidance, an important dimension of these services was the preparation of the student for working life. As with marriage guidance, the development of student counseling in universities occurred in the postwar context, which for the tertiary education sector saw an influx of ex-servicemen and a changing student population, one that was far more heterogeneous than before. In this context, student attrition became a particular problem. As with the use of psychology in industry to address issues of staff retention, the primary rationale for funding counseling services was to maintain student enrollment.

In addition to the perceived benefit psychologists could offer in helping students with study skills, "problems of minor psychological disturbance" came to be seen among a number of factors that could hinder academic success. The Australian Vice-Chancellors' Committee in 1960 thus recommended the expansion of services from those focused predominantly on issues of learning to also encompass attention to "personal problems."[38]

While the early period of student counseling was marked by an emphasis on medical models of behavior and concepts of normality, by the late 1960s there was a shift in the orientation of counselors towards the client, and their role as advocate and supporter became more important.[39] By the 1970s, many services had moved from a model predominantly focused on study skills and the administration of aptitude tests to one concerned primarily with providing counseling and therapy.[40]

The expansion of counseling in the 1970s reflected the intensification and institutionalization of what had been a growing therapeutic orientation across a variety of sectors. This involved both an expansion of services—in areas of health, education, and welfare in particular—and the development of new forms of analysis (as opposed to mere assessment and advice) in an approach that took greater heed of private life and the emotional realm. In the area of vocational guidance, aptitudes and preferences had been examined through psychological testing and interviews for many decades. But the new attention to the emotional dimensions of everyday life and relational problems—and the new privileging of communication and openness—marked a change from the concerns that had hitherto characterized applied psychology.

The advent of counseling and therapy on a broad scale bears an interesting relationship to developments in psychology within the academy. As Goff Barrett-Lennard, who taught psychology at the University of New England, recalls, counseling was up to the 1960s identified more with the field of marriage guidance and with educational and vocational guidance than with psychology. Nevertheless, he added, psychologists generally supervised the training of counselors.[41] Barrett-Lennard's observation raises two important points. First, that the training of counselors was provided by credentialed psychologists underscores the critical role of psychology in processes of the legitimation of counseling more broadly. Even though psychologists had been only one of a number of professional groups associated with the development of counseling services, the discipline and profession of psychology was instrumental to processes of expansion. Second, psychology itself—particularly counseling psychology—was in turn influenced by broader developments, notably those of marriage guidance and later, student counseling, both of which provided models of counseling for problems of everyday life.[42]

During the 1970s there was a significant expansion of training programs and counseling services. Psychologists working in the applied and academic fields were instrumental in these developments. By the mid-1970s counseling courses were established in universities across Australia and counseling psychology itself grew and professionalized. In 1977 the Australian Psychological Society (APS) established the division of "Counselling Psychology" and by the 1980s had established a professional journal, *Australian Counselling Psychologist*. During the following decades, psychological therapies and counseling services experienced tremendous growth. In addition to traditional face-to-face therapies, by 2010 there were also more than 500 telephone and e-counseling services in Australia, offering specialized counseling for victims of domestic violence, families, children, for drug and alcohol dependence, for stress, grief, and a range of other problems.[43]

Marriage guidance, to a large extent, paved the way for the emergence of a range of psychotherapeutic interventions, practices, and strategies aimed at problems of everyday life. That some of the earliest forms of counseling in Australia arose from or were aligned with Christian ministries provided a legitimizing moral element. The increasingly therapeutic orientation that followed reflected the changing interests of psychologists on the one hand, and the changing expectations of clients on the other, as demand for counseling services grew in the 1960s and 1970s. The domain of personal life and personal problems had been opened up to psychology during this period and it was in this context that the profession itself became increasingly interested in promoting its services to assist with problems of personal life. The value of psychology thus needed to be promoted to the general public and strategies of the APS increasingly came to be directed towards that end.

Marketing the Psychological

While the cultural diffusion of psychological knowledge has been critical to psychology's remarkable growth and success, it has also furnished a degree of professional anxiety. In 1970, in the context of increasing concern over its professional status, the APS formed a Public Relations Committee and charged it with improving public understanding of psychology. Despite the initial aims and high hopes of those involved, little progress was made, for according to Simon Cooke, the Committee "failed to move beyond the 'exchange of data-free opinion' on the question of how much the public already knew about psychology."[44] Research that purported to gauge the public perception of psychology was, however, published a few years later—with disappointing results. A 1975 survey confirmed what anecdotal evidence had already suggested: people were more than three times as likely to turn to the clergy or a medical doctor when faced with marital problems than they were to seek help from a psychologist, while less than ten percent of respondents nominated a psychologist as the professional they would turn to if feeling depressed or despondent.[45]

Disturbed by these findings, the promotion of greater public awareness of psychology and the work of psychologists became an important objective of the APS. A Community Relations Committee was formed in 1986, and a Marketing Committee in 1992, both to address what was clearly regarded as public ignorance. One part of their publicity campaign saw the APS become an agony aunt for the Melbourne newspaper, the *Age*.[46] In a regular column entitled, "Consulting Room," APS members would respond to questions such as: "When I'm depressed or bored, I find myself looking in the refrigerator for consolation. What causes this perverse temptation and how can I control it?" Or others, like: "I am a 38-year-old woman who has been given a good promotion, but instead of feeling elated, I feel depressed. Why?"

During the late 1980s and into the early 1990s, psychologists were enjoying a higher profile in the media. However, despite the efforts of the APS, promoting a greater understanding of psychology in the minds of the general public proved difficult. The results of a 1992 Newspoll survey of public perceptions of psychologists were interpreted as evidence that "few gains had been made since

1975."[47] Only three percent of male respondents and four percent of female respondents indicated they would seek help from a psychologist for relationship difficulties, while around 20 percent of men and 15 percent of women replied that they would not seek professional help at all. For a profession with high regard for its identity, it was perhaps the following finding that was most irksome—almost 28 percent of men and 40 percent of women indicated that they would seek help from a "counselor."

The APS's concern with public perception underscores the incongruity between the cultural impact of psychology and issues of professional identity. There is little doubt that psychological expertise is highly valued—evidenced by the growth of psychology as a discipline and its considerable professional power as a practice, and undoubtedly also the extent to which various forms of counseling have gained legitimacy as well. Academic, industrial, and educational psychologists established clearly demarcated terrains within institutional settings, but clinicians working in private practice have faced the competing interests of a range of other occupational groups providing similar services—psychiatrists, counselors, and psychotherapists in particular. Within the context of the increasing occupational power of counselors, who by the turn of the twenty-first century outnumbered psychologists in Australia by several thousand, an ongoing anxiety about professional identity and status is hardly surprising.[48]

An attempt to secure control over the provision of expert assistance for psychological difficulties and problems of everyday life continues to be an area of high priority for the APS. Following the success of its National Psychology Day initiative in 2002, it launched National Psychology Week the following year, with the aim of showcasing the benefits of psychology. The promotion of psychologists as the professionals of choice to assist with personal problems is evident in their marketing material—which asserts that consulting an APS psychologist is "good thinking."

The APS website advises potential client/consumers that: "Everyday problems, such as work stress, relationship troubles and coping with illness, can seriously affect your life. Addressing these concerns is vital to enjoying life and good relationships." The statement is accompanied by an exhaustive list of personal problems that psychologists can assist with, including marital, family, and relationship problems; stress or pain; fears, phobias, anxiety, and panic attacks; depression; loss and grief; sexual difficulties; sleeping difficulties; eating and weight control problems; children's learning, behavior, and management problems; addictions; making good relationships better; becoming better parents and teachers; personal growth; career planning, and so on.[49]

Since the 1990s, promoting the social and economic value of psychology has also constituted an important strategy. In the mid-1990s, the APS commissioned a study to ascertain psychology's contribution to health, wellbeing, and the "optimization of human performance," measured as gross domestic product (GDP). It purported to find that psychology contributed over $1.1 billion dollars per year to the Australian economy. A similar study conducted in 2001 suggested that the annual contribution of psychology to the national economy was, by that point, an estimated $8.6 billion.[50] In 1995, Peter Sheehan, a former APS president argued that it was "absolutely necessary" for the APS to engage in such economic analysis, arguing that it "demonstrates the value of psychology to others, and provides support for marketing our psychological skills."[51] Evidence of demonstrable economic and social benefits has buttressed the professional project, and APS psychologists have been extremely proactive in the expansion of their interests. This targeted strategy is evident most recently in the promotion of the value of psychologists in the area of mental health.

Within the contemporary environment of increasing government concern with rising rates of mental illness, psychology has been given greater fillip. As numbers of psychiatrists are far more limited (comprising around only twenty percent the number of psychologists), psychology has been able to make greater inroads into the area of mental health. After many years of lobbying by the APS, provision was made in the 2006 Federal Budget for clinical psychological services to be rebated under Medicare, Australia's publicly funded universal health care system.[52] While state support of psychology had long been established, the direct funding of psychological therapies in this way marks another important triumph for the profession.

The diverse interests of psychologists may have provided some challenges in relation to professional identity, but the heterogeneity of psychology has not diminished its professional power. Psychology's success has from the outset been largely achieved by underwriting the discipline with scientific method. Henry Laurie was lauding that approach in 1893, and Peter Sheehan was singing a similar tune in 1996.[53] Indeed, the practical application of scientific method—through psychometrics and later also through psychological therapies—has been central, both to the professional project, and to the ways in which psychology has been marketed.

As I have already indicated, an important strategy has been to promote the work of psychologists through the popular media. In 1999, the APS began a new initiative to train psychologists for such work. According to Hugh Mackay, the pressures of contemporary life mean that psychologists have a vitally important public role to play. As he put it: "Australians, in growing numbers, are asking someone (us?) to explain them to themselves, to help them understand themselves, to help them find strategies that will ease their anxieties and insecurities. Now, more than ever, the voice of psychologists should be heard. As a profession, we don't have all the answers, but we are certainly equipped to help people find their own answers."[54]

Though professional self-interest has clearly been a factor, the increasing public profile of psychologists has not always developed in ways that accord with the APS's vision, or indeed that of the psychologists directly involved. As the following discussion reveals, working with the media can be fraught with difficulty and psychologists' own views about their capacity to help people in times of distress is sometimes also marked by ambivalence.

Therapists as Public Experts

In the late 1970s, American social critic Martin Gross warned his compatriots that psychiatrists and psychologists had "appointed themselves the undisputed Solomons of our era, the sages of the Psychological Society." He went on to argue: "Their expertise covers an infinite variety of subjects that affect modern man: homosexuality, crime, sexual habits, marriage and divorce, psychosomatics, education, international relations, politics, child-parent relationships and psychobiography."[55] With cultural authority increasing in step with growing professional power, Gross expressed concern about the extent to which psychological experts were shaping policy, public opinion, and indeed American society more broadly.

In a mediated world the distinction between public expert and celebrity is not always clear. The United States is now home to a multitude of media psychologists and celebrity therapists, the most notable being "Dr Phil" McGraw who secured international fame through the *Oprah Winfrey Show*. Dr Phil's syndicated television talk show is broadcast in Australia, just as many of the self-help books sold in Australia are American. Though boasting no such equivalent, Australia has its own sagacious figureheads who disseminate psychological knowledge and know-how to millions through the mass media and therapeutic guides.

The following discussion draws on interviews I conducted in the mid 2000s with four prominent therapists from different intellectual and therapeutic traditions who have been actively involved in shaping therapeutic discourses in Australia. Former president of the APS and clinical psychologist, Amanda Gordon; author and psychoanalytic psychologist, Peter O'Connor; academic and clinical psychologist, Antony Kidman; and author, psychotherapist, and recently ordained Interfaith Minister, Stephanie Dowrick, discuss their roles as public experts and reflect on their experiences of working with the media. Their reflections offer an insight into the motivations driving the dissemination of psychological knowledge by experts in matters of the psyche. From the standpoint of these therapists at least, the desire to play an educative role is paramount, as is the belief that they can assist people in times of distress. Yet as the following account reveals, obligation to publishers, media imperatives, and other factors also come into play in shaping the therapeutic message.

The publication of a self-help book or therapeutic guide is often an entrée into the role of the psychologist as public expert. In the 1980s, Peter O'Connor and Antony Kidman both published popular psychological books that extended their careers beyond the academy and clinical practice to ones in which they developed prominent media profiles. For Peter O'Connor, teaching and clinical work had little prepared him for the experience of being propelled into the public eye with the publication in 1981 of *Understanding the Mid-Life*

Crisis. He said: "I remember being like a lamb to the slaughter. The book came out and I did this thing called an author's tour. I didn't even know what an author's tour was. I think that's when I started to get a sense of *being in the media*."[56]

For Antony Kidman, an Australian pioneer of Cognitive Behavioral Therapy (CBT), the publication of his first self-help book similarly cast him into the role of public expert. His first book, *Tactics for Change*, was tremendously successful. As he recalls: "It was one of the first around and it dealt with a whole range of things using CBT. The thing sold as fast as we could print them for a while there." Over the past twenty years, Kidman has made frequent appearances on radio and television and he uses the media to deliver public health messages, promote his books, and raise money for research. In his view, the electronic media has a vitally important role to play in the destigmatization of mental illness, and in bringing psychology to people who would otherwise not be exposed to it. As he stated: "It's the only way, the only vehicle. A lot of people don't read newspapers, don't even read books."

It is essential, according to Kidman, that experienced and qualified psychologists disseminate sound psychological advice. For him, it is thus a matter of professional obligation to provide information to the public about psychology, albeit an obligation that brings reciprocal benefits. As Kidman acknowledges: "You want publicity either for your book or fundraising, they want to fill the space with something of interest that will keep the audience." Clearly, psychology is a subject of broad appeal for contemporary audiences. As Kidman sees it:

> People are interested in behavior and personality disorder, you know what I mean, anxiety and depression, marital problems, obsessive compulsive disorder, and they turn up in magazines. The magazines write about them, and there is no shortage of people, some of them qualified, others unqualified, giving advice. There's all sorts of stuff pouring out into magazines and it seems to sell. I think the media likes these topics because they're sort of timeless in a way, anxiety and depression, all those issues.

Cultural Diffusion of the Analytic Attitude 159

As well as the public interest in these matters, Kidman recognizes the expansion of psychology itself as a factor in the growth of psychologically oriented stories in the popular media:

> There are also a lot of people doing good research all over the world, here, the US and UK. So there is a lot of data pouring out. And you know it gets the eye of the writers in the popular press, rather than discoveries in physiology, or biochemistry, which doesn't quite have the same appeal. Because I worked in neurobiology for a number of years…
>
> *And you weren't asked to speak on the radio about that?*
> Not quite so much, no (laughs), certainly not.

While Kidman generally views his work with the media in a positive light, Peter O'Connor is more ambivalent about his own public profile and the role of the psychological expert more generally. While he has had positive experiences with the national broadcaster, his encounters with other media, especially the print media, have disappointed him. As he candidly said:

> I'm very distrustful of print media, very distrustful, because my experience of them is that they ring up, and you sort of know intuitively that they have actually written the article and what they are using me for is to prop it up. And I really resent that. And I sort of feel, look, if you are interested in what I've got to say, come and see me. Don't ring me up for a quick grab. You feel like you're actually used in some system that's actually quick superficial grabs. They say things like: "We'd like a comment on men and the media." You know, to be perfectly honest, I haven't got a clue. Some people do that okay, I don't do it that way, nor would I feel comfortable doing that.

While Kidman holds the view that providing "some sensible advice," like giving a radio phone-in caller a useful tip, can be extremely helpful in times of distress, O'Connor's psychoanalytic orientation is perhaps less suited to the imperatives of the contemporary media. Both in therapy and also in his media work, O'Connor's intent has been to communicate a benevolent and therapeutic attitude, rather than to provide solutions. As he puts it: "I'm not very good at pop psychology, I don't really have the answers. For me, it is sort of an illusion that information will alter your behavior." Moreover, while his media work has ensured a steady supply of clients, O'Connor believes that it has, in some ways, made his clinical work more difficult:

> Having a public profile means I get, not huge numbers, but a number of people that turn up that have already got a fix that I have the answer. And I know I'm disappointing to them, because writing books is one thing, but seeing somebody is quite another. And I have to struggle a fair bit with that. If I had my life over again, I probably wouldn't do the media work. I think it has made it too difficult at times. I think it makes it more difficult to sustain the sort of philosophy I have with the sort clients you attract, who actually want an answer.

O'Connor's philosophical standpoint on therapy, that it is "about exploration, not explanation," sheds light on his ambivalence about his own role as an expert. As he explains: "I don't like telling people how to live their lives." The way in which the contemporary media contributes to the commercialization and marketing of psychology and therapy, therefore, does not sit well with him. As he sees it: "Therapy is marketed more, it's a product more. And I think the more you market it, the more factualized you have to become, the more simplistic you have to become in your ideas, and the more you have to promise."

In his capacity as Director of the Victorian Marriage Guidance Council in the 1970s, O'Connor would brief the media about marriage. In later years, following his success as an author, his public profile grew and he received more invitations to appear on television and radio. His media appearances have been in part driven by obligations to publishers, but he has also accepted invitations to speak on the radio and write for newspapers because of a deeply felt responsibility to communicate a therapeutic attitude:

Cultural Diffusion of the Analytic Attitude 161

I always felt that there was a role, an educative role that you could play, if you struggle with it, you know, without compromising your integrity. Which is the same for me when I would write the article for the *Good Weekend*, same thought. How do you straddle this line between actually introducing the community to some more or less useful ideas, without over-simplifying it and without compromising my own integrity?

While the intellectual traditions and theoretical orientations of those I interviewed differ significantly, a deeply felt commitment to helping people is shared by all. For O'Connor, the medium of radio has been more accommodating than television or print media because it allows for greater exploration of complex issues. When speaking on the radio, O'Connor says:

My conscious intention was that listeners would get an attitude towards themselves, but not an answer so much as a way of thinking about themselves that might have been more benevolent than they'd had before. I find it very important to talk about ambivalence, for example, in a world that's obsessed with clarity. Things are difficult sometimes and you can love and hate simultaneously. You know, dependency has a hostility in it, looking after your aged mum creates fantasies of wanting to kill her. And I just find that sort of, instead of it being restricted to the counseling room, if you put it in reasonably straightforward language, there is something that is quite liberating about that if people are ready to hear it.

The conviction that the therapeutic message can be liberating is shared by all the therapists I interviewed. As Kidman noted, the discussion of problems through a medium like the radio or television has the capacity to reach large numbers of people who may be suffering from a similar problem: "So you can give them a thumbnail sketch of what to do, challenge their thinking, advise them to consult a professional, buy a book, etcetera."

Like O'Connor and Kidman, Amanda Gordon describes her

public role as primarily educative, part of which has involved the promotion of psychology and the Australian Psychological Society. Prior to her election as President of the APS in 2004, she held the position of Director of Communications, a role that included responsibility for developing policies and procedures for the promotion and marketing of psychology and psychologists. Her own foray into the media began in the late 1980s after hearing a promotional segment for Tony Delroy's ABC radio program, *Nightlife*. The show was to feature various professionals—an accountant, a naturopath, a doctor—who would provide general advice to listeners and respond to callers. Gordon saw an opportunity: "So, I rang him and said that the program sounded great but he had a glaring hole in his line-up: he needed a psychologist." Delroy agreed and offered her a twenty-minute slot for a trial period of six weeks. The segment proved to be so popular that it was extended to one hour per week and her appearance on the program spanned some twelve years.

The weekly radio segment established Gordon's public profile and led to other work with the media. She was the agony aunt, "Dear Amanda" for Sydney's *Daily Telegraph* for seven years, she writes columns for newspapers and magazines, and makes regular guest appearances on television. As a prominent member of the APS, an important part of her media work has involved the promotion of psychology. While she also recognizes it as a useful way of building her private practice, she stresses that the paramount objective of her media work, and indeed its most rewarding aspect, is to reach people who would otherwise have no access to a psychologist:

> I like to demystify. I bring psychology into the lives of people who do not understand what it can do for them, or who do not have access to it. What I loved about the ABC was that we went all over Australia. So I was there for people in remote areas, people whose husbands would not let them talk to anyone, or consult anyone about their problems, people who were suffering in silence or who lived alone and had no access to anyone else.

The criticism often leveled at the popular psychological message—be it delivered via a prominent psychologist or through a self-help book—is that it is an illusory form of liberation. As a critique of the promise of miraculous transformation that characterizes some strands of popular psychology, particularly in the United States, this view is compelling. The Australian therapeutic landscape, however, is somewhat different. Though American discourses do shape those in Australia, the messages carried through the media by local therapists and psychologists reflect a different cultural sensibility, one that is arguably less geared towards the miraculous than much of the American market. Gordon, for example, has come to see the sort of advice she offers as a kind of "common sense":

> Someone once said to me, "I really like what you say Amanda. It's just such common sense." And I remember initially being quite offended, thinking, no, I have trained for years, I have read all the articles, I have done the research. What I say is not just common sense. It is psychological wisdom. And then I thought, no, I am actually communicating in a way people can hear, and that is what it is all about.

In critiques of the therapeutic society, a dimension commonly overlooked is the degree to which the dissemination of the psychological is driven by a genuine desire to provide a public service—indeed to help people. That this often intersects with professional and commercial interests, however, complicates the matter. Gordon provides a fine example of how altruism, professional obligation, self-interest, and commercial imperatives came together in an experience that helped her become "media savvy." In our interview, she described an early foray into commercial television as the psychological expert on Channel Ten's, *Sex/Life*. Following her initial appearance on the program, she tried to negotiate for a degree of editorial control, as well as an appearance fee. In her view, having some control over the way in which she was represented was important, both for her own reputation but also in terms of safeguarding the interests of her profession. Secondly, as a commercial venture, she considered it appropriate that the psychologist appearing on the program be paid, just as others working on the show were remunerated for their services. Unsuccessful in her negotiations on those two key issues, she declined further work. Soon after, she was approached again, this time, with the offer of an appearance fee. Gordon recounts, in her excitement of being paid, she forgot to ask for further details:

> I missed one vital part of the equation. I had been so excited that they had agreed to the appearance fee that I forgot about editorial control, and I forgot to ask what topic they wanted me to speak on. As it turned out, it was "why men are attracted to breasts," which I would never have done in a million years ... I was actually very good, I talked about Freud and the maternal and that sort of thing, but of course when it was produced the segment had become an excuse for soft porn and I was cut through with images of topless women. It was a very interesting lesson and I use it in teaching. I was so caught up in the appropriateness of being paid that I let go of the other issues. And I do not do anything over which I do not have some control anymore, because it was the worst possible experience. They really got me!

Understandably, Gordon felt betrayed and misrepresented, but later came to view it as an important learning experience. Her story highlights the difficulties faced by those entering the media fray. Over the years she has learnt how to work productively with the media. However, in promoting the scientific status of psychology, Gordon faces competing interests in the psychotherapeutic domain. Other strands of the therapeutic that hold widespread appeal are those that tap into bigger questions of spirituality and meaning.

Emblematic of this kind of message is author of numerous therapeutic guides and books on spirituality, Stephanie Dowrick.[57] For many years, Dowrick combined writing with her work as a psychotherapist; she provides regular media commentary on psychological and spiritual issues, and in 2005 was ordained as an Interfaith Minister. Dowrick sees the core of her work as a concern with "the self in relation to the world, that is as much spiritual as it is psychological and social, and as much outward looking as inward looking." She describes her public role as "a great privilege" and is strongly invested in it at a personal level. In reflecting on her media work, she says:

> I see it primarily as an educative role. I believe I have the capacity to be very encouraging of other people, without being, I believe anyway, facile. I think I am able to avoid that because I do actually understand the depth of people's experience and yet retain some hope. I truly believe that we can learn even from great suffering, and probably that's what underpins my spiritual bias: that we can learn and grow even from difficult and unwelcome experiences. But often we need help.

Though coming from a different intellectual standpoint, she shares with O'Connor a deep interest in the spiritual as well as the psychological and social dimensions of the human condition. For O'Connor, the psychoanalytic tradition embraces the complexity of subjectivity and he sees it as an important dimension of the therapeutic landscape. He is concerned therefore that an analytic position is becoming harder to sustain in an environment dominated by cognitive behavioral therapies and increasingly subject to commercial imperatives, not to mention, Americanization:

> I think it is going to be very difficult to sustain an analytical position in Australia, we've become so Americanized and this fantasy that people like me know things, really it's not so. It's rather that I see therapy as the space in which you will discover what *you* already know, not what *I* know.

By contrast to O'Connor's analytic position in which exploration is a core dimension of the therapeutic enterprise, Kidman regards an approach of "problem solving" more positively. In addition to offering some advice to listeners of a radio program or viewers of a television show, he regards the greater psychological awareness that the media has fostered as critically important in the destigmatization of mental illness. As he put it:

People do suffer terribly. The vast majority of people hate being depressed and absolutely abhor being profoundly disturbed with anxiety disorders. It is a terrible experience. There is a lot of suffering and if you can alleviate some small part of that it is worthwhile. I've had people who ring up who've heard something that helped them at a crucial time. Thus I think it's well worth it.

O'Connor, Gordon, and Dowrick share with Kidman an abiding concern with human suffering and a resolute belief in the capacity to reach people, not only through therapy but also through therapeutic guides and the media. From divergent professional positions and intellectual traditions, the stories provided by these therapists offer an insight into the motives driving the dissemination of the psychological from the standpoint of those actively involved in spreading the psychological word. In the following chapter, their thoughts on therapy itself are explored. Consideration of the differing viewpoints of psychologists and therapists with prominent media profiles sheds further light on the complexity of the therapeutic society. Critically, their roles bridge the public and private. As therapists, they are at the front line of emotional problems and personal difficulties. As public experts, they recognize the significance of their role in lifting the lid on private suffering—a process that has been escalating in Australia since the 1970s.

Lifting the Lid on Private Pain

In August 1974, then Australian Prime Minister Gough Whitlam announced the establishment of a government inquiry that would subject private life to political and public examination as never before: a Royal Commission on Human Relationships. The Commission's terms of reference were broad: "to inquire into the family, social, educational, legal and sexual aspects of male and female relationships."[58] That "relationships" should warrant such a major investigation signals the extent to which private life—as distinct from "the family"—had become by the 1970s a central concern of government. Certainly the issue of abortion was the precipitating factor, for as one of the Commissioners was to later write, the establishment of the Commission was essentially "a political

Cultural Diffusion of the Analytic Attitude 167

compromise" over moves to reform abortion laws.[59] Yet despite the motives driving the investigation, what resulted was the uncovering of aspects of private life that had up till then been subject to little, if any, scrutiny.

During their investigations, the Commissioners spoke on radio, television, and at public forums, encouraging ordinary people to share their views and experiences on a broad range of issues affecting individuals and families. Flyers were widely distributed and advertisements were carried in the press asking the Australian public: "What do you think?" The response included more than 1,200 written submissions, oral testimony from several hundred people, and informally gathered information from many more. The voices of women, children, migrants, people with disabilities, those from sexual minority groups, and indigenous Australians were publicly articulated and formally documented.

A comprehensive picture of widespread emotional pain and suffering in the personal domain emerged. The handing down of the *Final Report* in November 1977 effectively institutionalized a new kind of public concern for the private troubles of ordinary Australians, as it documented experiences of distress, fear, and abuse that had hitherto been largely hidden. Domestic violence and child abuse were two issues that the investigation of family life uncovered. Hundreds of cases of child abuse were revealed to Commissioners, including reports from parents who had "battered" their children. One parent confessed that:

> He'd have been 2 when I first really used to get stuck into him. I used to punch him. And I used to belt him hard. I can remember breaking wooden spoons on him. I used to get him around the throat, and I'd hit his head up against things, and I couldn't understand why I would do this to a child. I used to be all sort of tense inside. It was a terrible thing and was just terrifying, but I couldn't stop.[60]

Child abuse first emerged as a pressing social issue in the early 1960s. In a landmark article published in the *Journal of the American Medical Association* in 1962, Henry Kempe and his colleagues delineated the problem of the "battered child syndrome."[61] The article not only raised concerns about a hidden social problem, it argued that it was a physician's duty to protect children. Doctors were urged to investigate cases of unexplained injury and make accurate diagnoses, to report willful trauma to police or child welfare agencies, and to institute therapy in the hope of preventing future abuse. By 1967, legislation had been passed in all American states requiring health professionals to report suspected cases of abuse. Legislation was also introduced that criminalized caretakers' abuse of children.[62] Australian legislative reform followed. Some states had introduced mandatory reporting by the 1970s, but it took until the 1990s for legislation to be enacted in all states and territories.[63]

Cases of abuse brought to light by the Royal Commission on Human Relationships therefore arose in this context of increasing concern with family violence and the criminalization of child abuse, both in Australia and internationally. Growing public awareness also gave rise to recognition of the danger that feelings of aggression against children might escalate. Psychology furnished a language with which to express such concerns, and the therapeutic ethos gave license to do so. One woman who gave evidence to the Commission during a domestic violence phone-in said:

> I've never told anyone before, but I often feel violent towards my eldest, she's six. I lie wake at nights worrying that one day I might do serious harm. My danger period is just before tea-time when the children have only just come home and my husband's demanding his tea on time because he works at night. I feel I'm being torn in little pieces ... Where do you go when you want to talk about these things, to relieve the pressure? [64]

In the mid-1970s when counseling services were still limited in Australia, the Commission proved to be not only a means of gathering information but also provided an opportunity for people to voice their experiences of personal distress and seek advice on where to go for assistance. That the issue of child abuse arose and that parents had begun to seek help by the 1970s was understood by the Commissioners as having been brought about by a number of interrelated factors: "Change in public attitude has come about partly because of

HELP for PARENTS

IS YOUR PRE-SCHOOLER MAKING YOU ANGRY
FRUSTRATED, UPTIGHT? WANT SOME HELP?
THE PARENTS' HELP CENTRE OFFERS UNDERSTANDING
HELP TO PARENTS WHO FEEL THAT THEY ARE PAST
RUNNING OUT OF PATIENCE IN A DIFFICULT
SITUATION INVOLVING A PRE-SCHOOL CHILD

IF YOU EVER FEEL ANGRY ENOUGH TO WANT TO HURT A CHILD,

Ring 283266
24 HOURS A DAY !

**Parents' Help Centre
5 Glendower St
North Perth**

In 1976 the Child Life Protection Unit of the Western Australian Department for Community Welfare began operating a Help Centre for parents at risk of harming their children. As noted in the Report of the Royal Commission on Human Relationships, these posters were displayed in baby health clinics, medical centers, shopping malls, laundromats, and taxis.

a growing sensitivity to the legal and human rights of individuals, partly with improved knowledge of childhood development, and partly because of the increased importance of outside agencies to families. Private life is now more public."[65]

The rise of the therapeutic society is deeply implicated in the growing recognition of child abuse and family violence. Professional intervention into private life has not only subjected the less powerful and marginalized to disciplinary practices and control, as Jacques Donzelot and others have argued, but it has often done so in the name of those historically possessing even less power: women and children.

The Royal Commission on Human Relationships not only threw light on experiences of suffering but it revealed, as much sociological and psychological research has also done, that distress is not equally distributed throughout the population. Recent cultural critiques have correctly identified the changing relationship between the public and private spheres as central to the ascendancy of the therapeutic society. Yet the idealization of traditional authority that colors many analyses prevents recognition of the ways in which, especially for the less powerful, the therapeutic has been enabling. Speaking out about abuse and suffering constitutes a significant sociocultural transformation, one that reflects shifting relations of power on the one hand, and changing codes of conduct on the other.

A hallmark of the contemporary therapeutic society is a greater level of openness—in contrast to earlier reticence—about problems of personal life and mental health, often manifest in public accounts of private troubles. According to Nikolas Rose, the contemporary form of "speaking out" arose from a fusion of the 1960s radical political practice of consciousness raising with a therapeutic ethos of self-realization. Rose suggests that: "Rather than a sinner repenting, those who speak out today are increasingly survivors bearing witness to the hidden injuries done to them by others—or by fate."[66] The disclosure of experience of family violence as discussed above, and that of depression to which I now turn, aptly illustrate such forms of hidden injury that increasingly have a public presence.

The disclosure of experiences of depression—by celebrities, sporting personalities, politicians and other public figures—is an especially important expression of the therapeutic ethos. While public discussion of problems of emotional and mental health is not entirely new, what has changed in recent decades is the way in which these discourses have taken a personalized form. Letters to agony aunts and psychological experts in the popular media over many decades may have contributed to the normalization of discussions of personal problems, yet the cloak of anonymity ensured distance, detachment, and privacy. Similarly, accounts of private pain documented by the Royal Commission on Human Relationships opened the realm of domestic life to scrutiny, but the gathering of evidence generally occurred within a reasonably private context. The contemporary form of speaking out about emotional pain and mental distress is qualitatively different. It not only reveals the extent to which the therapeutic ethos has saturated social and cultural life. It also reflects changes in identity construction and personhood, and a radical transformation of traditional (notably masculine) assumptions governing conduct in the public sphere.

Revelations of depression by prominent footballers in recent years provides a striking example, not only of the degree to which therapeutic disclosure has escalated, but also of how this new form of public speech has challenged dominant ideals of masculinity. The first—and consequently perhaps the most significant—of such events occurred mid-way through the 2004 Australian Football League (AFL) season. At a press conference held in May that year, then vice-captain of the Hawthorn Football Club, Nathan Thompson, made public his "battle" with depression. Thompson revealed that he had been diagnosed with clinical depression, was on medication, and was receiving counseling. He went on to say: "I hope that by speaking today, that it helps people better understand depression and the importance of being open and honest with yourself, and those around you."[67]

Thompson's public disclosure sparked commentary in dozens of newspaper articles and radio reports, as well as reverent discussion on such televisual bastions of masculine culture as the *Footy Show*, *On the Couch*, and *Talking Footy*. Fox Sports' *Back Page* saw the "tough blokes of footy" endorsing the value of talking through feelings as they discussed what constituted depression. Following Thompson's statement, another prominent AFL player, Scott West, spoke about his own experience of depression. On the sports radio station SEN—described by the *Age* journalist Suzanne Carbone as "aimed at men aged 25 to 54 and their fixation with bum-slapping locker-room banter, corked thighs, strained groins, footballers' hairstyles and Gary Ablett's glory days" — West supported Thompson's disclosure by saying that his life had improved after revealing he had depression and seeking help.[68]

Calls to Lifeline and the National Depression Institute, Beyond Blue, increased in the wake of Thompson's revelation, with Beyond Blue spokesman, Brian Peck, stating that the response had been "quite dramatic," and that his story had struck a chord with men in particular.[69] Within days it was reported that each year more than 270 AFL players utilize the counseling services of the Players Association, a figure suggesting close to half the league were getting some form of "counseling."[70] On the *Footy Show* the same week, high-profile AFL player, Jason Akermanis spoke openly about his own psychological difficulties and revealed that he had worked extensively with the club psychologist, not just to improve his mental resolve, but essentially did therapy to get rid of "baggage" from his teenage years. Later in the year his autobiography was released with the wonderfully therapeutic title, *Aka: The Battle Within*.

In recent years, there has not only been increased policy attention to problems of mental health, but there have been a number of prominent Australians, like Thompson, who have publicly discussed experiences of depression. Early in 2006, Western Australian premier Geoff Gallop resigned, citing depression as the precipitating factor. In his resignation statement, he said: "My commitment to politics has always been 100 per cent plus. I now need that time to restore my health and wellbeing." Others in public office and with prominent public profiles have revealed similar struggles. In 2003, following an incident in which he reportedly abused a female Liberal Senator, former Democrat Senator Andrew Bartlett admitted to suffering from depression and drinking excessively. While Bartlett's disclosure may be interpreted as an excuse for behaving badly, others have spoken out as part of concerted campaigns to raise awareness of, and destigmatize, mental illness. Actor Garry McDonald, for example, has been actively involved with Beyond Blue. He has spoken candidly about his experiences of depression and anxiety and uses his public profile to encourage others — particularly men — to seek professional help if they suspect they are suffering from a mental health disorder.

It is widely acknowledged that depressive and anxiety disorders constitute a major world health problem. In 2001, the World Health Organization reported that "one person in every four will be affected by a mental disorder at some stage of life."[71] More recently, the Australian Bureau of Statistics painted an even graver picture, with figures suggesting that almost half of all Australians will experience a mental disorder at some stage in their lives. These statistics, based on 2007 data, include people who have experienced a range of mental health conditions, including anxiety, mood, and substance use disorders.[72]

Clearly, the contemporary willingness to speak out about emotional and psychological problems encompasses various kinds of discourses. Such discourses contain confessional and redemptive elements, as well as political and therapeutic dimensions. One may confess to suffering depression to explain seemingly aberrant behavior—like excessive drinking in Bartlett's case. Self-disclosure may be part of a political or social justice project of destigmatizing mental illness—as with Garry McDonald. The desire to talk publicly about such problems is clearly driven by a number of factors, one of them surely being that it is therapeutic to do so. As a society, we now subscribe to the belief that talking about our problems is important for the process of healing.

Yet it is also more than that. For the dissemination of therapeutic discourse affects not only those who do the talking, it also shapes the broader culture. To illustrate, it is useful to return briefly to the discussions within the football fraternity about mental health, counseling, and emotional life that occurred in the wake of Nathan Thompson's statement on depression. While it is true that his revelation was framed within a biomedical model of illness, it nevertheless provided a platform for discussions about emotional life more broadly. The coming together of sport—long noted as significant to national and male identity—and the emotional realm, with its traditional associations with the "feminine" and the private sphere, has far-reaching cultural implications.

Indeed, the case of footballers talking about depression points to more than just the extent to which the therapeutic saturates cultural life. During the same period that the psychological entered the football vernacular, there was extensive public scrutiny about acceptable forms of behavior. In 2004 a number of allegations concerning sexual assault by professional footballers were made public. Players from both major football codes in Australia, the National Rugby League (NRL) and the AFL, were implicated. Members of the NRL's Canterbury Bulldog's team faced allegations of rape and players from the AFL's St Kilda Football Club were accused of sexual misconduct.[73]

As Senator Kate Lundy, then shadow Minster for Sport and Recreation noted, the allegations in these codes "uncovered what seems to be a culture of accepting unacceptable behaviours." She went on to say: "Whether these alleged crimes are proven or not, what they bring to light is the existence in some sports of a very distasteful and disturbing sexist subculture that marginalizes, silences and disrespects women. That a sexist culture exists, particularly within the football codes, is beyond question. In fact officials have admitted that serious misbehaviours have been covered up for decades."[74]

Following the scandals of 2004, other women also came forward with stories of sexual assault by footballers that had not previously been reported. The public airing of these issues led to a number of developments. Fans mobilized and established the campaign, Football Fans Against Sexual Assault (FFASA) with the aim of urging the AFL and the NRL to actively work to challenge norms of tolerance for sexual violence.[75] The hidden culture of violence against women that was brought to light with the string of allegations against footballers also led to the development of a range of strategies by the AFL and the NRL, the clubs, and players' associations to regulate the conduct of players. Late in 2005, the AFL released a new social policy, amending its rules regarding "Conduct Unbecoming" to include allegations, charges, or convictions of sexual harassment and assault. This change in official policy was driven by a variety of social and cultural shifts that the AFL had to respond to, one of which was recognition of the psychological damage that follows sexual assault.

By enabling, indeed encouraging, discussion of emotional injury and private pain, the rise of the therapeutic society is deeply implicated in developments such as those within the AFL. To view these kinds of social and cultural changes as merely an enchantment with psychological and emotional life—as some commentators have—does not take into account that they are part of a response to changes in the social acceptability of men's behavior. Such changes have not simply been driven by a "pro-therapy lobby" but have emerged from within a broader context of social and cultural change that has forced organizations to take the emotional and psychological realms seriously. It is important too, when considering the spread of therapeutic ideas and practices, to acknowledge that that there are complex structural arrangements within which counseling, for example, has blossomed. That footballers or officials who are alleged to have sexually harassed or assaulted a woman may be forced to have counseling, for example, is arguably a positive development, but importantly it is only one of a number of strategies the club or the league may adopt. Players found guilty of an offence also face decidedly anti-therapeutic action: like being de-listed.

To be sure, therapeutic solutions should never replace social and political ones, but neither should they be regarded as antithetical to social action and politics. In furnishing a language and legitimacy to experiences of suffering, the therapeutic ethos provides an alternative social critique. Superficial characterizations of the rise of "victim culture" and excessive emotionalism pay insufficient heed to the reality that the burden of abuse and suffering has traditionally been borne more heavily by the less powerful members of society. The pressing question is not so much whether we are all "victims" now, but to what extent the ascendancy of a therapeutic ethos has engendered a shift in social acceptability of abuse and suffering. This issue is further elucidated when attention is paid to people's actual experience of therapy and counseling.

5

Therapy: Inside the Talking Cure

> *To be modern is to find ourselves in an environment that promises us adventure, power, joy, growth, transformation of ourselves and the world—and, at the same time, that threatens to destroy everything we have, everything we know, everything we are.*
> —Marshall Berman, 1982

At the turn of the twentieth century, Freud's modestly stated aim of psychoanalytic therapy was to turn "hysterical misery into common unhappiness."[1] A century later, therapy had undergone such transformation that most varieties bore little resemblance to Freudian analysis. No longer solely the province of the elite or of the seriously incapacitated, the intervening years saw therapy democratized and normalized. Indeed by the end of the twentieth century, it had not only become a common practice of everyday life, but it had been imbued with the potential to attend to almost every human difficulty—from severe mental distress to lofty aspirations for happiness.

Each week in Australia, up to half a million people will see some kind of therapist or counselor.[2] From psychiatry and clinical psychology to a variety of other forms of therapy and counseling, Australians, like millions of others in the Western world, are turning to psychological therapies in growing numbers. Broadly defined, therapy exemplifies the contemporary fascination with the self and with psychological life. It represents the central metaphor of the therapeutic society, of which the clinical encounter—be it psychoanalysis or a single counseling session—constitutes a critical dimension. Given the proliferation of various iterations of the talking cure, and its symbolic importance, understanding the dynamics of therapy is critical to understanding the therapeutic turn more broadly. Indeed, the therapeutic is not only an abstracted cultural form deriving from psychological knowledge, institutional practices, and media representations, but it is also engendered through lived experience. Without attention to the social processes involved in therapy, the significance of this cultural shift remains only partially understood.[3]

While the preceding chapters have documented some key ways in which the therapeutic society developed in Australia, and have considered some of its consequences, the following analysis takes therapy itself as the focal point in order to gain an understanding of people's own perceptions of turning to psychological experts. It draws on narrative accounts from people who have sought therapeutic intervention in the hope that it would offer relief from distress and perhaps, even, a measure of happiness. A better understanding of *why* people turn to therapy, as well as the processes involved in therapy as a social practice, calls into question some of the key criticisms of the therapeutic society.

A reading that takes people's experiences of therapy seriously, within the wider context of contemporary social life, casts therapy not as the harbinger of diminished and vulnerable selfhood in an era of cultural decline, but rather as a strategic personal and institutional response to some of the rapid social changes of our time. Transformations in the gender order and in personal life are critical issues in the accounts of therapy that follow. As Anthony Giddens reminds us, changes in the personal sphere have on the one hand given rise to new possibilities of personal freedom and self-expression, but on the other they have also entailed new risks and new dilemmas of self-making.[4] These themes emerge as central in the narratives of the people I interviewed, as did another subject that also has little prominence in accounts of late modernity and the therapeutic turn: the problem of suffering.

"Ordinary Suffering" & the Promise of Therapy

Stories from individuals who have received psychological assistance, and observations from those who provide it, offer a valuable insight into the therapeutic society. The following account draws on interviews I conducted with eight people who undertook counseling or therapy in the 1990s and the early to mid 2000s.[5] Reflections on therapy by the therapists already cited in Chapter Four also inform this analysis. Propelling the research was a desire to elucidate the experiences of therapy from the viewpoint of the therapist and the client. Why do people seek therapy or counseling? What happens during the sessions? Does it change people, does it make them happier, and is life better as a result? I was interested in the nature of the therapeutic alliance, questions of power and resistance, processes of self-making and re-making, and whether the notion of therapy as antithetical to politics and social action—compelling at a theoretical level—was borne out by empirical research.

Before the interviews, I was keenly interested in the connection between therapy and cultural ideals of happiness, but later came to see unhappiness and suffering as more important in understanding the promise of therapy. The stories told reveal the intense difficulties people encounter in trying to make, and re-make, a life. Central to the narratives are problems of identity and intimacy. I began then to think about how the particular conditions of modern life might give rise to such anxieties, and to consider how therapy might be connected to emancipatory projects of modernity, particularly democratic shifts in the gender order and in personal life.

Dominant accounts of the therapeutic society, however, have advanced a rather unflattering view of the therapeutic turn and indeed of the self that inhabits the contemporary therapeutic landscape. Lasch and Furedi, for example, respectively argue that narcissism and diminished selfhood characterize the psychotherapeutic self. The question then of how to understand the kinds of emotional suffering experienced by those who have not endured great tragedy, who are neither mentally ill nor materially impoverished, presents a certain difficulty if one is to avoid resorting to degrading depictions of the modern personality. The misery of poverty, social disadvantage, and tragedy engender an understandable empathy in the social analyst. The sociological imagination, indeed the history of the social sciences, renders such subjects "worthy" of analysis. But what about the smaller miseries of the so-called worried well, the middle-class neurotic, or the anxious narcissist?

In *The Weight of the World*, Pierre Bourdieu and his colleagues capture the complexity and multidimensionality of suffering—not only the "real" suffering of material poverty (*la grande misère*) but also ordinary misery (*la petite misère*), encompassing unprecedented forms of distress inflicted upon individuals in the contemporary era. Bourdieu notes that these forms of misery appear entirely relative, indeed inconsequential in comparison to the "real" suffering of material impoverishment. As he explains: "This is invariably the point of criticism ('You don't really have anything to complain about'), as for consolation ('You could be worse off you know')." Yet, as Bourdieu argues, this standpoint offers only a limited view, for "using material poverty as the sole measure of all suffering keeps us from *seeing* and understanding a whole side of the suffering characteristic of a social order."[6]

Bourdieu's concept of ordinary suffering is particularly illuminating. Slightly recast, I use it here specifically in relation to the kind of psychological distress exacerbated by what Elliott and Lemert have described as a "new sense of uncertainty."[7] The twentieth century ushered in radical changes in the personal and economic spheres. Insecurity now characterizes both work and private life. At work, rigid hierarchical organizations have given way to corporate re-engineering, flexible work practices, and short-term contracts.[8] In the private sphere, egalitarian shifts have given women and men greater choice in private life and personal relationships. Yet these new forms of freedom have also brought forth experiences of diminished security, as the certainty afforded by traditional forms of long-term attachment has been replaced with more fleeting ties, both at work and at home.

While Bourdieu's notion of ordinary suffering underlies the interpretive framework of this chapter, his methodological approach also inspires its spirit. In contrast to many analyses of the therapeutic society that understate the problem of suffering, what is foregrounded here are the struggles of ordinary people in trying to deal with the unhappiness, misfortunes, and difficulties faced in their lives. Qualitative research of this nature inevitably invokes anxieties about representation and interpretation, particularly when dealing with human distress. This apprehension is aptly captured by Bourdieu, again, in *The Weight of the World*: "We are offering here the accounts that men and women have confided to us about their lives and the difficulties they have in living those lives ... How can we not feel anxious about making *private* words *public*, revealing confidential statements made in the context of a relationship based on a trust that can only be established between two individuals?"[9]

The people in this study, as well as many seen by the therapists already mentioned in Chapter Four, are not on the margins of social and cultural life. They are for the most part educated and employed, but their stories nonetheless reveal that very real forms of distress propelled them into therapy and kept them there until it had been alleviated. For these people at least, the decision to go to therapy was made in desperation, and common to all was the hope that counseling or therapy held the possibility of relief from suffering and the promise of making life bearable.

Turning to Therapy

From Jessica's brief counseling with a new age therapist to Simon's decision to get serious and see a psychiatrist, four women and four men talk about their decisions to seek psychological help and reflect on their experiences of being in therapy. Though depression and anxiety loom large, their stories reveal that psychological distress also has an undeniably social dimension. The problematization of personal life in particular permeates these accounts. While new possibilities of choice and self-expression in the private domain are certainly welcomed, insecurity is also acutely felt. Moreover, this double-edged experience of contemporary life is not limited to the private domain, for a generalized uncertainty also permeates their working lives.

Those interviewed are, in some ways, characteristic of Giddens' subjects of late modernity. Their lives are precarious, contingent, and somewhat unencumbered by the ties that bind. They are neither affluent nor poverty-stricken, and, while able to navigate the contours of modern life, it has nonetheless created anxiety. Such individuals are emblematic of the therapeutic society: well versed in the confessional mode, able to articulate the practice of self-examination, techniques of self-management, and the various processes facilitating self-transformation.

Although the willingness to talk about intimate details of one's life reflects a central dynamic of the therapeutic, it would be inaccurate to characterize our discussions as opportunities for self-indulgence. Those interviewed may or may not have enjoyed talking about their experiences, but I was left in no doubt that they all, to varying degrees, felt uncomfortable discussing their personal inadequacies and their sometimes profound disappointments in life. And despite the increasing social acceptance of therapy and counseling as a means of dealing with personal problems, most felt a great deal of angst, ambivalence, and, more often than not, shame in admitting they needed psychological help.

– *Jessica* –

Jessica is 25, the youngest and most "untroubled" of those interviewed. After returning to study following work as a teacher, she recently qualified as a physiotherapist and plans to establish her own business. In many ways Jessica's life is unremarkable: she grew up on Sydney's north shore in a stable home with a loving family and has not experienced great disappointment, tragedy, or loss. Her life revolves around friends and family and she recently moved out of the family home into an apartment with a friend. At the suggestion of her mother, she saw a therapist for five sessions after the break-up of her first serious romantic relationship:

> I was feeling like it was all out of my control, like I was stuck in this spot and I couldn't see how I was going to get out of it. I had never really broken up with anyone before and I didn't know how I was going to get over it. You don't really understand how it's going to get better. Your mind is just saying, it's not going to get better and it's not going to change and you can't see how time is going to help. I really felt like everything was out of my control and I kept thinking, you know, what's it going to matter, what's the point, the next relationship could just be taken away from me like that, and how do I make that better?

— *James* —

James is 52 and lives with his partner in an inner-city suburb of Melbourne where he runs a vegan cafe. He grew up in suburban Brisbane and worked as a lawyer before moving to Melbourne. The interstate move was part of a series of major life changes James undertook in his thirties. The first time he sought therapy was around this time, as he was coming to terms with his sexuality, and trying to build a future in which he was not struggling with his own identity:

> I initially pursued law as kind of fulfilling this external ambition and sense of self, you know, the status that went with that. That was in Brisbane. And during that period of time it became quite apparent that my sexuality was an issue for me, that I needed to address that and start to engage with that, otherwise I'd be leaving a part of me dead. And as part of that too, Brisbane and law had to go. And so I sold out of the practice that I was in, I moved to Melbourne and I basically dismantled most of the things that shored me up in my sense of self-concept. The last thing I hadn't kind of pulled apart was the relationship that was going on at the time and for some reason I seemed to want to dismantle that too. And as I pushed John aside, I suddenly realized there was nothing holding up who I was. So the house of cards came tumbling down. And that was the first time that I actually sought therapy, sought help, because I now was left with a blank sheet of paper.

— *George* —

George is 36, single, and lives in Brisbane. He worked as a reporter for a local newspaper before retraining as a youth worker, but he now works in hospitality to "pay the bills." His real interest, however, lies in social justice activism. He found his work as a journalist "too one dimensional," saying, "All you are doing is reporting things, you are never solving problems, you are never taking them on, or doing anything about them, you are just communicating." It was after making the decision to change his career and become a youth worker, that he realized that something was amiss:

> It was around the time of my first placement at a youth center ... I was feeling emotional and sort of crying and things like that, for no rational reason. It was also when Mary and I had sort of broken up, or we were about to break up. During the placement I was going there and sort of crying, after work, that is, obviously not around the kids. And I'm thinking, what the hell is going on here, this is not right. And that is when I approached the counselor.

– Simon –

Simon is 29 and lives in Adelaide. He grew up in a rural area of South Australia and moved to the city after completing high school. Simon studied psychology at university and now works as a counselor in a local community center. His first experience of therapy was with his supervisor as he was completing the requirements for state registration as a psychologist. He describes what he was experiencing at the time as "the madness":

> Oh the madness ... I guess it was doing quite extreme things. The first thing that comes to mind is that I had an enormous sense of anxiety, a sense that something bad was going to happen, impending doom, I guess. I was feeling fragmented and I acted out sexually. Had I been someone else, I think I would have gone on a drinking binge, or a drug binge. But I went on a sex binge. It was later that I started to drink. So the madness to me would be acting erratically, not being able to sleep well, changing my mind about a lot of things, yeah the erraticism, I guess. And just a general feeling inside yourself that you don't have a full sense of integrity, sort of a bit fragmented, a bit all over the shop, and don't know what you're doing ... I was trying to stop ... I think that's the point, I couldn't stop.

In the following years, he saw several counselors, mostly short term. Two of these experiences were for relationship counseling—first with a former partner who was living with a life-threatening illness, and later with his current partner who is in Australia on a temporary visa. Recently, he started therapy with a psychiatrist, to finally resolve what he regarded as deep seated and ongoing problems. For Simon, the decision to seek therapy again was critical:

> I didn't want to go back to being a client again, to admitting that I had a problem and facing all this stuff ... but I realized that I wasn't happy and it wasn't changing and I really didn't want to be like that for the rest of my life. I realized that I needed to do something ... I think when you are a counselor and a psychologist, people have quite high expectations, or you have your own expectations that you should have it all together, or you shouldn't be fucked-up or you shouldn't smoke cigarettes or you shouldn't have problems in your relationship. You should be this very well adjusted, coping, understanding, together person. And most people aren't. I mean when you are a psychologist and you have your own stuff going on, there is some shame kind of involved in that, and there shouldn't be, but there is, and I don't tell many people that I'm seeing a psychiatrist cause they must think I'm crazy.

– *Svetlana* –

Svetlana, 37, is a beauty therapist. She moved to Australia from Russia when she was eleven. Svetlana is divorced and lives with her nine-year-old daughter in Sydney. She first saw a counselor when she was in her early twenties. Later she saw a therapist when she was separating from her husband:

> I guess both times were when I was kind of in the middle of a crisis. The first time I was just really feeling depressed and I wasn't sure why. I didn't know what I was doing with my life, what I wanted out of life, and I was doing stupid things. I don't know how much it was the counseling but things did get better ... The second time was six years ago. My life had just fallen apart. My husband left me and it was a real shock, very unexpected. I knew I had to keep myself going because of my daughter, but I was devastated. I didn't want to get out of bed in the mornings, I didn't want to do anything, but I had to, I kind of dragged myself though the day

but I was worried that if I didn't get help then it would get worse, or my daughter would suffer more than she already was suffering.

– Andrew –

Andrew, 35, is a naturopath and lives in Sydney with his partner of ten years. He describes himself as someone interested in personal development, and sees counseling as one part of his journey of self-discovery. Andrew has sought various forms of therapy and counseling, including some he associates with alternative medicine. He also practices what he describes, in effect, as forms of self-therapy:

> I've done everything from art therapy to family therapy to bark flower remedies, to just sitting down and working things out with my partner. We have had a few difficulties and now we have taken it upon ourselves to actually, I don't know, for want of a better word, have *active conversations*. I mean it might get to the stage where we get a counselor in, but so far we haven't needed to.

Although both Svetlana and Andrew have undergone several bouts of therapy, during their interviews both preferred to talk more about their roles as healer than client. They both believed the work they did assisted people in all manner of distress, including the psychological and emotional kinds, both through talk but more importantly, through care of the body.

– Maria –

Maria is 36, lives in Brisbane, and works as a teacher in a secondary school. She first started therapy when she was in her early thirties after noticing, she says, how desperately unhappy she was. She was having problems in her relationship and as she said:

> I just started feeling really, really unhappy. Well, I don't know if I felt *more* unhappy. I just noticed it, I acknowledged the unhappiness more, and I was getting into a bit of a downward cycle. So I thought, I'll go and see a therapist,

> and I went to a therapist who was a narrative therapist, for about 9 months. That was my first experience and it was full-on. It was all about, you know, tell me the stories of your family and your father, and I've always had issues with my parents, or my father basically, he's quite negative in his feedback to everyone. But as a child, I think I must have received that quite harshly and it really affected my self-esteem. So I worked mainly on all those stories with my father.

Her first experience of therapy, however, left her disappointed. She felt that it had provided her with insight, but not with strategies to effect change. As she put it, there was no "proactive action plan":

> I just felt that yes, I knew where I stood, I knew what was happening, I understood the dynamic one hundred percent, I could write a paper on it. But I didn't feel like I had any tools to deal with that. And maybe that's what the nature of the therapy was, to go deeper into it. But I didn't want to go deeper, I don't know, I felt like I'd gone deep enough into it. And I told her, I don't feel like I'm getting anywhere and I'm going to have to stop. I feel like I understand what's happening but there's nowhere else for me to go.

Maria recalls that in the midst of feeling "stuck," her depression intensified. A friend then recommended another therapist, someone with whom she immediately felt comfortable, someone she believed could help her, and she continued her therapy with him for two and a half years.

- *Amy* -

Amy is 31 and lives in Melbourne. She works part-time in information technology and has recently returned to university to study software engineering, after working for many years in the industry as a technician without formal qualifications. In her twenties she traveled and worked overseas and upon returning to Australia was married for a brief period. Before starting therapy, Amy was experiencing extreme anxiety and panic attacks:

> The episodes would last for half an hour to an hour. I'd be paralyzed and afterwards I'd throw up. It was like a combination of having a major heart attack and going crazy and I didn't understand what was happening to my body … I was feeling a lot of anxiety generally just in everyday life and I also had really morbid thoughts that were coming into everyday normal situations. I'd be driving along and I'd think, what if I turned the steering wheel and went into oncoming traffic. And I'd actually picture the car crash and I'd picture what my body would look like mangled up in the car crash. I'd then go through how my family would cope with my death, what my funeral would be like, how my friends would react, all that. I'd go through that whole scenario. Or if I was on a balcony at someone's house and it was high up, I'd walk to the end of the balcony and think, imagine if I jumped. And those thoughts were coming into my head a lot and it wasn't that I wanted to do it, and it wasn't that I was suicidal or anything like that, it was more like my brain playing games with me and testing out my common sense. And it got to the stage with things like driving, for example, when I was working in Sydney for a month, I'd have to drive through the harbor tunnel. And I'd get really claustrophobic and panicky and think I can't go through the tunnel, what if it collapsed. And it got to the point where I stopped going through the harbor tunnel. And it was then, when I was in Sydney, that I thought, if I am getting to the stage that thoughts are stopping me from doing something so mundane, I think I need to talk to someone, I need to see a psychologist.

Amy's story is a poignant example of how the burden of suffering leads people, often reluctantly, and in desperation, to seek therapy. Amy had tried various means of alleviating her distress, but to no avail. Like others interviewed, the decision to go to therapy for her was an admission of failure, that she lacked the resources to fix her own problems. But equally, therapy held the hope of resolution, of making life bearable, of curing, as Simon said, "the madness."

Turning to Therapy – The Therapists' View

The vignettes above provide some insight, from the point of view of those who seek psychological assistance, into why people are turning to therapy in increasing numbers. From very different professional standpoints, the therapists I interviewed describe what they regard as factors driving the increasing demand for therapy and counseling. In Amanda Gordon's view:

> Partly it is families dissipating. People don't take responsibility for themselves as early so they are looking for mentors and emotional support. People want quick fixes too. I think perhaps we tolerated a bit more pain, say 30 years ago. There are no role models in terms of how to deal with life now, and the world is very different. Most people's parents had them when they were in their early twenties, now people in their late twenties and early thirties are just starting to think about having a relationship. Their parents can't really help them with that because they already had three kids by that stage of life. Things are very different now. And also, people are generally more open about being depressed.

In reflecting on the growth of clinical services, the problem of mood disorder features prominently in the therapists' accounts. Antony Kidman, for example, cites rising rates of depression and anxiety as a significant factor. In addition, he sees greater public awareness of psychological issues as contributing to the destigmatization of therapy and the growing willingness of people to seek assistance. Stephanie Dowrick also identifies shifting levels of social acceptability as critical to generating demand: "It used to be that only a very educated or privileged elite would think of psychotherapy as a choice. And feel free to take it up for reasons that were not always the result of a psychological crisis. For most of the rest of the world it was something that was kind of forced upon you in dire circumstances. So that has changed radically."

Dowrick suggests that another factor in the destigmatization of therapy, and the increasing demand for it, is that "people's actual levels of tension and stress are very, very high currently." In her view: "The demands of work and home frequently leave little time for people to engage in community activities, introspective or relaxing hobbies or interests, or with something greater than themselves," a need she regards as genuine and one traditionally met by religion. In sum, she says: "People's inner worlds can feel as constricted as their external timetables."

By contrast to what is often portrayed as therapy's highly individualistic approach to the amelioration of problems, Dowrick recognizes the sociopolitical context in which therapy operates, and acknowledges the limitations of the therapeutic project. From a critical standpoint, she suggests that less individualistic approaches can be helpful both in understanding people's distress and in finding solutions for it:

> I think for a lot of people life is reduced to their career, immediate family—which may or may not be stable—and their financial anxieties. In that context, where do people turn for insight, never mind a transformative perspective on their inner pain or confusion? Isolation is also part of the problem, even when people are living intimately with others. A question that remains legitimate within the "therapeutic project" in all its manifestations is whether people can feel stable inwardly *without* engaging with the wider world in robust and enthusiastic ways.

Dowrick acknowledges that depression is a big problem and that many of her clients have come to her with a feeling of emptiness. Gordon makes a similar point, noting also that in her view the presenting problems have not really changed, but the way people express their distress has. As she observes: "I think the issues are the same but the currency they are using as their explanation is different. It used to be that people would come with a particular symptom. Now, generally not feeling good about what is happening in their life, or feeling that their life is not functioning is a good enough reason for people to come."

Peter O'Connor offers a slightly different take on this issue, as he articulates what he sees as the connection between changes in the social world and problems of the individual: "I think it would be foolish not to see it as an interaction between psyche and society.

I don't think we are seeing the sorts of issues that Freud saw. As society changes, so also does the typology change. We are not seeing so much sexual repression now, but what we are seeing a lot of is the loss of connection."

Clarifying the Issues

In the contemporary vernacular, one of the reasons people go to therapy is that they have "issues." The issues causing the most difficulty for the people I interviewed centered around identity and relationships. For both George and Maria, domineering, critical fathers were understood to be a source of their problems, while for Amy, an absent father was regarded as a cause of some of her difficulties. Clearly, these experiences are not uniquely contemporary. What has changed markedly, however, is people's expectations of family life and also the extent to which they connect their childhood experiences with problems faced in adulthood.

In many therapies, especially those in which psychodynamic approaches are employed, an excavation of the past constitutes a critical dimension of the therapeutic process. In other modalities, such as CBT oriented therapies which focus on thought and behavior patterns, talking about one's formative relationships may not be considered essential for therapeutic success, but developing self-understanding through self-examination certainly is. In John McLeod's view, all talking therapies are essentially narrative therapies. As he argues: "Whatever you are doing, or think you are doing, as therapist or client can be understood in terms of telling and re-telling stories."[10]

The personal narrative is central to psychotherapies of very different orientations. Amanda Gordon's work is informed by the view that "many people's scripts are deeply written." She sees one of her tasks as a psychologist as "trying to help people realign the scripts of their lives." Peter O'Connor makes a similar point: "You could even say re-store, you could play with the idea, because the story they've got is no longer making sense." He goes on to say: "I think bad therapy usually gives people another story, a therapeutic one, rather than them working it out for themselves. In many ways therapy *is* story telling but I don't think it's up to professionals to say, look, I've got a better story than yours."

In narratives developed in therapy, parental relationships often feature prominently. Indeed, blaming one's parents for difficulties in adult life is commonly cast as a stereotypical therapy story. While perhaps overly caricatured, it does raise as central the questioning of parental authority itself, made possible by wider democratic shifts in the personal sphere. In Giddens' analysis, the claim of children to be cared for emotionally and to have their views taken into account is no less of a human right than the right to be fed and clothed. As he argues: "Escaping from toxic parental backgrounds is inseparable from the assertion of certain ethical principles or rights. Individuals who seek to alter their relationship to their parents by means of looking back to childhood experience are in effect claiming rights."[11]

Much of George's therapy involved just this kind of reflection on his childhood. As he came to understand:

> That's where it all starts and that's where it all tends to go horribly wrong. So you know, I might talk about how I'm having problems with this manager at work and it seems like he's a bully, he doesn't let me speak and he doesn't listen. And the counselor would reflect back, and say, is there anyone else that that might sound like? And you go, well, it sort of actually does remind me of my father, you know, *again*! And you talk about what it was like with your father. My father was an alcoholic and a very aggressive person. It was a very fearful house and a very repressive house as well. And we grow up holding these feelings inside us. Counseling helps us to let these out, and to become conscious of what was really going on back then so that we don't have to be this scared child anymore.

Similarly, a central part of Maria's therapy involved processes of clarification of the dynamics of her relationship with her father. After developing the capacity to identify established behavioral patterns, Maria says that therapy allowed her to understand, and indeed change, the way she related to and interacted with her partner. She came to recognize, she says, how she in effect created some of their relationship problems and began to take responsibility for changing this.

Maria's interpretation perhaps lends support to critiques of adaptation as a particularly troubling problem of therapy, especially for women. But while such an interpretation is compelling, what must also be acknowledged is that changing behavior does not necessarily imply submission, just as adaptation does not simply mean the acceptance of unequal social relations. Perhaps an equally well-founded reading may be that therapy in this instance provides support for the process of negotiating new forms of relating. Through the analysis of her relationship with her father, Maria says she also developed an understanding of the dynamics of her relationship with her partner:

> My father was always telling me that I was no good, not telling me, but his reaction to me and to everybody is to be a bit negative and I was internalizing that I wasn't good enough. At the same time I was also quite dogmatic about what I wanted in my relationship with my partner. So I became my dad in my relationship with him, telling him that he wasn't good enough, at the same time I didn't feel good enough.

Maria believes that through recognizing these dynamics and using techniques suggested by her therapist, she was able to change the pattern of interaction, which altered the dynamics of her relationship. This developed, in part, through an understanding that her father's behavior was not "all about her." But equally, the techniques her therapist provided her with enabled her to disengage from what she came to see as an unhealthy way of relating. She illustrated this point with the following example:

> Well I'd go to my parents' house and I'd get the behavior and what I'd normally do would be to fight back. But instead I'd say, well I'm going to leave now, doesn't mean I don't love you, but I don't want to listen to this anymore. And I was able to just separate myself from what was happening, it wasn't really about me, it was about my dad and I had to let it go, walk out of the room or whatever, but in a very civilized way.

In therapy, Maria not only found new ways of relating, but she developed a new story of her past, one in which her father's negativity was no longer taken to be an evaluation of her.

That therapy may assist in the "reflexive mobilizing of self-identity," as Giddens suggests, is also evident in James' story.[12] In his case, it provided a means of support as he was forging his own identity as a gay man within the larger social context of shifting gender relations and sexual practices. His location in time and space affords greater freedom of self-expression, identity, and ways of "doing gender" than that which was available to previous generations, or indeed to him in the suburban area where he grew up.[13] But the social changes that have enabled greater openness in the sexual domain are complex and often difficult to negotiate. James' first bout of therapy assisted him with problems of identity. Later, as he approached fifty, a new problem emerged—how to grow older with dignity:

> The first of the two therapists was about my age. The second one, yes, there was another issue with him. He was an older man and I particularly wanted to see an older man. I wanted to see a man at least in his fifties if not sixties because there were some issues that I was having in my late forties about, what do you do when you get to this age. Not "life is over," but "life is changing" and what do you do now and how do you navigate that kind of thing. So I wanted to talk to an older person who'd been around the block a few times themselves. I was interested in that. Also because he was gay. Although, I seemed to have more anxiety about being older and being gay when I was forty than I did when I was fifty. I don't feel any of those issues now, well, not any, that's probably too black and white. But I don't feel driven by this need to stay young, or your life is over as a gay man once you get older. That kind of issue doesn't seem to concern me, whereas probably when I was forty, I was like, oh god!

The anchors of older social structures—a fixed gender order, traditional heterosexual marriage and children, relatively secure employment, and the nature of work itself—that provided a measure of stability during periods of life transition have undergone significant transformation. The repressive nature of these older regimes curtailed self-expression and self-identity, often in brutal fashion and at terrible cost. Democratic shifts in the personal sphere and diminished cultural authority have opened up new possibilities of autonomy and self-expression, for both men and women. Yet the flip side of greater freedoms appears to be manifest in a degree of instability and associated anxiety. Seen in this light, therapy becomes not only "the exemplary form of the reflexive project of the self," as Giddens has argued, but also an important mechanism of support and clarification in a cultural climate of reorganization.[14] In the exploration of these issues, the client's relationship with the therapist is of critical significance.

The Therapeutic Alliance

In the therapeutic encounter, the most intimate aspects of a person's biography provide the basis for a dialogue in which interpretation and analysis of a life and a self are explored devoid of the intricacies of personal relationships. Australian psychologist and social researcher Hugh Mackay suggests that: "For a fee, counsellors can provide the kind of intimacy, support, affirmation, clarification and willingness to listen non-judgmentally that can otherwise only be found in a rich and healthy personal relationship."[15]

With the exception of George, all those interviewed described having at least some very good personal relationships. That this changed throughout the course of George's therapy may well be attributable to the efficacy of treatment, yet it could also be a consequence of the passage of time. However, the important point here is that for most, therapy was not a substitute for healthy personal relationships. Rather, the level of support and assistance they required was often simply beyond the capacity of those close to them. Instead of viewing the therapeutic alliance as a substitute for friendship, then, we might well say that a friend is no substitute for a therapist. Perhaps the most important aspect differentiating the two is the uniquely non-reciprocal quality of the therapeutic relationship. As Jessica explains:

> I think it was almost like, a bit of self-indulgent, well not self-indulgent, but being able to have an hour where you would go, look, this is about me and this is how I'm feeling, and just being able to get that out with someone who didn't know me. And there was something about that that helped me get it out of my system, more so than I was able to with mum for some reason, and not because she wasn't listening or anything, just because it just kind of felt better.

Why talking to the counselor, rather than her mother, "just felt better" taps into an elusive dimension of therapy. Jessica's account attests to the importance of the therapeutic alliance, which since Freud has been understood as a critical dimension of therapy, and the most robust predictor of treatment success.[16] Whatever the modality, the relationship between the therapist and the analysand or client is regarded as paramount. As Antony Kidman says: "The great thing in any therapy is the therapeutic alliance. You give them confidentiality and if they think you are knowledgeable and can help them, then they will not only listen, they will hear. Whereas if a relative or a husband or a wife says it, they are less likely take any notice."

For Jessica, it was an indefinable quality that separated the relief she felt from therapy from that provided by those close to her. Amy, still more precisely, articulated what she believes sets her therapist apart from her friends:

> He's more objective. My friends have my welfare at heart and are emotionally involved in their responses to me. He can actually say, I think you're wrong, I don't think you behaved correctly in that situation, Amy. He's very honest and open with me. Or he'll say, you could've dealt with that better, whereas my friends would never say that. They would be more likely to try and make me feel better whereas he might make you feel worse to get you better in the long run. That's a massive difference. Also, I can tell him stuff and not be embarrassed about how he'll react. I can't tell my friends absolutely anything all the time. You can't do that with your friends. You have to censor yourself, out of respect.

Whether the primary driver of self-censorship is respect, or whether it is motivated by other factors, the therapeutic relationship nevertheless provides Amy with support of a particular kind. On the one hand, she can tell her therapist things she would not otherwise divulge, but equally important is that her therapist will challenge her in ways that her friends do not. Amanda Gordon's approach to therapy accords with Amy's account. Her therapeutic technique, she notes, includes softness and engagement, but she does not allow her clients "to sit still":

> Sometimes I challenge people using confrontational therapy. I will do that with clients that I know well. I recently did some telephone counseling with a woman who is in hospital withdrawing from prescription drugs to which she has been addicted. I actually told her that she was behaving like a drug addict. That really hit her. It was a slap across the face, metaphorically. I have to know my clients well before I do that. I would never do it in the first session. Along with that is the basic support you give people, but I don't let them sit still. I warn them that my goal is to be redundant in their lives.

From the client's point of view, being challenged may be one dimension, but whether through shame or embarrassment, or through concern about respecting the boundaries of friendship, therapy provides opportunities for disclosure that would otherwise be difficult or problematic. As Simon explained of the decision to seek couples counseling: "We were having a lot of problems in our relationship and we were basically draining our friends. And we both didn't want to continue to do that because it is such a downer, to be talking to your friends about your problems all the time. We had already exhausted one friendship and we didn't want to do that again."

As Dowrick observes, people's recognition of the limits of their own solutions or the repetition of unhelpful patterns are among a number of factors that lead people to therapy. This was true for Simon, who had tried in various ways to bring about a change in his life. But there are also other factors at play and for Simon in particular, shame has been an important one. As a therapist himself, Simon sees this play out in his relationship with his psychiatrist:

> There has been a whole thing with shame and I've seen in my thinking that I don't want to tell him certain things or I'm concerned about how he would think about me. And I keep thinking that this guy is a therapist, and I mean of course he has his own mind, but he is in a certain role and I know that he won't reject me. He will survive me. He won't humiliate me. He will accept me. And he is the strongest example I've ever had in my life of that. I've had some true friends like that too, that I knew would be there for me no matter what. But it's through that process of playing the game with him. The guy's a therapist, he's not my best friend or my father and I know that, but he is there for me in a professional sense.

Clearly, Simon understands the nature of the therapist-client relationship. Nevertheless, his therapist's acceptance of him is of critical importance for it has provided him with the strongest example of constancy and consistency he has experienced up to this point in his life. For Maria, the crucial element was feeling comfortable with her therapist, and so developing a connection with him was paramount. She stopped seeing her first therapist because she found her "too cold" and consequently did not manage to develop the kind of intimacy with her that she desired. Maria described what was different about her next therapist, whom she continued to see for two and a half years:

> It was like talking to an old friend, an old uncle, giving him information and then he'd give you a little bit of advice, but not in a preachy kind of way. It was well, not like a friendship, but it was choreographed that way. I knew I was paying him. I didn't want to call him at home or invite him over for dinner. Although I guess sometimes I would have liked it to be more like that.

While the complexities of the therapeutic alliance constitute an area of ongoing scholarly interest, the crucial theme to emerge from these interviewees is that the quality of the relationship is highly important.[17] Maria described her therapist as like "an artificial friend" and there was, as she says, sometimes a temptation to personalize the relationship. While she was able to manage her desire for greater intimacy, George found this more difficult. For him, it was strange and at times, painful:

> I think the whole crucial element in the relationship is I still don't know much about this person that I went and saw for these years, this counselor. I knew her name. I knew she had a couple of children. That's it! There was no engagement in a personal way throughout the therapy. And you are talking about such intimate things as well, and you know at the time, and maybe even now, there is probably no-one that knows me better than she does. But the reality is that there is no ongoing personal relationship. And sometimes you want that so much.

George's desire for greater intimacy with his therapist reveals a deep vulnerability as well as a potential hazard. The problem of therapists taking advantage of their clients, especially sexually, has rightly received widespread condemnation.[18] Yet while the potential for harm is well documented, what is less often acknowledged are the complex ways in which people negotiate their own desires, manage these interactions, and develop strategies to deal with problems encountered in client-therapist relationships.

George's first experience of therapy, for example, was with a woman he calls the "ghost therapist." As he recalls, he was experiencing difficulties in his relationship with his then girlfriend, Mary, and they decided to seek couple's counseling. Mary was attracted to new age philosophies and she attributed the problems they were having to the presence of spirits in their house; she thought ghosts were "affecting them." As George recalls, Mary engaged a "clairvoyant psychologist" who indeed confirmed the presence of otherworldly beings:

> So we go and see this person who confirms yes, there is nothing wrong with the two of you. It's all because there are spirits in this house affecting you (laughs). So anyway, we were all fixed after that because we knew there were ghosts there. They were creating all our problems. And I've just gone, oh god, this is fucking ridiculous! It was all just too bizarre.

George is philosophical about the experience:

> I mean look, I can laugh about it now but at the time it was all terribly serious. And if we had stuck with that, and I hadn't said, no, there is a problem here, there is something about me, or about us, well, who knows where I would be now. This is the nature of the industry, this is the problem with the industry. There are people who are very good and there are people who are dangerous.

George's encounter with the so-called ghost therapist provides a compelling example of one of the more damningly critiqued aspects of therapy, and by extension, the therapeutic society. Individual responsibility is absolved in favor of external blame—in this case ghosts, but equally this could have applied to other people, say his parents. Moreover, when people are in serious distress, indeed at their most vulnerable and seeking help, they are open to exploitation. As George says, disreputable therapists can be dangerous, and evaluations of therapy must be attuned to the potential for harm. But if analysis stops at that point then a vital part of the equation is missed. For a crucial point of this story is that George stopped seeing the "ghost therapist." He rejected the notion that there was nothing wrong with him or with his relationship. So as well as his story being a tale about the danger of the therapeutic society, it is also a story about the complex ways in which people navigate the terrain of therapy. People can and do take personal responsibility, and ideas that fail to resonate with the individual's worldview are often resisted, even in times of great personal distress.

While the case of the "ghost therapist" is perhaps an extreme example, George was not alone in experiencing counseling in which the lines between psychology, new-age spirituality, or alternative medicine were blurred. Amy's therapist used a mixture of talk therapy and acupuncture, while Jessica's used crystals and kinesiology. James says he looked for answers from clairvoyants before seeking therapy and Andrew says he has tried everything from Bach Flower remedies to art therapy and family therapy. For Amy, being able to refer to her therapist as an acupuncturist was important. Not only did it align with her belief in the value of a holistic approach to dealing with her problems, but it removed the problem of social stigma. She could openly say to friends and work colleagues that she had an appointment with her acupuncturist, omitting the detail that he was also a psychologist and she was "in therapy." For Jessica, on the other hand, the new age component of her counseling did not particularly interest her:

> She was a kinesiologist, this lady. I don't know whether she was a qualified psychologist, I know she had some sort of psychology background. I saw her, I think, four or five times. We'd sit down for the first half hour or so and we'd just basically talk about the relationship and how I was feeling about it. And then for the last half hour she would do some sort of kinesiology stuff. I don't know, it was a bit weird ... I would lie on the table and she would wave things above me. But really, I wasn't really going for that. I went basically to talk to her for that first half hour.

Clearly, the extent to which the worldview of the therapist is taken up by the client is highly variable. The experiences of the people in this study, however, does suggest that rejection of ideas and techniques put forward by therapists is not uncommon. The selective uptake of the psychological and other acts of resistance was highlighted in a number of ways throughout the interviews. Jessica, for example, was adamant that she is not interested in self-help books, but acknowledged that she looks for therapeutic themes and life lessons in the novels she reads. Similarly, Andrew and James both reject pop psychology and regard self-help books as ineffectual. In their view, they may provide some interesting insights, but unlike therapy they do not actually help in any significant way.

For Amanda Gordon, the critical difference between reading self-help books and undertaking therapy is the role of the therapist. As she explains: "I think there is a limit to how useful self-help books can be. If people only read and learn without the reflective part of them working, then it is not very helpful. Ultimately, the relationship people create with their therapist, their psychologist, is useful because it allows for both learning and reflection. And one without the other is not all that useful."

Many of those interviewed about their experience in therapy spoke of repeated times in which they dismissed a certain construction of events by their therapist. They also discussed terminating when they were ready, and just as therapists report "choosing" their clients, many had seen more than one therapist before they settled on someone with whom they felt comfortable working. These aspects of the therapeutic encounter suggest that contrary to the fantasy of the all-powerful therapist, even in times of great distress individuals can and do find the inner resources to resist and negotiate. Certainly, the people in this study possess a significant degree of cultural capital. The implications for those who are mentally ill, experiencing extreme distress, or are seriously disadvantaged are less straightforward and, clearly, far more serious.

Investing in the Self

For Freud, a financial exchange was essential to the business of therapy. In his view, reticence on the topic of money is much like that on the subject of sex; both are approached with "the same inconsistency, prudishness, and hypocrisy," and the therapist must deal with these issues frankly in order for therapeutic progress to be made. From Freud onwards, the payment of fees for therapy has been regarded as a critical dimension of the therapeutic process: it motivates the analysand, it formalizes a commitment to the real work involved in an intensely intimate, yet ultimately impersonal, relationship, and it creates boundaries necessary to overcome what might otherwise be problems of transference and countertransference.[19] These issues were illuminated in a number of my interviews. Particularly striking was the way some people spoke of their (at times intense) desire for a personal relationship with their therapist. As George said: "sometimes you want that so much." Not surprisingly, perhaps, the financial transaction was a source of great frustration for him:

> It shitted me, it gave me the shits. That I was paying someone to listen to me, absolutely. That I had to give money to somebody to listen to me talk about my problems and stuff, that this person was sitting there listening to me, not giving anything of themselves and I'm giving everything of me, yes, including my money!

In the face of his considerable agitation about the market logic of the exchange, many therapists would argue that the payment of fees was particularly important in George's case. Interestingly, however, not everyone paid the sort of financial premium that George did. Simon received "free therapy" from his supervisor during sessions that were ostensibly for professional training, while others negotiated very reduced rates during times of financial hardship. These arrangements sometimes continued for several years. For most others, however, the price ranged between $80 and $120 per session, a cost they were willing and able to meet. In spite of his frustrations over paying, George was typical in his view that therapy was an investment in himself:

> I made the decision was that this was actually a very important thing for me, and that while I could have pursued someone who was free, or gone to a psychiatrist and got a rebate or something like that, or some place where they didn't charge, I made the decision that look no, I was going to spend the money here, because this is important for me and I need to sort this problem out. So I made the decision then that I was going to spend whatever it took to find the right person and to work this through.

James, too, was committed to spending whatever it would take. Having sold out of his legal firm, he was in a financial position to do so:

> I had quite a lot of cash lying around and my view was, because I was in such a disheveled and vulnerable state, my view was that it was money well spent. It was an investment. And I kind of thought, well look, this will go on for probably a year, I'll reappraise it at that stage. But while I was in that turmoil there was no issue for me about the cost.

The next time James sought therapy, his needs were not so acute. He was grappling with questions of meaning—or more accurately meaninglessness—rather than trying to alleviate unbearable distress. He describes himself on this occasion as more strategic; he discussed cost and timeframes with the therapist, and committed only to short-term counseling. Of his other therapeutic encounter, relationship counseling, he commented:

> I can unequivocally say that it was money well spent! The parameters were set at the start, "the outcome of this is not necessarily to get you back together again, but to make whatever this process is for you as beneficial as possible so that you two can move either forward together or apart with the necessary insight and dignity." And we certainly got that. It ensured that after a sufficient passage of time, to get over the relationship issue, it's allowed our friendship to go on. It gave respect to what the other person needed and what they couldn't give, if you like. It enabled the pain, the dirty pain—the counselor used the term dirty pain for when you compromise below your line—and certainly for me, and I think for Evan too, that has allowed that side to evaporate and for a friendship to sort of evolve.

For James, as with most others interviewed, therapy was predominantly about the alleviation of suffering—just as Freud had initially envisaged it. This was evident when they spoke of relationship counseling, and it was also true of individual therapy. At $120 per hour, Maria's therapy put her under considerable financial strain. She prioritized therapy over other expenditure and ceased abruptly when she no longer regarded it as necessary. Clearly, economic reality does curtail the duration of therapy. But while the logic of the market economy is certainly evident in private practice therapeutics—that is, it has to be value for money—the complexity of this issue is lost if the nature of the exchange is read merely as just another consumer choice. In the context of competing demands, paying demonstrates a commitment to the therapeutic enterprise and the values it entails. Rather than a self-indulgence of the chattering classes, therapy, at least for these people, involved dealing with enduring dilemmas of life—questions of how to ease their emotional suffering, and how to live with dignity.

Meaning, Morality & Responsibility

For those involved in the provision of psychological support, the idea that therapy builds character is not a particularly radical one. Indeed, the entire institution of therapeutics is built upon various articulations of how the self can be fortified. Broadly speaking, psychoanalysis seeks to strengthen the ego, humanist approaches are concerned with insight and self-development, while cognitive behavioral modalities are oriented towards developing resilience and life-skills. In many social theoretical interpretations of the therapeutic society, however, therapy is understood to have grown out of an amoral social order, and as such is interpreted as an unseemly repudiation of older repressive forms of dignified conduct.[20]

Philip Rieff was particularly concerned about the anti-religious doctrine he deemed to be at the heart of psychotherapy. He wrote: "As the aristocratic Roman summoned his philosopher when he was ill, as the Christian went to his pastor, so the dispirited modern visits his analyst. But the psychoanalyst does not compete with older therapists; his is not a therapy of belief but one which instructs how to live without belief."[21] Living without belief, in Rieff's view, is akin to a life that is bereft of moral purpose. The dissolution of a common system of belief, of faith, in Rieff's terms, is another facet of the issues dealt with in therapy. James highlights this issue as he recalls the circumstances precipitating his decision to return to therapy:

> I think it was in the late '90s and I had about four sessions. A lot of it was centered around meaning, the meaninglessness of life. And when I look back at it, it's kind of like I had

strayed off the track a bit and needed someone to nudge me back ... I came away thinking, ah, yes and no. But you see I didn't go in it with a great sense of despair. I was concerned about the meaning of life, or my life, and I was trying to find ways of evaluating what I was doing and probably kick-start myself a little. Things were just a little too easy, you know, I was working 20 hours a week, I was playing the share market quite a bit, but I was drifting. There seemed to be no core or meaning.

At this point in his life, James appears to be the embodiment of Rieff's "dispirited modern," seeking counsel on how to live without belief. Yet perhaps what Rieff's analysis overlooks is that for some therapy actually entails the search for meaning which itself may be understood—contra Rieff—as part of a moral quest. In the cultural context of secularization and detraditionalization, diminishing imperatives of responsibility, and shifting notions of morality, James was searching for meaning and purpose. Rather than using therapy as a means of avoiding responsibility, moreover, it was for him part of a quest to find and accept it.

Zaretsky makes a similar point in relation to the historical development of psychoanalysis. He argues that by: "Encouraging the capacity to look at oneself objectively—'analytically'—and to enter empathically into another person's inner world, analysis promoted an enormous expansion of the moral capacity. The vanguard of an epochal social transformation, it generated a new ethic, one that assumed that a meaningful life necessitated self-reflection in depth."[22]

Zaretsky's standpoint on responsibility and moral capacity offers an important counterpoint to prevailing social theoretical assessments of the therapeutic society. The ethos of responsibility as a prevailing ideology of therapy has been largely obscured, overshadowed by pronouncements of moral failure and analyses of therapy as complicit in the construing of social problems as individual ones. An examination of therapeutic approaches, both in therapy and therapeutic literature, however, reveals a more complex picture. Stephanie Dowrick, for example, is adamant that social responsibility comprises an important dimension of her approach, as a therapist and as an author. She argues that her books emphasize this, rather than focusing on individual solutions. Antony Kidman also holds this view, rejecting the notion of therapy as an entirely individualistic enterprise. In response to the claim that therapy is individualizing, he says: "CBT has been criticized for being an individualistic therapy that fits with economic rationalism. It's not really true, it's about people taking responsibility when they can, for their actions. Being willing to put up with discomforting situations at times. This fits quite well with social responsibility in my view."

The critical dimension of self-responsibility has also been obscured by depictions of the therapeutic enterprise as a "blame game" in which people excavate the past and find fault with early attachment figures. More accurate perhaps is that in many therapeutic approaches clarification of present problems usually entails a re-examination of the past. Blaming one's parents may certainly be part of this process. Taking responsibility for present difficulties and working towards change, however, is not only as important as understanding childhood experience, but is almost universally regarded as essential for therapeutic progress.

Therapy in the contemporary world is, for most people who choose to undertake it, not simply interminable talk. From the point of view of the client, it is work. It is often painful and embarrassing, for the whole point of therapy is to lay bare the self. Its material is problems, inadequacies, failures, and disappointments, at times in relation to significant others, but also in relation to the self. For Simon, and perhaps others, this entailed feelings of shame. As such, it is quite clearly not a pleasurable experience. On the contrary, it is a process that requires strength and a commitment to constructing new understandings and re-fashioning one's life. Maria described therapy as "hard work." Similarly, George's therapist referred to his therapy as "the work." "And it was," George said, "it was work. What I learnt from my experience was that the times when I most wanted to leave were the times when I most needed to go."

During our interview, George recounted feelings of extreme disappointment when a new girlfriend told him she was not interested in pursuing the relationship. He was reluctant to go to therapy that week because he was too distressed. After revealing this to his therapist, she responded: "Well, you don't realize George, this is the work, this is it." For George, this involved acknowledging his pain and finding the capacity to move forward. Similarly, part of Simon's therapeutic work has centered around understanding the cause of his anxiety and his feelings of fragmentation, an understanding that allowed him to take control over the behavior he described as erratic. As he said, the critical issue for him in deciding to seek therapy was that he had wanted to make changes in his life but had been unable to do so.

Simon's story, like that of George and others, seriously calls into question the notion that therapy reflects a failure of responsibility. Certainly, as has been widely noted, therapy does have the potential to encourage self-indulgence, but in the context of a continuing level of social stigma, perhaps the more important point is that it represents a commitment to building a life. Often this entails people's desire to alleviate experiences of suffering, but equally it is about learning how to live with purpose and finding ways to foster good relationships. This signals, perhaps, a crucial difference between therapy as a clinical practice and the dissipated effects of the therapeutic ethos in society more broadly. The work involved in therapy makes demands of the individual that therapeutic culture does not. That is not to say, however, that a more diffuse therapeutic ethos cannot function in a similar way. An important question that has yet to be addressed, is whether the rise of the therapeutic society has reduced some forms collective denial, through the recognition and public acknowledgement of injustice and suffering—an issue I consider in the concluding chapter.[23]

Therapy & Self-Change

The contingent conditions of the lives of those interviewed form the backdrop of the story of therapy told here. Uncertainty and risk feature prominently.[24] Yet uncertainty itself was not generally recognized as a precipitating factor in seeking therapy. Nevertheless, participants acknowledged that therapy could equip them with skills to better navigate the uncertain conditions of their lives. Jessica captures something of this ordinary uncertainty as she reflects: "There is not one thing in my life that is permanent. I'm living in an apartment that is great, but I'm not going to stay there forever. I'm in a career that I'm not sure I want to do forever, and I'm in a relationship that is pretty good, but I'm not sure it will last. There is nothing in my life that is like, that's forever."

Importantly, the people interviewed for this study do have the capacity to navigate uncertainty in relation to changing labor markets—generally they have not encountered difficulties in securing employment—but the contingency of their connection to the world of work and other core aspects of their lives, in particular personal relationships, is experienced to greater or lesser degrees as fragmentation. Therapy can help to alleviate the anxiety of this fragility, as Simon explained:

> The structure provided by therapy came at a time in my life when, you know, I have a temporary job, I have a temporary relationship, I'm living in temporary accommodation. There is so much going on and I know all of that can change and my therapist will still be there at 9.00 o'clock every Monday ... I don't know whether my job is going to be there. I don't know whether my partner is going to be there, whether I'm going to be living in the same house. There is nothing else in my life like that ... it makes me feel a bit safe.

Simon was most articulate about the ways in which therapy provided him with structure amid uncertainty. But feelings of fragmentation were not uncommon. George explained how therapy helped shift his worldview to one better suited to the conditions of contemporary life:

> I went from searching for the answers, to the realization that there is a much better way of looking at the world, that there is nothing laid out, there is nothing preordained. What it comes down to really is our choices and how we respond to the situations and things that happen to us. That tends to be a much better measure of how, for want of a better word, how you cope with life and whether you're happy and fulfilled.

Clearly, the conditions of contemporary life are experienced in a multitude of ways. Democratic shifts in the personal and sexual domains, for example, allow for the expression and exploration of sexual identity in ways not available to earlier generations of men and women. As a result, relationships have become, according Giddens, more democratic.[25] James, for example, has the freedom to explore same-sex relationships, while Andrew and his partner epitomize Giddens' notion of the "pure relationship." Theirs is a partnership that is constantly negotiated, one that has been uncoupled from the expectations of traditional marriage:

> It's a relationship we both actively work on. It's not something that every six months we have a little bit of a discussion and say you aren't doing the dishes or you don't do, whatever it is. I suppose really it's about actively deciding if we want to actually be with the person on a day-to-day, week-to-week level. I don't want to wake up, neither of us want to wake up going, well, I missed the last 20 years. I don't want to do that and she doesn't want to do that either. We've actively decided not to have children. We choose, we actively choose our friends, we choose to stay in Australia. I suppose what characterizes the life that I wish to create for myself is that every day is a decision.

Andrew's portrayal of his relationship resonates with Rose's notion of the modern self as a "choosing individual." The kinds of freedom and choice characteristic of contemporary life, particularly in the personal domain, however, necessitate finding ways of living with uncertainty. And for some, the flip side of liberation is anxiety.

In relation to the place of therapy in dealing with problems of intimate life, Simon's story is a useful one to return to. He has twice sought relationship counseling and continues to explore relationship issues in therapy. Putting questions of individual psychology aside, Simon's difficulties are acutely social, and contemporary. His experience of couples counseling is a case in point, as his former partner was living with a life-threatening illness, and his current partner does not have Australian residency. It is clear that attempting to establish long term bonds under these conditions is inherently problematic. The question, then, of how this is managed becomes important. In a cultural climate of greater openness about private life, talking things through has become a key means by which problems are dealt with. Yet, as Simon says, discussing such issues with friends can too easily exceed the boundaries of those relationships. It is in this context that alternative means of support assume greater significance.

Despite high levels of psychological literacy, most interviewees could not articulate with clarity the dynamics of therapeutic change. Not surprising, given the question of "how" therapy works is an area of continuing research.[26] What is evident, however, is that a central facet of therapy involves the construction of particular forms of self-understanding. As Maria put it:

> Now, after therapy, I feel like I can see the patterns, I can identify what's going on, the good things and the bad things. I can identify what is beneficial to me and what is not and how to actually change the negative patterns, or the negative things, to make my life better. So I'm happier … Therapy is not an overnight thing. It is something that stays with you. I think that I have become a problem solver in my own life. Not just fixing problems, but also accepting things that I can't change.

When asked to identify the most valuable thing therapy did for him, James said:

> It helped me put Humpty together again, is the way I would describe it. Because when Humpty Dumpty fell off the wall, who fell off was an external creation of who I thought I was. So it wasn't real. What got put back together again was an understanding of that, and the need to understand who I was, more than who I wanted to be. And it gave me a lot of the tools to be able to do that.

George offered a similar observation. In his view, therapy equipped him with strategies to get through difficult situations and it helped him develop greater self-understanding. But it did more than that; it enabled him to mature. As he sees it: "In many ways I guess at that time I was still a child and I hadn't been able to grow up properly and I guess I did through that process." Yet therapy provides more than an alternative framework for development. The dispositions and skills it fosters include particular forms of self-monitoring and a consonant language with which to understand feelings and behaviors. When I asked George what he does now when he is "feeling down," George responded:

> The other thing therapy does is help you put words on your emotions. So "down" is not a word I would use. I would say I'm feeling frustrated, or not sure of the direction I'm heading. I can put it in quite clear words, the reality of what I am experiencing. I gradually had to completely change my words, the words I was using for how I was feeling and experiencing things ... because once you know how you're feeling, then you can come up with rational ways of responding.

What George describes is akin to the development of what is now popularly known as emotional intelligence (EI), that is, a keen awareness of one's own and others' emotional life, the capacity to regulate one's emotions, and to think, feel and act in appropriate ways.[27] EI has become part of the great armory of self-help literature, but it is essentially a popularized form of the kind of understandings and skills learned in therapy. Changing ways of relating to self and others, by recognizing "patterns" and altering them, is fundamental to therapeutic outcomes. Amy, Maria, Simon, and George all spoke of the ways therapy helped them to recognize, and ultimately, change, thoughts, feelings, and behaviors. As Amy put it: "There are patterns that I now understand, in terms of what I do and being aware of them, being able to see it when it's happening, and change my response, because I've got a better understanding of where it's coming from."

Amy clearly recognizes how self-understanding has enabled her to develop a greater measure of control over her thoughts and behavior. Her comment suggests too that while she appreciates the benefits of therapy she also understands its limits; it may not bring about wholesale changes in one's life or in one's personality, but nevertheless that such insights into the self can be exceedingly powerful. Peter O'Connor's rather sober view of the capacity of people to actually change reflects another, albeit not dissimilar, standpoint. In his view, what therapy can do effectively is change how people attend to themselves. As a therapist, he believes that people do not actually change very much:

> You can't change their history, but I think what happens is that if you give people enough space to reflect on themselves then they can change the feeling towards themselves, in a sense they have another way of being with themselves, warts and all. I often say to people that history is fixed, it's nailed to the floor, it's in this room called your psyche and you can go round that room with the lights out and keep stumbling over the same chair, or we could start by lighting a match and getting them to that chair every time. And we might finish up with a candle. Now, the chair's going to be in the same position, but you have a way of negotiating yourself.

O'Connor's figurative depiction offers an insight into key dimensions of the therapeutic process, in particular the importance of developing of self-understanding. Sixteen years after undertaking Jungian therapy, James reflects on the experience:

> It provided sort of lovely insights and foundations for me to, even now, I suppose, to feel comfortable standing on. That there is a solid foundation of my understanding of my inner world, and my acceptance of my inner world, when I have to deal with whatever current crisis or issues that's coming up. I think that it gave me the tools to push me in the direction to search for my own self-identity, at a very turbulent time. Now the question that I suppose that stands juxtaposed to is would that have not occurred spontaneously had I done nothing? Who knows?

Despite some speculation about what may have happened in the absence of therapeutic intervention, there was a general consensus amongst interviewees that therapy had played a critical role in helping them through some very difficult times in their lives. In Stephanie Dowrick's view, therapy can be of enormous assistance in helping people to "re-engage more hopefully with the world." This certainly appears to have been the case for George. As he put it:

> Life before therapy was pretty dark. It was a pretty dim place to be really. I was not making good choices about my life. I was lonely. I had no idea about entering into a relationship that was respectful. I was looking for the meaning of life, looking for answers in bizarre places. I had no idea about the emotions that I was experiencing. So that was life before therapy. And after therapy? Well, completely different! I think I am a reasonably self-aware person now. I'm happy. I can make good choices about my life. I've got friends. I've got good relationships. I guess, as I said before, this inner peace thing, which sounds a bit wanky, but so many people are looking for it. People are trying Buddhism and Christianity and crystals and all this sort of stuff. But it really just comes from being self-aware, through getting rid of the issues and the angst and the anger and all that sort of stuff that was there in childhood and undoing all the damage, so that you can live consciously making good choices for yourself.

Both Rose and Giddens point to the centrality of choice and the capacity to choose as imperatives of modern life. For Rose: "Selves unable to operate the imperative of choice are to be restored through therapy to the status of a choosing individual." Giddens advances something of a related argument, suggesting that therapy should be understood primarily as "a methodology of life-planning." In an environment characterized by plurality of choice, Giddens argues that 'the capable individual' of today not only has a developed self-understanding, but is able to harmonise present concerns and future projects with a psychological inheritance from the past."[28]

In light of this analysis, the importance of the process of clarification—particularly of emotional life and of issues around self-identity and relationships—is worth revisiting. Not only is it often regarded by those in therapy as revelatory, but it also offers an important insight into the relationship between the therapeutic society and therapy. The therapeutic ethos, broadly diffused at the cultural level, certainly encourages self-analysis. It expounds a psychological worldview that promotes inwardness, but by and large it does not actually equip people with the resources to make sense of such self-analysis and facilitate change. Therapy, by contrast to psychotherapeutic cultural forms, provides a relational dimension. It yields insights generated through interaction, and for many, practical strategies and tools which can be used to effect change.

In the Final Analysis

Freud—and his patients—recognized from the outset the limits of therapeutic intervention. That the aims of therapy were modest was one element. Another was the problem of the relationship between psychological distress and the material reality of the patient's life. Freud wrote:

> When I have promised my patients help or improvement by means of a cathartic treatment I have often been faced by this objection: "Why, you tell me yourself that my illness is probably connected with my circumstances and the events of my life. You cannot alter these in any way. How do you propose to help me, then?" And I have been able to make this reply: "No doubt fate would find it easier than I do to relieve you of your illness. But you will be able to convince yourself that much will be gained if we succeed in transforming your hysterical misery into common unhappiness."[29]

But it is with the following remark, in which he notes: "With a mental life that has been restored to health you will be better armed against that unhappiness," that he pre-empts the most strident and long-lasting critique of therapy that was to follow.

The complicity of therapy in the individualization of social problems constitutes a major point of criticism. That the aim of therapeutic intervention is primarily to bring about self-change rather than social transformation, has cast therapy as a practice antithetical to politics and social action. Underpinning this line of analysis, however, is the presumption that this entails "adjustment" to oppressive social conditions, and/or unequal social relations. While it would naïve to suggest that therapy never encourages such dispositions, the assumption that it only works in this fashion is overly simplistic and partial. Moreover, it is important to also consider the multifaceted social arrangements that it might foster adaptation to. To be sure, there are many aspects of contemporary life that remain inequitable and oppressive. Yet, if one is to accept the proposition that the contemporary era is, at the same time, marked by democratic shifts, notably in the gender order and in private life, it is important to be attuned to the possibility that adjustment also involves finding ways of living with more equitable social relations.

A related point regards the presumption of a dichotomous relationship between therapy—and indeed the broader therapeutic society which it exemplifies—and social action. It is difficult to say whether Freud believed that material changes might follow the restoration of mental health, but in the alleviation of distress, therapy does open the possibility for greater social engagement. Clearly, self-transformation does not in itself bring about social change, as some currents of new age thought contend, but equally it does not preclude it. An important point to consider is whether people have already turned inward before seeking therapy. At least for those interviewed here, therapeutic intervention appears to have enabled them to re-engage with the world and, moreover, develop solutions which go beyond "self-adjustment" and in fact change the circumstances of their lives.

To be sure, the extent to which the accounts of therapy I have presented can be generalized is limited by the socioeconomic characteristics of the participants. Therapy, in the terms discussed here, is generally only an option for people who have the financial resources to pay for it. Yet there are exceptions to this, even within this small cohort. Nevertheless, my intention was not to evaluate therapy and counseling for different social groups and engage in comparative analysis, nor was it to document the sinister forms that, clearly, therapy can take. Rather, my interest was in exploring how therapy itself might throw light on the therapeutic society. The narratives recounted here suggest an alternative reading to that which prevails in the social theoretical literature: instead of moral decline and disempowerment, what emerges is a story of the struggles of men and women trying to build a life and live with dignity.

6

Reflections on the Therapeutic Turn

The "triumph of the therapeutic" has been a complex and contradictory development. Psychological knowledge, therapeutic techniques, and a pervasive analytic attitude emerged amidst the widespread social, economic, and technological transformations of the late nineteenth and twentieth centuries. Historicizing the therapeutic society brings to light its multifaceted and paradoxical dimensions. It reveals that the ascendancy of a therapeutic ethos has gone hand-in-hand with procedures that have sought to classify and manage populations, that it fosters, at times, an excessive concern with the self, and that it has been associated with processes of depoliticization. Yet, in addition to those insidious effects that have long been emphasized, what it also reveals is that the therapeutic imperative works in ways that have enhanced social, political, and personal life.

That therapeutic strategies arose in response to emergent social and personal dilemmas suggests that the therapeutic turn was never simply the result of capitalist expansion, a proxy for lost communal faiths, or a new regime of control and regulation. Rather, it was through a series of disparate strategies and shifting knowledges directed towards improving various dimensions of social, economic, and personal life that the therapeutic came into its own. From late nineteenth century approaches to dealing with "nerves" to contemporary modalities of therapy and counseling, individuals and groups of professionals have embraced psychological knowledges and therapeutic techniques in attempting to manage anxieties generated under the rapidly changing conditions of modern and late modern life.

A historical analysis of the therapeutic society demonstrates that the changing social management of emotional suffering, transformations in the gender order, and the role played by ordinary people and professionals in driving cultural change must be given due consideration. Attention to these dimensions suggests that some elements of traditional theorizing may be misplaced, particularly those concerning the decline of traditional authority, the blurring of the boundaries between the public and private spheres, and the rise of a so-called victim culture.

There can be no doubt that the therapeutic has been instrumental in the disruption of the older order of society—in which there was a clear separation between public and private life, and in which authority was powerfully embodied in the social and cultural elite, and in men within family households. It has similarly destabilized a set of arrangements that ensured the powerful had a public voice, while the marginalized did not. Much disquiet about the therapeutic has accordingly centered upon a perceived diminishment of public life on the one hand, and an apparent impoverishment of private life on the other. The seeping of the "private" into the public domain constitutes a central concern, as does the intrusion of experts into the domestic realm. In addition to subverting repressive codes of conduct governing public life, these processes have been read as undermining intimate relationships and threatening the development of autonomous selfhood, both of which are said to require the sanctity of a protected private sphere.

Concerns about the delicacy of private life are not entirely misplaced. Yet, unqualified denunciation of greater openness about matters once considered personal is itself problematic, for it ignores the burden of suffering historically veiled by the cloak of privacy. The intense focus on the depoliticizing effects of the therapeutic, moreover, has tended to obscure the ways in which new forms of confessional practice and increased attention to emotional and psychological life have underwritten the politicization of the private realm. Indeed, in making private pain public, the therapeutic—especially the confessional mode—has been instrumental to the legitimation of emotional suffering. Particularly for women and other marginalized groups, public recognition of psychological and emotional trauma has, moreover, enabled the exposure of widespread experiences of violence and abuse.

Accounts lamenting the emergence of a "victim culture" posit that pain and suffering in the pre-therapeutic era were simply viewed as a part of everyday life—experiences to be welcomed, even, for the strengthening of character and the attainment of virtue they entailed. Such a stance, however, not only ignores the fact that suffering is not equally distributed amongst the population, it overlooks the emancipatory potential of the therapeutic in buttressing claims of injustice.

Rather than escalating claims of victimization representing cultural diminishment, an alternate view is that the blurring boundaries between public and private life and the rise of confessional culture has finally provided a means of expression for those who have been marginalized, abused, and oppressed. It may legitimately be argued that the therapeutic has been instrumental in the exposure of abuse against some of the least powerful in society, by providing knowledge to understand emotional pain, a language with which to articulate injury to the self, and the expertise with which to redress the damage.

Clearly, a cultural sensibility that accords a certain reverence to the self and privileges emotional life may engender a degree of self-centeredness, or encourage self-pity. Yet it also reflects changing social and cultural values in relation to what may be damaging to the self, and this in turn has implications for codes of conduct and the just treatment of individuals. The established reading of the therapeutic as antithetical to politics is thus problematic. Indeed, to view therapeutic solutions as disconnected from social action and politics is to misread the complexity of the therapeutic society.

It is no coincidence that the same period in which the therapeutic imperative intensified also witnessed the emergence of politics of recognition and the rise of social movements seeking redress for past injustices. Over the second half of the twentieth century, from the level of the state to that of the individual, there have been moves to acknowledge the ongoing cultural, social, and psychological costs of abuse and injustice.[1] Emerging from social struggles, many claims of victimization have been underwritten by a therapeutic ethic that has given legitimacy to experiences of suffering that were previously denied, ignored, or covered up. As Elazar Barkan notes: "The move to publicize private feelings, as performance and a display of individual pain, has become part of the political agenda for victims' rights."[2]

The capacity to bring experiences of suffering into public discussion, to give voice to marginalized and oppressed groups, has been one of the most powerful, yet under-recognized, dimensions of the therapeutic turn. Through the opening up of a discursive space in which personal pain can be openly discussed, psychology has furnished a language and a therapeutic ethic has given legitimacy to experiences of injustice in new ways. This has enabled recognition of forms of suffering which were institutionalized, systemic, and, most importantly, avoidable. Evidently, then, while the therapeutic can work in ways that individualize and depoliticize, it also works the other way. Cultural acceptance of a therapeutic ethic has been critical to the elevation of such issues in the public realm, issues that until recently were subject to little public scrutiny and almost no public discussion. This is not to advance a utopian view of the therapeutic, but rather to highlight how it has been marshaled in ways that are not "merely therapeutic," depoliticizing, or hedonistic.

Excavating the past and bringing painful experiences into the present in the hope of making a better future, is a process that in recent years has not only been taking place in therapy but also at the wider societal and political levels in a variety of international contexts. In Australia, there has been far-reaching examination of the darker side of the nation's history, especially in relation to injustices suffered by vulnerable children and Indigenous Australians. Government initiated inquiries have revealed widespread experiences of trauma resulting from past policies of the state and the past and present practices of institutions charged with responsibility for the care of young people.

The Australian Human Rights and Equal Opportunity Commission's 1997 report, *Bringing Them Home*, exposed the devastating impact that Australia's past laws and policies have had on its Indigenous peoples. The report laid bare the brutality of past practices of the forcible removal of children from their families and communities, "often in the absence of the parent but sometimes even by taking the child from the mother's arms." It acknowledged the intergenerational trauma that resulted, and documented the abuse experienced by many children after being removed.[3] *Bringing Them Home* was one of several major reports that in recent years have revealed terrible injustices suffered by Australian children, and in many cases their families and their communities, during the twentieth century.

Another damning report, *Lost Innocents*, exposed the tragic consequences of unassisted child migration.[4] For many children who arrived in Australia under child migration schemes, the hopes and promises of a better life soon gave way to the reality of depravation and isolation as they were placed in barrack style institutions away from the broader community. A similar story of suffering also emerged through an inquiry into the abuse of children in state and religious orphanages. *Forgotten Australians*, the report which examined experiences of institutional or out-of-home care represented what the Committee of Inquiry referred to as the third part of a trilogy documenting the hidden history of the treatment of children in Australia.[5]

In the move to recognize and make reparation for past injustices, the therapeutic has clearly aligned with a social justice agenda. A notable feature of the abovementioned reports is that all three inquires were underwritten by a therapeutic ethic that legitimated people's experiences of suffering: an ethic that recognized the ongoing and intergenerational legacies of abuse and victimization, an ethic that gave voice to some of the most marginalized people in Australian society, an ethic that has forced both governments and a range of other institutions to take seriously the welfare of those for whom they have a duty of care.

That these issues are being addressed underlines an important political dimension of the therapeutic society. Research in this area may well bring to light the limitations of therapeutic politics, but it may also reveal that there are real benefits that as yet have been under-recognized.[6] Clearly, the issues are complex, but the extent to which the therapeutic has given language and legitimacy to claims of suffering and abuse calls out for further investigation. That it is now widely accepted that maltreatment, especially of children, leads to psychological and emotional damage is unquestionably one of the more significant cultural consequences of the therapeutic turn. Moreover, that these matters have currency, that victims have a public voice, and that government and other institutions implicated in unjust practices are being held accountable points to a highly significant cultural shift, especially in terms of changing relations of authority and power.

The exposure of child sexual abuse in the Catholic Church provides another example of how a therapeutic ethic has underwritten a dramatic challenge to traditional authority. It is highly improbable that the uncovering of this form of institutional abuse and violence would have been possible in the pre-therapeutic era. For the religious authority of the church to be challenged in such a way required a movement so profound that we may well call it, as Philip Rieff did, a cultural revolution. Certainly, the claim of victimization was central. So too was the capacity to speak out publicly about matters that had hitherto been unspeakable. It required recognition of the vulnerability of children, and the capacity to assert individual rights to bodily autonomy—even in the face of an institution as powerful as the Catholic Church.

By deflecting attention from the odious reality of victimization, unflattering characterizations of "victim culture" are liable to shield perpetrators of abuse and violence from due responsibility. That it is acceptable and even encouraged that victims once silent challenge the authority of the usually more powerful perpetrator calls into question bleak assessments of diminishing authority. And as with institutional abuse, the politicization and criminalization of domestic violence and sexual assault in the private sphere also became possible in an era of in which therapeutic authority destabilized traditional authority.

The transformation of intimate relations is a subject to which it is perhaps useful to return at this point. Giddens' analysis of the democratization of family life is instructive. As he argues, the liberalization of the personal sphere does not entail the disappearance of authority altogether, "rather, coercive power gives way to authority relations which can be defended in a principled fashion."[7] In line with Giddens' view that changing patterns of authority and the opening up of the personal sphere represent a democratic current, it becomes possible to start to delineate the ways in which the therapeutic has enabled a different set of moral questions to be posed from those associated with traditional social order.

Difficult questions remain. While cultural critics since Lasch have recognized the depoliticizing tendency of the therapeutic, lifting the lid on pain has itself been a political development. The stories told by people in the course of the investigations of the Royal Commission on Human Relationships in the 1970s, for example, had not only legislative consequences, such as in the criminalization of family violence, but contributed to a search for practical solutions, as with the establishment of women's refuges. No doubt a culture of therapy can and does operate in ways that are depoliticizing and individualizing. But the therapeutic itself furnishes an alternative social critique, and as such it can also—both at the individual and collective levels—be emancipatory. Indeed, the complexity of the therapeutic means that it plays out in myriad ways, both at the level of culture and at that of the individual. On the personal level, the therapeutic on the one hand may be read as promoting narcissism or inciting vulnerability, but equally we might assert that in individualized secular cultures it also provides resources for building a life and managing difficult circumstances.[8]

Though there has been wide ranging analysis of the therapeutic, little of it has engaged with people's actual experiences. Empirical evidence from therapists and clients presented in the preceding chapters throws light on the complex ways in which therapy shapes the lives of modern individuals. Amid wide ranging social changes that include the weakening of cultural authority and the destabilization of the private sphere, accounts of therapy do point to a generalized anxiety brought about by the contingent conditions of contemporary life. In work, the promise of freedom under the guise of flexibility has forced individuals to adapt to a climate of employment marked by insecurity. Instability also characterizes changes in the personal sphere. The democratic currents involved in the breaking down of a fixed gender order, more openness regarding sexuality, and the imperative of relationships of choice have produced a range of uneven and contradictory effects, for both men and women. The uncertainty that accompanies greater freedom necessitates the finding of new ways of living that involve not simply the pursuit of happiness, but that also help to alleviate emotional pain and provide answers to questions of how to live with dignity.

As with the therapeutic society more broadly, therapy embodies contradictions that are quintessentially late modern. It encourages introspection and at times casts social problems as individual ones. Therapy can be dangerous, it may involve adaptation and "self-adjustment" and it mostly offers only an individualized solution for problems that are often not of the individual's making. But it can also be experienced as transformative. Not only can it assist with mental health problems, but it can also be a mechanism of support amid social and personal upheaval, a resource for navigating uncertainty.

In addition to the interview material presented in Chapter Five, my thoughts on the therapeutic have also been shaped by many people who spoke informally to me of their views on therapy. In a variety of social situations, enquiries about the nature of my research often led people to candidly discuss experiences of counseling, as well as the personal problems that led them to seek professional help. During these encounters I heard numerous accounts of how "nerves," depression, and anxiety have plagued people's lives. Many of these stories were poignant and deeply moving, and I recount three of them here: one from a middle-aged finance executive who attended group counseling following the breakdown of his marriage, and two from women who suffered from problems of "nerves."

One woman's "nervous breakdown" in the 1960s following the death of her mother, necessitated the "farming out" of her four children to relatives. It was only as her mother lay dying in hospital, she said, that she had her first "real conversation" with her. Her father had been killed during the Second World War and she remembers her childhood as one in which no expression of grief was permitted. She never saw her mother cry, and when she herself at the age of five wept for her dead father, she was scolded and told "not to be silly." As she describes it, high levels of repression were expected, an environment one suspects Rieff would favor. While she says she has worked hard over the years to overcome what she now regards as ongoing problems with anxiety, she wonders if things would have been different for her had she been allowed, as a child, to openly express her grief, had she known then that it was normal to feel devastated by the death of her father.

One elderly woman I met revealed that she had been utterly debilitated with nerves for many decades and it was not until she was in her eighties that she spoke of her condition to anyone except her doctor, after organizations like Beyond Blue and Sane Australia began public campaigns to destigmatize depression and anxiety. Another memorable encounter for me involved an unexpected discussion about emotional life with a middle-aged man who works in high-end finance. He spoke with great compassion about the struggles of men dealing with the emotional fallout of marriage breakdown. His experience of group counseling was in the company of working-class men with whom in the course of his daily life he had virtually no contact. It was an experience that stayed with him, he said, bringing about a greater understanding of the commonality of human suffering. In his words: "In that room, we all had the same problems, we were all hurt, we were all sad, and we were all angry. We were all the same."

Such anecdotal stories, prompted in social exchanges by the subject of my research, strengthened my views about the complexity of the therapeutic society and the need, moreover, for a more nuanced reading of its ambivalent legacy. For while disdainful critique of the therapeutic may be compelling at the theoretical level, people's lived experiences tell another story, one that must take its place alongside critical readings of social and cultural change. Perhaps what also deserves consideration is the extent to which overly negative accounts of the therapeutic turn have been colored by generational—and indeed gendered—discomfort about the ascendancy of the emotional realm and concerns that were formerly confined to women's culture and the domestic sphere.

In tracing the multifaceted dimensions of sociohistorical change, as well as in theorizing its implications, I have suggested the need for a conceptual framework that recognizes what is largely missing in debates on this subject—the acknowledgement of emotional suffering and struggles for human dignity. The therapeutic does not simply reflect rampant desires for self-fulfillment and happiness, nor is it simply a mechanism of internalized social control. Indeed, it is a deeply contradictory historical project. Attention to those aspects of the therapeutic society often overlooked, including people's experiences of therapy, offers new insights into the cultural and personal issues at stake. In further developing our understanding of these processes, deeper examination of the parallels between therapy and the therapeutic society suggests another vantage point from which to assess sociocultural change. When assessing the many consequences of the "triumph of the therapeutic," then, further consideration must be given to the question of whether we are now as a society, like reflexive individuals, in less denial about human suffering.

Notes

Introduction

1. Julie McLeod and Katie Wright, "The Talking Cure in Everyday Life: Gender, Generations and Friendship," *Sociology* 43, no. 1 (2009): 122–39.
2. In 2004, Australia had an estimated 58 psychologists and 17 psychiatrists per 100,000 population. The comparative estimate for the United States for the same year was 33.5 psychologists and 5.2 psychiatrists per 100,00 population. See Australian Institute of Health and Welfare, *Mental Health Services in Australia 2004–05* (Canberra: Australian Institute of Health and Welfare, 2007), xii; and M. Dionne, J. Moore, D. Armstrong, and R. Martiniano, *The United States Health Workforce Profile* (Rensselaer, NY: Center for Health Workforce Studies, School of Public Health, SUNY Albany, 2006), 136.
3. Philip Rieff, *The Triumph of the Therapeutic: Uses of Faith After Freud* (1966; Chicago: University of Chicago Press, 1987); Christopher Lasch, *The Culture of Narcissism: American Life in an Age of Diminishing Expectations* (1979; New York: Norton, 1991); Frank Furedi, *Therapy Culture: Cultivating Vulnerability in an Uncertain Age* (London: Routledge, 2004). See also James Nolan, *The Therapeutic State: Justifying Government at Century's End* (New York: New York University Press, 1998).
4. Dana Cloud, *Control and Consolation in American Culture and Politics: Rhetoric of Therapy* (Thousand Oaks, CA: Sage, 1998); Dana Becker, *The Myth of Empowerment: Women and the Therapeutic Culture in America* (New York: New York University Press, 2005).
5. Nikolas Rose, *Inventing Our Selves: Psychology, Power, and Personhood* (Cambridge: Cambridge University Press, 1996); *Governing the Soul: The Shaping of the Private Self*, 2nd ed. (London: Free Association Books, 1999).
6. For an analysis of this issue drawing on interviews from another study, see McLeod and Wright, "The Talking Cure in Everyday Life."
7. Michel Foucault, "Two Lectures," in *Power/Knowledge: Selected Interviews and Other Writings*, ed. Colin Gordon (New York:

Pantheon, 1980), 78–108; "Nietzsche, Genealogy, History," in *The Foucault Reader*, ed. Paul Rabinow (New York: Pantheon, 1984), 76–100; "Problematics," in *Foucault Live (Interviews, 1961–1984)*, 2nd ed., trans. John Johnston, ed. Sylvère Lotringer (New York: Semiotext(e), 1996), 416–22.

8. Katie Wright, "Theorizing Therapeutic Culture: Past Influences, Future Directions," *Journal of Sociology* 44, no. 4 (2008): 321–36. See too Eva Illouz, *Saving the Modern Soul: Therapy, Emotions, and the Culture of Self-Help* (Berkeley: University of California Press, 2008).

1 The Therapeutic Society & Its Discontents

Epigraph is from Philip Rieff, *The Triumph of the Therapeutic: Uses of Faith After Freud* (1966; Chicago: University of Chicago Press, 1987), 240.

1. Philip Rieff, "The Emergence of Psychological Man," in *Freud: The Mind of the Moralist*, 3rd ed. (1959; Chicago: University of Chicago Press, 1979), 329–57; *The Triumph of the Therapeutic*.
2. Lasch, *The Culture of Narcissism*; Jacques Donzelot, *The Policing of Families*, trans. Robert Hurley (New York: Pantheon, 1979); Andrew Polsky, *The Rise of the Therapeutic State* (Princeton, NJ: Princeton University Press, 1991); Cloud, *Control and Consolation*; Rose, *Inventing Our Selves*; *Governing the Soul*.
3. Lasch, *The Culture of Narcissism*; Furedi, *Therapy Culture*; Nolan, *The Therapeutic State*.
4. Wright, "Theorizing Therapeutic Culture."
5. Rieff, "The Emergence of Psychological Man."
6. Rieff, *Triumph of the Therapeutic*, 62.
7. Rieff, *Triumph of the Therapeutic*, x.
8. Rieff, *Triumph of the Therapeutic*, 4. In his conceptualization of interdicts, Rieff followed Durkheim in arguing that religious prohibitions form a foundational element of the sacred order and also constitute the basis of a moral demand system. See Emile Durkheim, *The Elementary Forms of Religious Life*, 2nd ed., trans. Joseph Ward Swain (1912; London: Allen & Unwin, 1976).
9. Rieff, *Triumph of the Therapeutic*, 17.
10. Rieff, *Triumph of the Therapeutic*, 2.
11. Rieff, *Triumph of the Therapeutic*, 24–25.
12. For critical feminist analyses of the public/private split, see Jean Bethke Elshtain, *Public Man, Private Woman: Women in Social and*

Political Thought (Princeton, NJ: Princeton University Press, 1982); Carol Pateman, *The Disorder of Women: Democracy, Feminism, and Political Theory* (Cambridge: Polity Press, 1989), Chap. 6; and Joan Landes, ed., *Feminism, the Public and the Private* (Oxford: Oxford University Press, 1998). For a concise overview of the separation of public and private life under capitalism, see Eli Zaretsky, *Capitalism, the Family, and Personal Life* (London: Pluto Press, 1976).
13. Nolan, *The Therapeutic State*.
14. Nolan, *The Therapeutic State*, 7.
15. Nolan, *The Therapeutic State*, 306.
16. John Carroll, *Puritan, Paranoid, Remissive: A Sociology of Modern Culture* (London: Routledge & Kegan Paul, 1977); *Ego and Soul: The Modern West in Search of Meaning* (Pymble, NSW: HarperCollins, 1998).
17. Carroll, *Ego and Soul*, 92.
18. Maurice North, *The Secular Priests* (London: Allen & Unwin, 1972); see too Paul Halmos, *The Faith of the Counsellors* (London: Constable, 1965); and Eva Moskowitz, *In Therapy We Trust: America's Obsession with Self-Fulfillment* (Baltimore: Johns Hopkins University Press, 2001).
19. Michael Casey, "Authority, Crisis, and the Individual," *Society* 39, no. 2 (2002): 82.
20. Rieff, *Triumph of the Therapeutic*, x.
21. Martin Gross, *The Psychological Society: A Critical Analysis of Psychiatry, Psychotherapy, Psychoanalysis, and the Psychological Revolution* (New York: Simon & Schuster, 1979), 4.
22. Gross, *The Psychological Society*, 92.
23. See especially Lasch, *The Culture of Narcissism*. Also, *Haven in a Heartless World: The Family Besieged* (New York: Basic Books, 1977); and *The Minimal Self: Psychic Survival in Troubled Times* (New York: Norton, 1984).
24. Lasch, *Culture of Narcissism*, Chap. 2. See too *The Minimal Self*.
25. Furedi, *Therapy Culture*, 107.
26. Furedi, *Therapy Culture*, 113.
27. Furedi, *Therapy Culture*, 21.
28. Furedi, *Therapy Culture*, 72.
29. Rieff, *Triumph of the Therapeutic*, x.
30. Robert Bellah et al., *Habits of the Heart: Individualism and Commitment in American Life*, rev. ed. (1985; Berkley: University of California Press, 1996), 98.
31. Whereas the political and economic barely register on Rieff's radar, he does note that the therapeutic is not only an anti-religion but it is also anti-political.

32. See T.J. Jackson Lears, "From Salvation to Self-Realization: Advertising and the Therapeutic Roots of the Consumer Culture, 1880–1930," in *The Culture of Consumption: Critical Essays in American History, 1880–1980*, ed. Richard Wightman Fox and T.J. Jackson Lears (New York: Pantheon, 1983), 3–38. See also Lasch, *Culture of Narcissism*; Cloud, *Control and Consolation*; and Moskowitz, *In Therapy We Trust*.
33. Lears, "From Salvation to Self-Realization," 4.
34. Stuart Ewen, *Captains of Consciousness: Advertising and the Social Roots of the Consumer Culture* (1976; New York: Basic Books, 2001).
35. Philip Cushman, *Constructing the Self, Constructing America: A Cultural History of Psychotherapy* (Boston, MA: Addison-Wesley, 1995), 68.
36. Lears, "From Salvation to Self-Realization," 4.
37. Lears, "From Salvation to Self-Realization," 10.
38. See David Riesman, with Reuel Denney and Nathan Glazer, *The Lonely Crowd: A Study of the Changing American Character* (1950; New Haven, CT: Yale University Press, 2001); Richard Sennett, *The Fall of Public Man* (Cambridge: Cambridge University Press, 1977); and *The Corrosion of Character: The Personal Consequences of Work in the New Capitalism* (New York: Norton, 1998). See too Lasch, *Culture of Narcissism*; and *The Minimal Self*.
39. Riesman, *The Lonely Crowd*, 25.
40. Lasch, *Culture of Narcissism*, 27, 65; *Minimal Self*.
41. Lasch, *Culture of Narcissism*, 68–69.
42. Lasch, *Culture of Narcissism*, 13.
43. Lasch, *Culture of Narcissism*, 3.
44. Lasch, *Culture of Narcissism*, 13–14.
45. Cloud, *Control and Consolation*, xii.
46. Cloud, *Control and Consolation*, xvi.
47. Cloud, *Control and Consolation*, 3.
48. Furedi, *Therapy Culture*.
49. Kathleen Lowney, *Baring Our Souls: TV Talk Shows and the Religion of Recovery* (New York: Aldine de Gruyter, 1999), 23.
50. See Wendy Kaminer, *I'm Dysfunctional, You're Dysfunctional: The Recovery Movement and Other Self-Help Fashions* (Reading, MA: Addison-Wesley, 1992); Wendy Simonds, *Women and Self-Help Culture: Reading Between the Lines* (New Brunswick, NJ: Rutgers University Press, 1992); and Micki McGee, *Self-Help Inc.: Makeover Culture in American Life* (New York: Oxford University Press, 2005).
51. Kaminer, *I'm Dysfunctional, You're Dysfunctional*, 152.
52. Aric Sigman, *New, Improved? Exposing the Misuse of Popular Psychology* (London: Simon & Schuster, 1995); Ewen, *Captains of Consciousness*.
53. Cloud, *Control and Consolation*, xx.

54. David Ingleby, "Editor's Introduction," in *Critical Psychiatry: The Politics of Mental Health*, ed. David Ingleby (1980; London: Free Association Books, 2004), 8.
55. James Hillman and Michael Ventura, *We've Had a Hundred Years of Psychotherapy and the World's Getting Worse* (San Francisco: HarperSanFrancisco, 1993), 156.
56. See especially the works of Rose, *The Psychological Complex*; *Inventing Our Selves*; and *Governing the Soul*. See too Donzelot, *The Policing of Families*; and Polsky, *The Rise of the Therapeutic State*.
57. See especially Michel Foucault, *Madness and Civilization: A History of Insanity in the Age of Reason*, trans. Richard Howard (London: Tavistock, 1967); *The Order of Things: An Archaeology of the Human Sciences* (London: Tavistock, 1970); *Discipline and Punish: The Birth of the Prison* (New York: Pantheon, 1977); "Technologies of the Self," in *Technologies of the Self: A Seminar with Michael Foucault*, ed. Luther Martin, Huck Gutman, and Patrick Hutton (Amherst, MA: University of Massachusetts Press, 1988), 16–49; and *History of Sexuality, Vol. 1: An Introduction*, trans. Robert Hurley (1978; New York: Vintage, 1990).
58. Donzelot, *The Policing of Families*.
59. Donzelot, *The Policing of Families*, xxi.
60. Rose, *Inventing Our Selves*, 2.
61. Rose, *Governing the Soul*, 7.
62. Rose, *The Powers of Freedom*, 90.
63. Rose, *Powers of Freedom*, 91.
64. Foucault, *History of Sexuality, Vol. 1*, 67.
65. Foucault, "Technologies of the Self," 49.
66. Polsky, *Rise of the Therapeutic State*, 4.
67. Rose, *The Powers of Freedom*, 52.
68. Anthony Elliott, *Concepts of the Self*, 2nd ed. (Cambridge: Polity Press, 2008), 104.
69. Elliott, *Concepts of the Self*, 109. See too his discussion of the limitations of Foucault's theorization of the subject, 100–01.
70. Lois McNay, *Foucault and Feminism: Power, Gender and the Self* (Cambridge: Polity Press, 1992), 3.
71. See McNay, *Foucault and Feminism*; Tina Besley, *Counseling Youth: Foucault, Power, and the Ethics of Subjectivity* (Westport, CT: Praeger, 2002), 63; and Helen O'Grady, "An Ethics of the Self," in *Feminism and the Final Foucault*, ed. Dianna Taylor and Karen Vintges (Urbana: University of Illinois Press, 2004), 91–117.
72. See Virginia Held, *The Ethics of Care: Personal, Political, and Global* (Oxford: Oxford University Press, 2006); and Ruth Groenhout,

Connected Lives: Human Nature and the Ethics of Care (Lanham: Rowman & Littlefield, 2004).
73. Cloud, *Control and Consolation*, 129–30.
74. Phyllis Chesler, *Women and Madness*, rev, ed. (1972; New York: Palgrave Macmillan, 2005); Elaine Showalter, *The Female Malady: Women, Madness and English Culture 1830–1980* (London: Virago, 1987); Jane Ussher, *Women's Madness: Misogyny or Mental Illness?* (Amherst, MA: University of Massachusetts Press, 1992).
75. Jill Matthews, *Good and Mad Women: The Historical Construction of Femininity in Twentieth-Century Australia* (Sydney: Allen & Unwin, 1984); Judith Allen, *Sex and Secrets: Crimes Involving Australian Women Since 1880* (Melbourne: Oxford University Press, 1990).
76. See Linda Blum and Nena Stracuzzi, "Gender in the Prozac Nation: Popular Discourse and Productive Femininity," *Gender and Society* 18, no. 3 (2004): 271; and Jane Ussher, "Are We Medicalizing Women's Misery? A Critical Review of Women's Higher Rates of Reported Depression," *Feminism and Psychology* 20, no. 9 (2010): 10.
77. Celia Kitzinger, "Therapy and How it Undermines the Practice of Radical Feminism," in *Radically Speaking: Feminism Reclaimed*, ed. Diane Bell and Renate Klein (Melbourne: Spinifex Press, 1996), 92–101.
78. Susan Faludi, *Backlash: The Undeclared War Against Women* (London: Vintage, 1992), 371.
79. See Simonds, *Women and Self-Help Culture*, 227.
80. Franny Nudelman, "Beyond the Talking Cure: Listening to Female Testimony on the Oprah Winfrey Show," in *Inventing the Psychological: Toward a Cultural History of Emotional Life in America*, ed. Joel Pfister and Nancy Schnog (New Haven, CT: Yale University Press, 1997), 297.
81. See Helen Wood, *Talking with Television: Women, Talk Shows, and Modern Self-Reflexivity* (Urbana: University of Illinois Press, 2009); and Janice Peck, "TV Talk Shows as Therapeutic Discourse: The Ideological Labor of the Talking Cure," *Communication Theory* 5, no. 1 (1995): 58–81.
82. Becker, *The Myth of Empowerment*, 10.
83. Becker, *The Myth of Empowerment*, 2.
84. Becker, *The Myth of Empowerment*, 1.
85. Becker, *The Myth of Empowerment*, 35.
86. See Wright, "Theorizing Therapeutic Culture; and McLeod and Wright, "The Talking Cure in Everyday Life."
87. Cloud, *Control and Consolation*, 6.
88. See Miriam Greenspan, *A New Approach to Women and Therapy*, 2nd ed.

(Blue Ridge Summit, PA: TAB Books, 1993); Judith Worell and Pamela Remer, *Feminist Perspectives in Therapy: An Empowerment Model for Women*, 2nd ed. (New York: Wiley, 2002); and Mary Ballou, Marcia Hill, and Carolyn West, ed. *Feminist Therapy Theory and Practice: A Contemporary Perspective* (New York: Springer, 2008).

89. Ellen Herman, *The Romance of American Psychology: Political Culture in the Age of Experts* (Berkley: University of California Press 1995), 313.
90. Illouz, *Saving the Modern Soul*, 114.
91. Katie Wright, "Therapy Culture," in *Reflected Light: La Trobe Essays*, ed. Peter Beilharz and Robert Manne (Melbourne: Black Inc., 2006), 302–12; McLeod and Wright, "The Talking Cure in Everyday Life."
92. For a critique of the dominance feminism perspective and an alternative conceptualization, see Joan Williams, *Unbending Gender: Why Family and Work Conflict and What to Do About It* (New York: Oxford University Press, 2000), 254.
93. Williams, *Unbending Gender*, 253.
94. R.W. Connell, *Gender* (Cambridge: Polity Press, 2002).
95. In elucidating the complexity of the self-society relationship and the contradictory nature of late modern culture, the works of Anthony Giddens, Anthony Elliott, and Eli Zaretsky have been especially useful to the development of my account. See Anthony Giddens, *Modernity and Self-Identity: Self and Society in the Late Modern Age* (Stanford, CA: Stanford University Press, 1991); *The Transformation of Intimacy: Sexuality, Love and Eroticism in Modern Societies* (Stanford, CA: Stanford University Press, 1992); Anthony Elliott, *Subject to Ourselves: Social Theory, Psychoanalysis and Postmodernity*, 2nd ed. (Boulder, CO: Paradigm, 2004); *Concepts of the Self*, 2nd ed. (Cambridge: Polity Press, 2007); "Therapy Culture and Its Discontents," *Meanjin* 63, no. 4 (2004): 47–52; and Eli Zaretsky, *Secrets of the Soul: A Social and Cultural History of Psychoanalysis* (New York: Vintage, 2005). I should also like to acknowledge the importance of the new cultural sociology in developing my analysis of the therapeutic. See Jeffrey C. Alexander, *The Meanings of Social Life: A Cultural Sociology* (New York: Oxford University Press, 2003); and Lyn Spillman, ed., *Cultural Sociology* (Malden, MA: Blackwell, 2002).
96. For a critique of Lasch's "mythic family" and his theory of narcissism, see Michèle Barrett and Mary McIntosh, "Narcissism and the Family: A Critique of Lasch," *New Left Review* 135 (Sep–Oct 1982): 35–48.
97. Jessica Benjamin, *The Bonds of Love: Psychoanalysis, Feminism, and the Problem of Domination* (New York: Pantheon, 1988), 137.
98. See Jane Flax, "Political Philosophy and the Patriarchal Unconscious: A Psychoanalytic Perspective on Epistemology and Metaphysics," in

Discovering Reality: Feminist Perspectives on Epistemology, Metaphysics, Methodology, and Philosophy of Science, 2nd ed., ed. Sandra Harding and Merrill Hintikka (Dordrecht: Kluwer Academic Publishers, 2003), 245–81. See also Benjamin, *The Bonds of Love*; and Nancy Chodorow, *The Reproduction of Mothering: Psychoanalysis and the Sociology of Gender*, 2nd ed. (1978; Berkley: University of California Press, 1999); *Feminism and Psychoanalytic Theory* (New Haven, CT: Yale University Press, 1989).

99. McNay, *Foucault and Feminism*, 10.
100. Elliott, *Concepts of the Self*, 100–01.
101. Elliott, *Concepts of the Self*, 101.
102. Chodorow, *Feminism and Psychoanalytic Theory*.
103. Zaretsky, *Capitalism, the Family and Personal Life*, Chap. 3.
104. Benjamin uses this term to refer to social critique that has emanated from both the left and the right "that celebrates the private world of female nurturance and criticizes social rationality while accepting this division, and indeed all gender polarity, as natural and inevitable," *Bonds of Love*, 198.
105. Zaretsky, *Capitalism, the Family, and Personal Life*.
106. Zaretsky, *Capitalism, the Family and Personal Life*, 57.
107. Wright, "Therapy Culture."
108. Giddens, *Modernity and Self-Identity*; John Scanzoni, "A Continuing Revolution: The 1950s to the Present," in *Designing Families: The Search for Self and Community in the Information Age* (Thousand Oaks, CA: Pine Forge Press, 2000), 39–72.
109. Anthony Giddens, *The Third Way: The Renewal of Social Democracy* (Cambridge: Polity Press, 1998), 93–94.
110. Yvette Solomon, Jo Warin, Charlie Lewis, and Wendy Langford, "Intimate Talk between Parents and their Teenage Children: Democratic Openness or Covert Control?" *Sociology* 36, no. 4 (2002): 965–83; Lynn Jamieson, "Intimacy transformed? A Critical Look at the 'Pure Relationship,'" *Sociology* 33, no. 3 (1999): 477–94.
111. McLeod and Wright, "The Talking Cure in Everyday Life."
112. Giddens, *Modernity and Self Identity*, 33.
113. Giddens, *Modernity and Self Identity*, 34. See too McLeod and Wright, "The Talking Cure in Everyday Life."
114. Elliott, *Subject to Ourselves*, 58.
115. Elliott, *Subject to Ourselves*, 57.
116. Elliott, *Concepts of the Self*, 85.
117. Zaretsky, *Secrets of the Soul*, 5. I take Zaretsky's view on the contradictory legacy of psychoanalysis as my starting point for a broader analysis of the ascendancy of the therapeutic society.

118. Zaretsky, *Secrets of the Soul*, 1.
119. Zaretsky, *Secrets of the Soul*, 10.
120. Jeffrey Weeks, *The World We Have Won: The Remaking of Erotic and Intimate Life* (London: Routledge, 2007); *Invented Moralities: Sexual Values in an Age of Uncertainty* (New York: Columbia University Press, 1995); Jeffrey Weeks, Brian Heaphy, and Catherine Donovan, *Same Sex Intimacies: Families of Choice and Other Life Experiments* (London: Routledge, 2001).
121. Weeks, *Invented Moralities*, 13. See too Giddens, *Transformation of Intimacy*.
122. Anthony Elliott and Charles Lemert, *The New Individualism: The Emotional Costs of Globalization* (London: Routledge, 2006), 131.
123. R.W. Connell, *Masculinities* (1995; Berkley, CA: University of California Press, 2005), 194.
124. Connell, *Masculinities*, 64.
125. Illouz's, *Saving the Modern Soul*, is a notable exception.

2 Modernity, Medicine & the Problem of "Nerves"

Epigraph is from, "Psycho-Analytic Methods," *Medical Journal of Australia* (May 1924), 516.

1. Kerreen Reiger, *The Disenchantment of the Home: Modernizing the Australian Family 1880–1940* (Melbourne: Oxford University Press, 1985); Katie Spearritt, "New Dawns: First Wave Feminism 1880–1914," in *Gender Relations in Australia: Domination and Negotiation*, ed. Kay Saunders and Raymond Evans (Sydney: Harcourt Brace Jovanovich, 1992), 226; Michael Gilding, *The Making and Breaking of the Australian Family* (Sydney: Allen & Unwin, 1991).
2. Katie Wright, "Engendering a Therapeutic Ethos: Modernity, Masculinity & Nervousness," *Journal of Historical Sociology* 22, no. 1 (2009): 84–107.
3. Janet Oppenheim, *"Shattered Nerves": Doctors, Patients, and Depression in Victorian England* (New York: Oxford University Press, 1991), 141–80.
4. James Smith, *The Nervous System: Its Use and Abuse* (Melbourne: Australian Health Society, 1881), 3–4; see too "Australian Health Society," *Argus*, 5 October 1881, 10.
5. Smith, *The Nervous System*, 4.
6. See also James Smith, "Worry as a Factor of Disease," *Victorian Review* (June 1880): 203–12.
7. David Walker, "Modern Nerves, Nervous Moderns: Notes on Male

Neurasthenia," in *Australian Cultural History*, ed. S.L. Goldberg and F.B. Smith (Cambridge: Cambridge University Press, 1988), 131.
8. George Beard, "Neurasthenia, or Nervous Exhaustion," *Boston Medical and Surgical Journal* 3, no. 13 (1869): 217–21.
9. George Beard, *American Nervousness: Its Causes and Consequences* (New York: GP Putnam's Sons, 1881), 96.
10. F.G. Gosling, *Before Freud: Neurasthenia and the American Medical Community, 1870–1910* (Urbana, IL: University of Illinois Press, 1987), x.
11. Gosling, *Before Freud*, 9.
12. Roy Porter, "Nervousness, Eighteenth and Nineteenth Century Style: From Luxury to Labour," in *Cultures of Neurasthenia from Beard to the First World War*, ed. Marijke Gijswijt-Hofstra and Roy Porter (Amsterdam: Rodopi, 2001), 39.
13. David Schuster, "Neurasthenia and a Modernizing America," *Journal of the American Medical Association* 290 (2003): 2327–28; "Personalizing Illness and Modernity: S. Weir Mitchell, Literary Women, and Neurasthenia, 1870–1914," *Bulletin of the History of Medicine* 79, no. 4 (2005): 695–722.
14. Emile Durkheim, *Suicide: A Study in Sociology*, trans. John A. Spaulding and George Simpson, ed. George Simpson (1897; New York: The Free Press, 1997), 181. There was considerable intellectual interest in problems of nervousness around this time. German sociologist Georg Simmel reflected medical opinion and social thought of the day in his view that the stimulation of the city strained the nervous system; see "The Metropolis and Mental Life," in *The Sociology of Georg Simmel*, trans. and ed. Kurt H. Wolff (1903; New York: The Free Press, 1950), 409–24. By contrast, Freud's view, as outlined in an 1893 memorandum to Wilhelm Fliess, was that "it may be taken as a recognized fact that neurasthenia is a frequent consequence of abnormal sexual life." Sigmund Freud, "The Aetiology of the Neuroses," in *The Freud Reader*, ed. Peter Gay (New York: Norton, 1995), 56.
15. Ruth Taylor, "The Death of Neurasthenia and Its Psychological Reincarnation," *British Journal of Psychiatry* 179 (2001): 550–57.
16. Oppenheim, *"Shattered Nerves,"* 99.
17. Dona Davis, "George Beard and Lydia Pinkham: Gender, Class, and Nerves in Late Nineteenth Century America," in *Gender, Health, and Illness: The Case of Nerves*, ed. Dona Davis and Setha Low (New York: Hemisphere, 1989), 1–22. See too Ann Douglas Wood, "'The Fashionable Diseases': Women's Complaints and their Treatment in Nineteenth Century America," *Journal of Interdisciplinary History* IV, no. 1 (1973): 25–52.

18. There were, nonetheless, important differences in perceived aetiology and prevalence. For an overview of the British and continental European context, see Gijswijt-Hofstra and Porter *Cultures of Neurasthenia*; for the American context, see Gosling, *Before Freud*.
19. See Walker, "Modern Nerves, Nervous Moderns"; and "Continence for a Nation: Seminal Loss and National Vigour," *Labour History* 48 (May 1985): 1–14. See too "Mind and Body," in *Australians 1938*, ed. Bill Gammage and Peter Spearritt (Sydney: Fairfax, Syme & Weldon, 1987), 223–34.
20. Porter, "Nervousness," 40.
21. Oppenheim, *"Shattered Nerves,"* 99.
22. Beard, *American Nervousness*, 8.
23. V. Marano, "On Neurasthenia," *Australasian Medical Gazette* (October 1890), 21.
24. Marano, "On Neurasthenia," 23.
25. Walker, "Modern Nerves, Nervous Moderns," 130.
26. T.C. Allbutt, "Neurasthenia," *Australasian Medical Gazette* (February 1912): 149.
27. As noted by Matthew Thomson, "Neurasthenia in Britain: An Overview," in *Cultures of Neurasthenia*, 81.
28. Michael Neve, "Public Views of Neurasthenia: Britain, 1880–1930," in *Cultures of Neurasthenia*, 141–59.
29. For an analysis of the "psychological reincarnation" of neurasthenia see Taylor, "The Death of Neurasthenia." Taylor notes that, "particularly striking are its abrupt appearance in 1886 and equally sudden disappearance after 1930," 555.
30. J. Montgomery Mosher, "The Treatment of Mental Disease in the Early Stage," *Australasian Medical Gazette* (February 1912): 154.
31. Neve, "Public Views of Neurasthenia," 157.
32. See, for example, J.V. McAree's discussion of Freud and use of Freudian terms, "Notes on Applied Psychology and Suggestive Therapeutics," *Medical Journal of Australia* (April 1920): 355–61; and "Notes on Psycho-Therapeutic Practice," *Medical Journal of Australia* (May 1923): 543–47.
33. Walker, "Continence for a Nation"; Robert Darby, "William Acton's Antipodean Disciples: A Colonial Perspective on His Theories of Male Sexual (Dys)Function," *Journal of the History of Sexuality* 13, no. 2 (2004): 157–82.
34. Walker, "Continence for a Nation," 3.
35. Walker, "Continence for a Nation," 6.
36. Stephen Garton, *Medicine and Madness: A Social History of Insanity in New South Wales 1880–1940* (Sydney: New South Wales University

238   Notes

   Press, 1988). See also Darby, "William Acton's Antipodean Disciples"; and Walker, "Continence for a Nation."
37. Marano, "On Neurasthenia," 22.
38. Walker, "Continence for a Nation," 13.
39. John W. Springthorpe, "On the Psychological Aspects of Sexual Appetite," *Australasian Medical Gazette* (October 1884): 11.
40. Springthorpe, "On the Psychological Aspects of Sexual Appetite," 9.
41. Springthorpe, "On the Psychological Aspects of Sexual Appetite," 11.
42. There was, therefore, an historical dimension to the perceived problem of male sexuality that fed these fears. While there was variation between states, Carmichael notes that patterns of immigration saw men outnumber women by a ratio of roughly three to one until around 1830, and that the gender imbalance continued into the twentieth century. See Gordon Carmichael, "So Many Children: Colonial and Post-Colonial Demographic Patterns," in *Gender Relations in Australia: Domination and Negotiation*, ed. Kay Saunders and Raymond Evans (Sydney: Harcourt Brace Jovanovich, 1992), 103–43.
43. Allbutt, "Neurasthenia," 151.
44. Philippa Martyr, *Paradise of Quacks: An Alternative History of Medicine in Australia* (Sydney: Macleay Press, 2002), 100.
45. Oppenheim, *"Shattered Nerves,"* 144.
46. Christopher Lukinbeal and Stuart Aitken, "Sex, Violence and the Weather: Male Hysteria, Scale and the Fractal Geographies of Patriarchy," in *Places Through the Body*, ed. Heidi Nast and Steve Pile (London: Routledge, 1998), 359; Cynthia Weber, *Faking It: U.S. Hegemony in a "Post-Phallic" Era* (Minneapolis: University of Minnesota Press, 1999).
47. Stephen Garton, "Freud Versus the Rat: Understanding Shell Shock in World War I," *Australian Cultural History* 16 (1997/1998): 48. See also Michael Tyquin, *Madness and the Military: Australia's Experience of the Great War* (Loftus: Australian Military History Publications, 2006).
48. "Treatment of Soldiers: Case of W. Perry," *Age*, 10 September 1915, 6.
49. "Soldiers in Hospital: Charge Against Doctor," *Argus*, 10 September 1915, 6.
50. "Case of Gunner Perry: Defence Minister Requests Investigation," *Age*, 13 September 1915, 13.
51. See "Alleged Malingering," *Medical Journal of Australia* (December 1915): 537–38.
52. "Alleged Malingering," 538.
53. "Neuroses and Psychoses," *Medical Journal of Australia* (August 1918): 94.

54. "War and What It Means," *Medical Journal of Australia* (July 1917): 55.
55. Tyquin, *Madness and the Military*.
56. Garton, "Freud Versus the Rat," 49.
57. Walter Summons, "Medical Work Seen in the Australian Military Hospitals," *Medical Journal of Australia* (September 1917): 246.
58. E.T.C. Milligan, "Medical Experience in the War Zone," *Medical Journal of Australia* (March 1917): 203.
59. A. Jefferis Turner, "Medical Gleanings in War Time," *Medical Journal of Australia* (April 1919): 294.
60. Springthorpe wrote: "The neuromimetic (badly called hysteric) — with dominant ideas, producible and removable by suggestion." See John W. Springthorpe, "War Neuroses and Civil Practice," *Medical Journal of Australia* (October 1919): 281.
61. Garton, "Freud Versus the Rat," 49.
62. Berthold Gersons and Ingrid Carlier, "Post-traumatic Stress Disorder: The History of a Recent Concept," *British Journal of Psychiatry* 161 (1992): 744.
63. Garton, "Freud Versus the Rat." See too Joy Damousi, *Freud in the Antipodes: A Cultural History of Psychoanalysis in Australia* (Sydney: University of New South Wales Press, 2005), especially Chap. 2.
64. See Springthorpe, "War Neuroses and Civil Practice."
65. A.C. Fraser, "Notes on Three Cases of Functional Disease of the Nervous System Seen During the Voyage from England to Australia," *Medical Journal of Australia* (November 1919): 436.
66. Garton, "Freud versus the Rat," 51.
67. Neve, "Public Views of Neurasthenia," 142.
68. See, for example, "Theories in Psychology," *Medical Journal of Australia* (February 1918): 150.
69. See Review, "Psychiatry," *Medical Journal of Australia* (July 1917): 27.
70. Springthorpe, "War Neuroses and Civil Practice," 280.
71. See Review, "Psychiatry," *Medical Journal of Australia* (July 1917): 27; contrast with "Psycho-Analytic Methods," *Medical Journal of Australia* (May 1924): 516.
72. M.C. Lidwill, "Some Notes on the Diagnosis and Treatment of the Neuroses," *Medical Journal of Australia* (January 1923): 57.
73. Lidwill, "Some Notes," 59.
74. McAree, "Notes on Applied Psychology," 355.
75. McAree, "Notes on Applied Psychology," 361.
76. John W. Springthorpe, "Psychology: Its Basis and Application," Inaugural Address delivered before the Section on Neurology and Psychiatry of the Victorian Branch of the British Medical Association, *Medical Journal of Australia* (October 1922): 461.

77. Stephen Garton, "Asylum Histories: Reconsidering Australia's Lunatic Past," in *"Madness" in Australia: Histories, Heritage and the Asylum,"* ed. Catharine Coleborne and Dolly MacKinnon (St Lucia, Qld: University of Queensland Press, 2003), 11.
78. Andrew Davidson, "Mental Diseases from a Sociological Point of View," *Australasian Medical Gazette* (September 1908): 456.
79. Milton Lewis, *Managing Madness: Psychiatry and Society in Australia 1788–1980* (Canberra: Australian Government Publishing Service, 1988), 39.
80. Cited in Lewis, *Managing Madness*, 40.
81. Garton, *Medicine and Madness*, 92.
82. Mark Finnane, "From Dangerous Lunatic to Human Rights?: The Law and Mental Illness in Australian History," in *"Madness" in Australia*, 23–33.
83. Walker, "Modern Nerves, Nervous Moderns," 132.
84. These kind of advertisements appeared in newspapers and periodicals across Australia. Examples are taken from the *Sydney Morning Herald, Sun-Herald, Australian Women's Weekly* and the *Bulletin*.
85. Walker, "Modern Nerves, Nervous Moderns," 126.
86. Davis, "George Beard and Lydia Pinkham."
87. Davis, "George Beard and Lydia Pinkham,"108.
88. *Medical Journal of Australia Advertisers* (June 1919): vi.
89. Walker, "Mind and Body," 228.

3 The Legitimation of Psychological Expertise

Epigraph is from Henry Laurie, "Recent Progress and Present Position of Mental Science," Presidential Address to Section J: Mental Science and Education. Report of the 5th Meeting of the Australasian Association for the Advancement of Science, (Adelaide: The Association, 1893), 206.

1. Ronald Taft and Ross Day, "Psychology in Australia," *Annual Review of Psychology* 39 (1988): 376; Ronald Taft, "Psychology and Its History in Australia," *Australian Psychologist* 17, no. 1 (1982): 38. For a historical overview of psychology in Australia, see also W.M. O'Neil, *A Century of Psychology* (Sydney: Sydney University Press, 1987).
2. Peter Sheehan, "Anticipations Ahead for Psychology: Looking from Past to Future," *Australian Psychologist* 31 (1996): 184.
3. Alison Turtle, "Education, Social Science and the 'Common Weal,'" in *The Commonwealth of Science: ANZAAS and the Scientific Enterprise in Australasia 1888–1988,* ed. Roy Macleod (Melbourne: Oxford University Press, 1988), 223.

4. Laurie, "Recent Progress", 196.
5. Laurie, "Recent Progress," 198.
6. Turtle, "Education, Social Science and the 'Common Weal,'" 225.
7. Henry Laurie, et al., "Report of the Committee on the Best Means of Encouraging Psychophysical and Psychometrical Investigation in Australasia," Report of the 6th Meeting of the Australasian Association for the Advancement of Science (Brisbane: The Association, 1895), 842.
8. Laurie et al., "Report."
9. For an overview of developments in child welfare, see Robert van Krieken, *Children and the State: Social Control and the Formation of Australian Child Welfare* (Sydney: Allen & Unwin, 1992).
10. Reiger, *The Disenchantment of the Home*, 165–66; David McCallum, *The Social Production of Merit: Education, Psychology and Politics in Australia 1900–1950* (London: Falmer Press, 1990), 14–19.
11. A.W. Rudd, "The Scientific Study of the Child," Report of the 12th Meeting of the Australasian Association for the Advancement of Science (Brisbane: The Association, 1909), 763–64.
12. The first psychology major was offered at the University of Sydney in 1925 with the first endowed Chair established soon after. Similar developments occurred at the University of Western Australia in the 1930s and universities in other states followed suit during the 1940s and 1950s. O'Neil, *A Century of Psychology*; Taft and Day, "Psychology in Australia."
13. Alison Turtle, "The Development of Institutionalized Psychology in Australia Between the Wars: Bibliographical Compendium and Commentary," *Historical Records of Australian Science* 9, no. 3 (1992): 242. See also Alison Turtle, "Psychology in the Australian Context," in *Psychology Moving East: the Status of Western Psychology in Asia and Oceania*, ed. Geoffrey Blowers and Alison Turtle (Sydney: Sydney University Press, 1987), 312.
14. Turtle, "Psychology in the Australian Context," 312.
15. "From the Editor's Chair," *Australasian Journal of Psychology and Philosophy* 1, (1923): 59.
16. Cited in Simon Cooke, *A Meeting of Minds: The Australian Psychological Society and Australian Psychologists 1944–1994* (Melbourne: The Australian Psychological Society, 2000), 34.
17. W.M. O'Neil and K.F. Walker, "Psychology in the Universities," *Australian Journal of Psychology* 10, no. 1 (1958): 18.
18. Cooke, *A Meeting of Minds*, 34–35. Cooke notes that Australian university enrollments increased fourfold in the two decades following the Second World War, from 25,000 in 1946 to 100,000 in 1968.

19. Turtle, "The Development of Institutionalized Psychology," 241; Taft, "Psychology and Its History in Australia," 34.
20. Cooke, *A Meeting of Minds*, 35.
21. Sidney Lovibond, "Undergraduate Teaching in Psychology in Australian Universities," in *Psychology in Australia: Achievements and Prospects*, ed. Ronald Taft and Mary Nixon (Sydney: Pergamon Press, 1977), 101.
22. O'Neil, *A Century of Psychology*, 106.
23. Anthony Giddens notes that the professions almost trebled in advanced capitalist societies between 1950 and 1970. See *The Class Structure of the Advanced Societies*, 2nd ed. (London: Hutchison, 1981), 186.
24. The first professional association representing Australian psychologists, the Australasian Association of Psychology and Philosophy (AAPP), was formed in the early 1920s. See O'Neil, *A Century of Psychology*, 77.
25. David Mellor, *The Role of Science and Industry* (Canberra: Australian War Memorial, 1958), 195.
26. See Mellor, *The Role of Science and Industry*, 186; and D.E. Rose, "Psychology in the Armed Forces," *Australian Journal of Psychology* 10, no. 1 (1958): 43.
27. Cooke, *A Meeting of Minds*, 20. These figures should be treated with some caution as those already working in the armed services were not required to register. See too Mellor, *The Role of Science and Industry*, 195.
28. O'Neil, *A Century of Psychology*, 77.
29. O'Neil, *A Century of Psychology*, 78.
30. Cooke, *A Meeting of Minds*, 22.
31. Cooke, *A Meeting of Minds*, 31.
32. See Australian Psychological Society, "Past Presidents and Chairmen of the APS," http://www.psychology.org.au
33. Cooke, *A Meeting of Minds*, 220–22.
34. Alison Turtle, "The First Women Psychologists in Australia," *Australian Psychologist* 25, no. 3 (1990): 252.
35. Leonie Martin, "Psychology in the Clinic," *Australian Journal of Psychology* 10, no. 1 (1958): 49–53.
36. Cooke, *A Meeting of Minds*, 101.
37. Nikolas Rose, "Power in Therapy: Techne and Ethos," Academy for the Study of the Psychoanalytic Arts, http://www.academyanalyticarts.org/rose2.htm.
38. For an overview of these developments see McCallum, *The Social Production of Merit*, 1–12.

39. McCallum, *The Social Production of Merit*, 5.
40. McCallum, *The Social Production of Merit*, 13.
41. McCallum, *The Social Production of Merit*, 23; Reiger, *The Disenchantment of the Home*, 165.
42. P. Board, "Mental Science and Education," Presidential Address to Section J: Mental Science and Education, Report of the 12th Meeting of the Australasian Association for the Advancement of Science (Brisbane: The Association, 1909), 705.
43. O'Neil, *A Century of Psychology*, 42.
44. Laurie, "Recent Progress," 196.
45. Turtle, "Education, Social Science and the 'Common Weal,'" 233.
46. David McCallum, "Educational Expansion, Curriculum Reform and Psychological Theory: Australia in the 1930s," *Australian and New Zealand Journal of Sociology* 22, no. 2 (1986): 225–37.
47. Turtle, "Education, Social Science and the 'Common Weal,'" 233.
48. John Smyth, "Five Years' Experience with Testing the Intelligence of New Students at the Teachers' College, Melbourne," Report of the 18th Meeting of the Australasian Association for the Advancement of Science (Perth: The Association, 1926), 709.
49. Turtle, "Psychology in the Australian Context," 311.
50. Reiger, *The Disenchantment of the Home*, 167.
51. For an historical overview of ACER, see W.F. Connell, *The Australian Council for Educational Research, 1930–1980* (Melbourne: Australian Council for Educational Research, 1980).
52. Connell, *The Australian Council for Educational Research*, 133.
53. Connell, *The Australian Council for Educational Research*, 134.
54. O'Neil, *A Century of Psychology*, 60.
55. Kathryn Dixon, "Vocational and Career Education in Schools: A Historical Perspective 1920–2001," *Curriculum Perspectives* 22, no. 3 (2002): 44.
56. Norman Jenkins, "Training and Work: Inservice Training for Psychologists in State Education Departments," in *Psychology in Australia*, 138.
57. Cooke, *A Meeting of Minds*, 210.
58. See Matthew Thomson, "The Psychological Body," in *Medicine in the Twentieth Century*, ed. Roger Cooter and John Pickstone (Amsterdam: Harwood Academic Publishers, 2000), 301; Donald Blocher, *The Evolution of Counseling Psychology*, (New York: Springer, 2000), 165.
59. Monica Thielking, "An Investigation of Attitudes Towards the Practice of School-Based Psychological Services" (PhD diss., Melbourne: Swinburne University of Technology, 2006), 8.
60. McCallum, *The Social Production of Merit*, 71.

61. John Hall, "Educational Psychology in Public Service," in *Psychology in Australia*, 164.
62. Hall, "Educational Psychology," 170–71.
63. Nancy Wear Burton, "The Child Guidance Clinic" (PhD diss., Sydney: The University of Sydney, 1939).
64. David Ivison, "Clinical Psychology in Public Service," in *Psychology in Australia*, 176.
65. J.A. Johnson, "The New Psychology and the Schools," Presidential Address to Section J: Mental Science and Education, Report of the 16th Meeting of the Australasian Association for the Advancement of Science (Wellington, NZ: The Association, 1923), 697.
66. G.R. Giles, "Vocational Guidance in Australia in 1932," *International Labour Review* 26 (1932): 530.
67. See McCallum, *The Social Production of Merit*.
68. J. Nangle, "Vocational Guidance," Presidential Address to Section J: Mental Science and Education, Report of the 17th Meeting of the Australasian Association for the Advancement of Science (Adelaide: The Association, 1924), 625.
69. Nangle, "Vocational Guidance," 617.
70. New South Wales Department of Public Instruction, "Report of the Minister of Public Instruction for the Year 1925" (Sydney: Government Printer, 1926), 3–4.
71. Giles, "Vocational Guidance," 530.
72. Nora Hales, "Sydney's Worry Clinic," *Rydge's* (January 1936): 27–28.
73. Giles, "Vocational Guidance," 535.
74. Giles, "Vocational Guidance," 542.
75. John Hughes, "Harold Wyndham and Educational Reform in Australia 1925–1968," *Education Research and Perspectives* 29, no. 1 (2002): 40.
76. "Teachers Confer: Vocational Guidance Discussed: Department's System Opposed," *Age*, 23 January 1930, 13.
77. W.M. O'Neil, *From School to Work: A Plea for Vocational Guidance* (Melbourne: Australian Council for Educational Research, 1944), 15.
78. J.F. Clark, "Psychology in the Public Service, Business and Industry," *Australian Journal of Psychology* 10, no. 1 (1958): 30.
79. D.J.A. Verco, "Psychology Services in Education Departments," *Australian Journal of Psychology* 10, no. 1 (1958): 26.
80. Verco, "Psychology Services in Education Departments." For an overview of legislation and education policy with reference to students with a disability, see Ian Dempsey, Phil Foreman, and Josephine Jenkinson, "Educational Enrolment of Students with a Disability in New South Wales and Victoria," *International Journal of*

Disability, Development and Education 49, no. 1 (2002): 31–46.
81. Jenkins, "Training and Work", 138.
82. Hall, "Educational Psychology," 163.
83. Michael Faulkner, "School Psychologists or Psychologists in Schools?" *InPsych* 29, no. 4 (2007): 10.
84. Kevin Blackburn, "The Quest for Efficiency and the Rise of Industrial Psychology in Australia, 1916–29," *Labour History* 74 (1998): 122–36.
85. F.W. Taylor, *The Principles of Scientific Management* (1911; New York: Dover, 1998).
86. See Lucy Taksa, "The Cultural Diffusion of Scientific Management: The United States and New South Wales," *Journal of Industrial Relations* 37, no. 3 (1995): 427–61; and Blackburn, "The Quest for Efficiency."
87. Rose, *Governing the Soul*, 59.
88. Blackburn, "The Quest for Efficiency," 124.
89. See Bernard Muscio, *Lectures on Industrial Psychology* (Sydney: Angus & Robertson, 1917).
90. Blackburn, "The Quest for Efficiency," 125.
91. Blackburn, "The Quest for Efficiency," 127.
92. See "Mental Hygiene in Industry," *Medical Journal of Australia* (December 1924): 629–30; and "The Industrial Clinic," *Medical Journal of Australia* (April 1924): 393–94.
93. "Mental Hygiene in Industry," 629.
94. H.M.L. Murray, "Pre-Employment Medical Examination," *Industrial Psychology and Personnel Practice* 2, no. 1 (1946): 33.
95. Alison Turtle, "Institution, Ideology, Icon: Psychology at Sydney 1921–1996," *Australian Journal of Psychology* 49, no. 3 (1997): 121.
96. Ronald Walker, "Some Recent Developments in Industrial Psychology," Report of the 19th Meeting of the Australasian Association for the Advancement of Science (Hobart: The Association, 1928), 540.
97. Walker, "Some Recent Developments in Industrial Psychology," 541.
98. Rose, *Governing the Soul*, 58.
99. "Mental Hygiene in Industry," 629.
100. Mellor, *The Role of Science and Industry*, 185.
101. Mellor, *The Role of Science and Industry*, 187.
102. Cooke, *A Meeting of Minds*, 18.
103. Mellor, *The Role of Science and Industry*, 188.
104. Mellor, *The Role of Science and Industry*, 188.
105. By 2002, it was reported that more than six million working days were lost annually due to depression and that depression goes untreated in more than 60 percent of cases. The article reported on

new initiatives developed to encourage people to seek treatment. University of Queensland Professor, Harvey Whiteford appealed to companies to become proactive in the diagnosis and treatment of depression because "it has an economic outcome." Melissa Sweet, "Out of the Blue," *Bulletin*, 12 November 2002, 38.
106. Stella Lees and June Senyard, *The 1950s: How Australia Became a Modern Society, and Everyone Got a House and a Car* (Melbourne: Hyland House, 1987), 70.
107. Lees and Senyard, *The 1950s*, 69.
108. Christopher Wright, *The Management of Labour: A History of Australian Employers* (Melbourne: Oxford University Press, 1995), 47.
109. "To Win Friends," *Sun Herald*, 9 September 1962, 2; Tony Abbott, "Self-Improvement: Inside a Modern Growth Industry," *Bulletin*, 3 November 1987, 38.
110. Charles Higham, "The Young Executives," *Bulletin*, 29 April 1967, 26.
111. Higham, "The Young Executives," 28.
112. Higham, "The Young Executives," 26.
113. Higham, "The Young Executives," 27.
114. Wright, *The Management of Labour*, 126. See too Alex Carey, "Industrial Psychology and Sociology in Australia," in *The Professions in Australia* (St Lucia, Qld: Queensland University Press, 1976), 231.
115. Wright, *From Personnel to Human Resource Management*.
116. Rose, *Governing the Soul*, 112.
117. James Tucker, *The Therapeutic Corporation* (New York: Oxford University Press, 1999).
118. Daniel Goleman, *Emotional Intelligence* (New York: Bantam Books, 1995).
119. Helen Trinca and Catherine Fox, *Better Than Sex: How a Whole Generation Got Hooked on Work* (Sydney: Random House Australia, 2004).

4 Cultural Diffusion of the Analytic Attitude

Epigraph is from a newspaper article entitled, "You and the Psychiatrist," *Sunday Herald*, 28 May 1950, 15.

1. Eric Hobsbawm, *The Age of Extremes: A History of the World, 1914–1991* (New York: Vintage Books, 1996).
2. Joy Damousi, *The Labour of Loss: Mourning, Memory and Wartime Bereavement in Australia* (Cambridge: Cambridge University Press, 1999); *Living with the Aftermath: Trauma, Nostalgia and Grief in Postwar Australia* (Cambridge: Cambridge University Press, 2001).

3. John Murphy, *Imagining the Fifties: Private Sentiment and Political Culture in Menzies' Australia* (Sydney: Pluto Press, 2000), 16.
4. Gilding, *The Making and Breaking of the Australian Family*, 120.
5. Kerreen Reiger, "The Coming of the Counsellors: The Development of Marriage Guidance in Australia," *Australian and New Zealand Journal of Sociology* 23, no. 3 (1987): 375–87.
6. Damousi, *Freud in the Antipodes*, 100–01.
7. Clifford Adams, "What Your Husband Really Thinks of You," *Australian Women's Weekly*, 15 March 1947, 27.
8. "These Restless Modern Women," *Sydney Morning Herald Magazine*, 11 March 1947, 9.
9. John Rigby, "Men are So Vain," *Sun-Herald*, 12 May 1957, 31.
10. Universal Opportunity League, "Wake Up and Live: Get Rid of that Inferiority Complex and the World Is Yours!" (Advertisement) *Australian Women's Weekly*, 8 March 1947, 47.
11. *Sun Herald*, July 1954, 61. These advertisements appeared frequently in Australian newspapers during the 1950s and early 1960s.
12. Damousi, *Freud in the Antipodes*, 102.
13. *Sun-Herald*, 16 November 1952, 15.
14. John Gibson, "Anxious, Ritualistic, Indifferent: Your Eating Betrays You," *Sydney Morning Herald*, 30 November 1957, 15. See too, "Do You Have Illusions About Your Eating?" *Sydney Morning Herald*, 26 July 1953, 20.
15. "At Home with Margaret Sydney," *Australian Women's Weekly*, 19 September 1962, 53.
16. See for example, "It's Better to Let Off Steam," *Sun-Herald*, 16 April 1967, 40.
17. "No Kiss in the Ring for Us!" *Sun-Herald*, 16 April 1967, 4–5.
18. Though the first full-time psychoanalyst began practicing in Australia in 1931, and a decade later the first psychoanalytic institute was established, psychoanalysis itself never achieved more than marginal status as a clinical therapy. For the founding of psychoanalysis as a profession and the establishment of psychoanalytic institutes, see Damousi, *Freud in the Antipodes*, 8. On the first full-time psychoanalyst, see, Damousi, *Freud in the Antipodes*, 49–51.
19. Murphy, *Imagining the Fifties*, 31.
20. Gilding, *The Making and Breaking of the Australian Family*, 120.
21. Reiger, "The Coming of the Counsellors," 377; Paul Simmons, "Relationship and Family Counselling in Australia: A Review of Our History and Current Status," *International Journal of Psychology* 41, no. 3 (2006): 180–88.
22. W.L. Carrington, *The Fine Art of Human Partnership: A Talk on Modern*

Marriage (Melbourne: Marriage Guidance Council of Victoria for The National Marriage Guidance Council of Australia, 1954); "Marriage Guidance Lectures," *Argus*, 27 January 1949, 9.
23. The Melbourne Marriage Guidance Council (Melbourne: The Council, 1951).
24. Reiger, "The Coming of the Counsellors," 379.
25. W.L. Carrington, *Education for Marriage and Parenthood*, The John Williams Memorial Foundation Lectures, 1951 (Melbourne: Methodist Book Depot, 1952).
26. Nancy Miller, "Introduction," in *An Oral History of Marriage Counselling in Australia: From Meaning Well to Doing Well*, ed. David Fox and Nancy Miller (Canberra: Les Harvey Foundation, 2000), 6.
27. Miller, "Introduction," 7.
28. Simmons, "Relationship and Family Counselling," 182.
29. Reiger, "The Coming of the Counsellors," 379.
30. Allen Stoller, "Sexual Conflict in Marriage," *Marriage and Family* (March 1964): 4–5.
31. Barry Nurcombe, "Neurotic Relationships," *Marriage* (June 1963): 4.
32. Pat Pentony, "Client Centred Therapy and the Communications Analysis Position," *Marriage and Family* (June 1965): 8.
33. Les Harvey, "Conjoint Counselling: How Does it Apply to Marriage Guidance?" *Marriage and Family* (March 1965): 10–12.
34. Church of England Marriage Guidance Council, Unpublished 2 pp. Archives of August, 1981. Personal papers of Kerreen Reiger.
35. ABC Radio National, "Alan Walker Remembered," *Religion Report*, Australian Broadcasting Commission, 5 February 2003.
36. Lifeline Australia, *Annual Report 2009*, http://www.lifeline.org.au/learn_more/publications
37. Anne Deveson, *Australians At Risk* (Sydney: Cassell, 1978), 137.
38. Neil Quintrell and Margaret Robertson, "Student Counselling in Australian Universities: Forty Years of Development," *International Journal for the Advancement of Counselling* 18 (1996): 208.
39. Brian Hazell, "The Counselling Profession," in *The Professions in Australia: A Critical Appraisal*, ed. Paul Boreham, Alec Pemberton, and Paul Wilson (St Lucia, Qld: University of Queensland Press, 1976).
40. Quintrell and Robertson, "Student Counselling," 208.
41. George Wills, "A Brief History of Counselling Psychology in Australia, 1945–1975," *Australian Journal of Counselling Psychology* 1, no. 1 (1999/2000): 22.
42. Wills, "A Brief History of Counselling Psychology," 22.
43. "Helplines Australia," http://helplines.org.au
44. Cooke, *A Meeting of Minds*, 230.

45. J. Small and U. Gault, "Perceptions of Psychologists by the General Public and Three Professional Groups," *Australian Psychologist* 10, no. 1 (1975): 26–27.
46. Cooke, *A Meeting of Minds*, 231.
47. Cooke, *A Meeting of Minds*, 232.
48. Australian Bureau of Statistics, "Classification Counts: Occupation by Sex," Catalogue no. 2022.0 (Canberra: Australian Bureau of Statistics, 2002).
49. Australian Psychological Society, "Consulting an APS Psychologist." http://www.psychology.org.au/community/consult
50. Jeff Patrick, "The Economic Value of Psychology in Australia: 2001," *Australian Psychologist* 40, no. 3 (2005): 149–58.
51. Peter Sheehan, "Anticipations Ahead for Psychology: Looking from Past to Future," *Australian Psychologist* 31, no. 3 (1996): 186.
52. Ruth Pollard and Mark Metherell, "Mentally Ill Get a Medicare Lifeline," *Sydney Morning Herald*, 6 April 2006, 1.
53. Sheehan, "Anticipations Ahead for Psychology"; Laurie, "Recent Progress."
54. Hugh Mackay, "Psychologists in the Age of Discontinuity," *Australian Psychologist* 34, no. 1 (1999): 3.
55. Martin Gross, *The Psychological Society*, 56.
56. O'Connor's *Understanding the Mid-Life Crisis* (1981) has been enormously successful, with sales exceeding 100,000 copies. See "The Wisdom Interviews: Peter O'Connor," *Big Ideas: The Wisdom Interviews*, ABC Radio National, broadcast 12 May 2002. His other books include, *Dreams and the Search for Meaning* (1986), *The Inner Man* (1993), *Understanding Jung* (1996), and *Looking Inwards* (2003).
57. Dowrick's books include: *Intimacy and Solitude* (1991), *Forgiveness and Other Acts of Love* (1997), *The Universal Heart* (2000), and *Choosing Happiness* (2005).
58. Australia, Royal Commission on Human Relationships, *Final Report*, vol. 1 (Canberra: Australian Government Publishing Service, 1977), 17.
59. Deveson, *Australians At Risk*, 2–3.
60. Australia, Royal Commission on Human Relationships, *Final Report*, vol. 4, 156.
61. C. Henry Kempe, Frederic Silverman, Brant Steele, William Droegemueller, and Henry Silver, "The Battered-Child Syndrome," *Journal of the American Medical Association* 181, no. 1 (1962): 17–24.
62. Stephen Pfohl, "The 'Discovery' of Child Abuse," *Social Problems* 24, no. 3 (1977): 310–23; Deveson, *Australians at Risk*, 124.
63. Thea Brown and Renata Alexander, *Child Abuse and Family Law:*

Understanding the Issues Facing Human Service and Legal Professions (Sydney: Allen & Unwin, 2007), 88.
64. Deveson, Australians at Risk, 135.
65. Australia, Royal Commission on Human Relationships, Final Report, vol. 4, 160.
66. Rose, Governing the Soul, 268.
67. Nathan Thompson, Press Conference, 26 May 2004.
68. Suzanne Carbone, "Talking of Sport," Age, 31 January 2004, 3; Jon Pierik, "West Backs Hawk's Move," Herald Sun, 28 May 2004, 107.
69. Shaun Phillips, "Flood of Support for Hawk's Revelation," Herald Sun, 28 May 2004, 13.
70. Chris Lines, "Sport Helps Hawk Stay Above Water," Newcastle Herald, 27 May 2004, 74.
71. World Health Organization, The World Health Report 2001: Mental Health: New Understandings, New Hope (Geneva: World Health Organization, 2001), x.
72. Australian Bureau of Statistics, "Mental Health," Australian Social Trends 4102.0 (Canberra: Australian Bureau of Statistics, 2009).
73. "Foul Play," Insight, SBS Television, 16 March 2004.
74. Kate Lundy, "Sexism in Sport," Adjournment Speech, The Australian Senate, 1 April 2004, http://www.katelundy.com.au/2004/04/01/sexism-in-sport/
75. "Football Fans Against Sexual Assault," Aware, ACSSA Newsletter no. 4, September 2004, 4.

5   Therapy: Inside the Talking Cure

Epigraph is from Marshall Berman, All That is Solid Melts into Air: The Experience of Modernity (London: Verso, 1983), 15.

1. Sigmund Freud, "The Psychotherapy of Hysteria," in Studies in Hysteria, Josef Breuer and Sigmund Freud, trans. James Strachey (1895; New York: Basic Books, 1957), 305.
2. Hugh Mackay, "The Best Intimacy Money Can Buy," Age, 8 June 2002, 14. Mackay notes that: "Psychiatrists alone make 1.6 million appointments for their patients each year" and that "a conservative estimate would be that, in the course of a year, well over one million Australians seek some form of psychotherapy."
3. Readers should note that I am using "therapy" here as a non-specific generic term to describe clinical interventions undertaken with psychologists, psychiatrists, psychotherapists, and counselors. While I recognize the problem in employing therapy to encompass

a variety of "talk cures," for the present discussion, what unites various orientations and approaches is more important than what distinguishes them. In the accounts of therapy presented here, the terms therapy and counseling are often used interchangeably by those interviewed.
4. See Giddens, *Modernity and Self Identity*; and *The Transformation of Intimacy*.
5. Four women and four men aged between 25 and 52 were interviewed. Among the group there was a mix of types of therapeutic intervention undertaken, and variations in the length of time "in therapy." Most had engaged in some form of therapy (either continuously or intermittently) for periods of between one and five years. All lived in capital cities of Australia, five were of Anglo Australian background, and the remainder were of continental European descent. Most were tertiary educated, and at the time of interview most were contingently attached to the labor force. Five were in committed relationships, one had children, but none were married.
6. Pierre Bourdieu, "The Space of Points of View," in *The Weight of the World: Social Suffering in Contemporary Society*, Pierre Bourdieu et al. (Oxford: Polity Press, 1999), 4.
7. Elliott and Lemert, *The New Individualism*, 8.
8. See Richard Sennett, *The Corrosion of Character: The Personal Costs of Work in the New Capitalism* (New York: Norton, 1998).
9. Bourdieu, "To the Reader," in *The Weight of the World*, 1.
10. John McLeod, *Narrative and Psychotherapy* (London: Sage, 2004), x.
11. Giddens, *The Transformation of Intimacy*, 109.
12. Giddens, *Modernity and Self Identity*, 33.
13. See Candace West and Don Zimmerman, "Doing Gender," *Gender and Society* 1, no. 2 (1987): 125–51; and Weeks et al., *Same Sex Intimacies*, 138.
14. Giddens, *Modernity and Self-Identity*, 202. See too Elliott, *Subject to Ourselves*, 57.
15. Mackay, "The Best Intimacy Money Can Buy."
16. Jeremy Safran and J. Christopher Muran, *Negotiating the Therapeutic Alliance: A Relational Treatment Guide* (New York: Guilford Press, 2000), 1.
17. See Adam Horvath and Lester Luborsky, "The Role of the Therapeutic Alliance in Psychotherapy," *Journal of Consulting and Clinical Psychology* 61, no. 4 (1993): 561–73; and Janice Krupnick et al., "The Role of the Therapeutic Alliance in Psychotherapy and Pharmacotherapy Outcome: Findings in the National Institute of Mental Health Treatment of Depression Collaborative Research Program," *Focus* 4, no. 2 (2006): 269–77.

18. See Glen Gabbard, ed., *Sexual Exploitation in Professional Relationships* (Washington: American Psychiatric Press, 1989).
19. Sigmund Freud, "On the Beginning of Treatment: Further Recommendations on the Technique of Psychoanalysis," in Vol. 12 of *The Standard Edition of the Complete Psychological Works of Sigmund Freud*, ed. and trans. James Strachey (1913; London: Hogarth Press, 1958), 122–44. See too William Herron and Sheila Rouslin Welt, *Money Matters: The Fee in Psychotherapy and Psychoanalysis* (New York: Guilford Press, 1992).
20. See Rieff, *The Triumph of the Therapeutic*; Lasch, *The Culture of Narcissism*; and Furedi, *Therapy Culture*.
21. Rieff, *Freud: The Mind of the Moralist*, 305.
22. Zaretsky, *Secrets of the Soul*, 333.
23. Katie Wright, "Social Justice and the Therapeutic Ethic," paper presented at the conference, *Therapy Culture Revisited: The Impact of the Language of Therapy on Public Policy and Societal Resilience*, Centre of Excellence for National Security, S. Rajaratnam School of International Studies, Nanyang Technological University, Singapore, October 2009.
24. See Zygmunt Bauman, *Society Under Siege* (Cambridge: Polity Press, 2002); Ulrick Beck, *Risk Society: Towards a New Modernity* (London: Sage, 1992); Giddens, *Modernity and Self-Identity*; Elliott, *Subject to Ourselves*; and Elliott and Lemert, *The New Individualism*.
25. See Giddens, *Modernity and Self-Identity*; and *The Transformation of Intimacy*.
26. Jane Ryan, ed., *How Does Psychotherapy Work?* (London: Karnac Books, 2005).
27. See Daniel Goleman, *Emotional Intelligence*.
28. Rose, *Governing the Soul*, 231; Giddens, *Modernity and Self-Identity*, 180.
29. Freud, "The Psychotherapy of Hysteria," 305.

6 Reflections on the Therapeutic Turn

1. Elazar Barkan, *The Guilt of Nations: Restitution and Negotiating Historical Injustices* (New York: Norton, 2000), 315.
2. Barkan, *The Guilt of Nations*, 316.
3. National Inquiry into the Separation of Aboriginal and Torres Strait Islander Children from their Families, *Bringing Them Home: Report of the National Inquiry into the Separation of Aboriginal and Torres Strait Islander Children from their Families* (Sydney: Human Rights and Equal Opportunity Commission, 1997), 5.

4. Australian Parliament, *Lost Innocents: Righting the Record: Report on Child Migration* (Canberra: Senate Community Affairs References Committee, 2001).
5. Australian Parliament, *Forgotten Australians: A Report on Australians who Experienced Institutional or Out-of-home Care as Children* (Canberra: Senate Community Affairs References Committee, 2004). See too Australian Parliament, *Lost Innocents and Forgotten Australians Revisited: Report on the Progress with the Implementation of the Recommendations of the Lost Innocents and Forgotten Australians Reports* (Canberra: Senate Community Affairs References Committee, 2009).
6. Wright, "Social Justice and the Therapeutic Ethic," See note 23 in previous chapter.
7. Giddens, *The Transformation of Intimacy*, 109.
8. McLeod and Wright, "The Talking Cure in Everyday Life."

Bibliography

Alexander, Jeffrey C. *The Meanings of Social Life: A Cultural Sociology*. New York: Oxford University Press, 2003.
Allbutt, Thomas Clifford. "Neurasthenia." *Australasian Medical Gazette* (February 1912): 149–53.
Allen, Judith. *Sex and Secrets: Crimes Involving Australian Women Since 1880*. Melbourne: Oxford University Press, 1990.
Australia. Royal Commission on Human Relationships. *Final Report*. Canberra: Australian Government Publishing Service, 1977.
Australian Bureau of Statistics. "Classification Counts: Occupation by Sex." Catalogue no. 2022.0. Canberra: Australian Bureau of Statistics, 2002.
_____. "Mental Health." *Australian Social Trends* 4102.0. Canberra: Australian Bureau of Statistics, 2009.
Australian Institute of Health and Welfare. *Mental Health Services in Australia 2004–05*. Canberra: Australian Institute of Health and Welfare, 2007.
Ballou, Mary, Marcia Hill, and Carolyn West, ed. *Feminist Therapy Theory and Practice: A Contemporary Perspective*. New York: Springer, 2008.
Barkan, Elazar. *The Guilt of Nations: Restitution and Negotiating Historical Injustices*. New York: Norton, 2000.
Barrett, Michèle, and Mary McIntosh. "Narcissism and the Family: A Critique of Lasch." *New Left Review* I/135 (September–October 1982): 35–48.
Bauman, Zygmunt. *Society Under Siege*. Cambridge: Polity Press, 2002.
Beard, George. *American Nervousness: Its Causes and Consequences*. New York: GP Putnam's Sons, 1881.
_____. "Neurasthenia, or Nervous Exhaustion." *Boston Medical and Surgical Journal* 3, no. 13 (1869): 217–21.
Beck, Ulrick. *Risk Society: Towards a New Modernity*. London: Sage, 1992.
Becker, Dana. *The Myth of Empowerment: Women and the Therapeutic Culture in America*. New York: New York University Press, 2005.
Bellah, Robert, Richard Madsen, William Sullivan, Ann Swidler, and Steven Tipton. *Habits of the Heart: Individualism and Commitment in American Life*. Rev. ed. Berkley: University of California Press, 1996. First published 1985.

Benjamin, Jessica. *The Bonds of Love: Psychoanalysis, Feminism, and the Problem of Domination*. New York: Pantheon, 1988.
Berman, Marshall. *All That Is Solid Melts into Air: The Experience of Modernity*. London: Verso, 1983.
Besley, Tina. *Counseling Youth: Foucault, Power, and the Ethics of Subjectivity*. Westport, CT: Praeger, 2002.
Blackburn, Kevin. "The Quest for Efficiency and the Rise of Industrial Psychology in Australia, 1916–29." *Labour History* 74 (1998): 122–36.
Blocher, Donald. *The Evolution of Counseling Psychology*. New York: Springer, 2000.
Blum, Linda, and Nena Stracuzzi. "Gender in the Prozac Nation: Popular Discourse and Productive Femininity." *Gender and Society* 18, no. 3 (2004): 269–86.
Board, P. "Mental Science and Education." Report of the 12th Meeting of the Australasian Association for the Advancement of Science, 703–12. Brisbane: The Association, 1909.
Bourdieu, Pierre, et al. *The Weight of the World: Social Suffering in Contemporary Society*. Translated by Priscilla Parkhurst Ferguson. Oxford: Polity Press, 1999.
Brown, Thea, and Renata Alexander. *Child Abuse and Family Law: Understanding the Issues Facing Human Service and Legal Professions*. Sydney: Allen & Unwin, 2007.
Burton, Nancy. "The Child Guidance Clinic." PhD diss. Sydney: The University of Sydney, 1939.
Carey, Alex. "Industrial Psychology and Sociology in Australia." In *The Professions in Australia: A Critical Appraisal*, edited by Paul Boreham, Alec Pemberton, and Paul Wilson, 220–55. St Lucia, Qld: Queensland University Press, 1976.
Carmichael, Gordon. "So Many Children: Colonial and Post-Colonial Demographic Patters." In *Gender Relations in Australia: Domination and Negotiation*, edited by Kay Saunders and Raymond Evans, 103–43. Sydney: Harcourt Brace Jovanovich, 1992.
Carroll, John. *Ego and Soul: The Modern West in Search of Meaning*. Pymble, NSW: HarperCollins, 1998.
———. *Puritan, Paranoid, Remissive: A Sociology of Modern Culture*. London: Routledge & Kegan Paul, 1977.
Casey, Michael. "Authority, Crisis, and the Individual." *Society* 39, no. 2 (2002): 78–82.
Chesler, Phyllis. *Women and Madness*. New York: Palgrave Macmillan, 2005. First published 1972.
Chodorow, Nancy. *Feminism and Psychoanalytic Theory*. New Haven, CT: Yale University Press, 1989.

———. *The Reproduction of Mothering: Psychoanalysis and the Sociology of Gender*. 2nd ed. Berkley: University of California Press, 1999. First published 1978.
Clark, J.F. "Psychology in the Public Service, Business, and Industry." *Australian Journal of Psychology* 10, no. 1 (1958): 30–41.
Cloud, Dana. *Control and Consolation in American Culture and Politics: Rhetoric of Therapy*. Thousand Oaks, CA: Sage, 1998.
Coleborne, Catharine, and Dolly MacKinnon, ed. *Madness in Australia: Histories, Heritage and the Asylum*. St Lucia, Qld: University of Queensland Press, 2003.
Connell, R.W. *Gender*. Cambridge: Polity Press, 2002.
———. *Masculinities*. 2nd ed. Berkley, CA: University of California Press, 2005. First published 1995.
Connell, W.F. *The Australian Council for Educational Research, 1930–1980*. Melbourne: Australian Council for Educational Research, 1980.
Cooke, Simon. *A Meeting of Minds: The Australian Psychological Society and Australian Psychologists 1944–1994*. Melbourne: The Australian Psychological Society, 2000.
Cushman, Philip. *Constructing the Self, Constructing America: A Cultural History of Psychotherapy*. Boston, MA: Addison Wesley, 1995.
Damousi, Joy. *Freud in the Antipodes: A Cultural History of Psychoanalysis in Australia*. Sydney: University of New South Wales Press, 2005.
———. *The Labour of Loss: Mourning, Memory and Wartime Bereavement in Australia*. Cambridge: Cambridge University Press, 1999.
———. *Living with the Aftermath: Trauma, Nostalgia and Grief in Post-War Australia*. Cambridge: Cambridge University Press, 2001.
Darby, Robert. "William Acton's Antipodean Disciples: A Colonial Perspective on His Theories of Male Sexual (Dys)Function." *Journal of the History of Sexuality* 13, no. 2 (2004): 157–82.
Davidson, Andrew. "Mental Diseases from a Sociological Point of View." *Australasian Medical Gazette* (September 1908): 449–57.
Davis, Dona. "George Beard and Lydia Pinkham: Gender, Class and Nerves in Late Nineteenth Century America." In *Gender, Health and Illness: The Case of Nerves*, edited by Dona Davis and Setha Low, 1–22. New York: Hemisphere, 1989.
Dempsey, Ian, Phil Foreman, and Josephine Jenkinson. "Educational Enrolment of Students with a Disability in New South Wales and Victoria." *International Journal of Disability, Development and Education* 49, no. 1 (2002): 31–46.
Deveson, Anne. *Australians at Risk*. Sydney: Cassell, 1978.
Dixon, Kathryn. "Vocational and Career Education in Schools: A Historical Perspective 1920–2001." *Curriculum Perspectives* 22, no. 3 (2002): 43–48.

Donzelot, Jacques. *The Policing of Families*. Translated by Robert Hurley. New York: Pantheon, 1979.

Durkheim, Emile. *The Elementary Forms of Religious Life*. 2nd ed. Translated by Joseph Ward Swain. London: Allen & Unwin, 1976. First published 1912.

_____. *Suicide: A Study in Sociology*. Translated by John A. Spaulding and George Simpson, edited and with an introduction by George Simpson. New York: The Free Press, 1997. First published 1897.

Elliott, Anthony. *Concepts of the Self*. 2nd ed. Cambridge: Polity Press, 2008.

_____. *Subject to Ourselves: Social Theory, Psychoanalysis and Postmodernity*. 2nd ed. Boulder, CO: Paradigm, 2004.

_____. "Therapy Culture and Its Discontents." *Meanjin* 63, no. 4 (2004): 47–52.

Elliott, Anthony, and Charles Lemert. *The New Individualism: The Emotional Costs of Globalization*. London: Routledge, 2006.

Elshtain, Jean Bethke. "Aristotle, the Public-Private Split, and the Case of the Suffragists." In *The Family in Political Thought*, edited by Jean Bethke Elshtain, 51–65. Amherst, MA: University of Massachusetts Press, 1982.

Ewen, Stuart. *Captains of Consciousness: Advertising and the Social Roots of the Consumer Culture*. New York: Basic Books, 2001. First published 1976.

Faludi, Susan. *Backlash: The Undeclared War Against Women*. London: Vintage, 1992.

Faulkner, Michael. "School Psychologists or Psychologists in Schools?" *InPsych* 29, no. 4 (2007): 10–13.

Finnane, Mark. "From Dangerous Lunatic to Human Rights? The Law and Mental Illness in Australian History." In *"Madness" in Australia: Histories, Heritage and the Asylum*, edited by Catharine Coleborne and Dolly MacKinnon, 23–33. St Lucia, Qld: University of Queensland Press, 2003.

Flax, Jane. "Political Philosophy and the Patriarchal Unconscious: A Psychoanalytic Perspective on Epistemology and Metaphysics." In *Discovering Reality: Feminist Perspectives on Epistemology, Metaphysics, Methodology, and Philosophy of Science*. 2nd ed., edited by Sandra Harding and Merrill Hintikka, 245–81. Dordrecht: Kluwer Academic Publishers, 2003.

Foucault, Michel. *History of Sexuality, Vol. 1: An Introduction*. Translated by Robert Hurley. New York: Vintage, 1990.

_____. "Nietzsche, Genealogy, History." In *The Foucault Reader*, edited by Paul Rabinow, 76–100. New York: Pantheon, 1984.

_____. "Problematics." In *Foucault Live (Interviews, 1961–1984)*. 2nd ed., translated by John Johnston, edited by Sylvère Lotringer, 416–22. New York: Semiotext(e), 1996.

———. "Technologies of the Self." In *Technologies of the Self: A Seminar with Michael Foucault*, edited by Luther Martin, Huck Gutman, and Patrick Hutton, 16–49. Amherst, MA: University of Massachusetts Press, 1988.

———. "Two Lectures." In *Power/Knowledge: Selected Interviews and Other Writings*, edited by Colin Gordon, 78–108. New York: Pantheon, 1980.

Fraser, A.C. "Notes on Three Cases of Functional Disease of the Nervous System Seen During the Voyage from England to Australia." *Medical Journal of Australia* (November 1919): 436–38.

Freud, Sigmund. "The Aetiology of the Neuroses" [1893]. In *The Freud Reader*, edited by Peter Gay, 56–60. New York: Norton, 1995.

———. "On the Beginning of Treatment: Further Recommendations on the Technique of Psychoanalysis." In Volume 12 of *The Standard Edition of the Complete Psychological Works of Sigmund Freud*, translated and edited by James Strachey, 122–44. London: Hogarth Press, 1958. First published 1913.

———. "The Psychotherapy of Hysteria." In *Studies on Hysteria*, Sigmund Freud and Josef Breuer, translated and edited by James Strachey, 253–305. New York: Basic Books, 1957. First published 1895.

Furedi, Frank. *Therapy Culture: Cultivating Vulnerability in an Uncertain Age*. London: Routledge, 2004.

Gabbard, Glen, ed. *Sexual Exploitation in Professional Relationships*. Washington, DC: American Psychiatric Press, 1989.

Garton, Stephen. "Asylum Histories: Reconsidering Australia's Lunatic Past." In *"Madness" in Australia: Histories, Heritage and the Asylum*, edited by Catharine Coleborne and Dolly MacKinnon, 12–21. St Lucia, Qld: University of Queensland Press, 2003.

———. "Freud Versus the Rat: Understanding Shell Shock in World War I." *Australian Cultural History* 16 (1997/1998): 45–59.

———. *Medicine and Madness: A Social History of Insanity in New South Wales 1880–1940*. Sydney: New South Wales University Press, 1988.

Gersons, Berthold, and Ingrid Carlier. "Post-traumatic Stress Disorder: The History of a Recent Concept." *British Journal of Psychiatry* 161 (1992): 742–48.

Giddens, Anthony. *The Class Structure of the Advanced Societies*. 2nd ed. London: Hutchison, 1981.

———. *Modernity and Self Identity: Self and Society in the Late Modern Age*. Stanford, CA: Stanford University Press, 1991.

———. *The Third Way: The Renewal of Social Democracy*. Cambridge: Polity Press, 1998.

_____. *The Transformation of Intimacy: Sexuality, Love and Eroticism in Modern Societies*. Stanford, CA: Stanford University Press, 1992.

Gijswijt-Hofstra, Marijke, and Roy Porter, ed. *Cultures of Neurasthenia from Beard to the First World War*. Amsterdam: Rodopi, 2001.

Gilding, Michael. *The Making and Breaking of the Australian Family*. Sydney: Allen & Unwin, 1991.

Giles, G.R. "Vocational Guidance in Australia in 1932." *International Labour Review* 26 (1932): 530–43.

Goleman, Daniel. *Emotional Intelligence*. New York: Bantam Books, 1995.

Gosling, F.G. *Before Freud: Neurasthenia and the American Medical Community, 1870–1910*. Urbana, IL: University of Illinois Press, 1987.

Greenspan, Miriam. *A New Approach to Women and Therapy*. 2nd ed. Blue Ridge Summit, PA: TAB Books, 1993.

Groenhout, Ruth. *Connected Lives: Human Nature and the Ethics of Care*. Lanham: Rowman & Littlefield, 2004.

Gross, Martin. *The Psychological Society: A Critical Analysis of Psychiatry, Psychotherapy, Psychoanalysis, and the Psychological Revolution*. New York: Simon & Schuster, 1979.

Hales, Nora. "Sydney's 'Worry Clinic.'" *Rydges* (January 1936): 27–28.

Hall, John. "Educational Psychology in Public Service." In *Psychology in Australia: Achievements and Prospects*, edited by Mary Nixon and Ronald Taft, 163–74. Sydney: Pergamon Press, 1977.

Halmos, Paul. *The Faith of the Counsellors*. London: Constable, 1965.

Harvey, Les. "Conjoint Counselling: How Does It Apply to Marriage Guidance?" *Marriage and Family* (March 1965): 10–12.

Herron, William, and Sheila Rouslin Welt. *Money Matters: The Fee in Psychotherapy and Psychoanalysis*. New York: Guilford Press, 1992.

Hazell, Brian. "The Counselling Profession." In *The Professions in Australia: A Critical Appraisal*, edited by Paul Boreham, Alec Pemberton, and Paul Wilson, 196–219. St Lucia, Qld: University of Queensland Press, 1976.

Held, Virginia. *The Ethics of Care: Personal, Political, and Global*. Oxford: Oxford University Press, 2006.

Herman, Ellen. *The Romance of American Psychology: Political Culture in the Age of Experts*. Berkley: University of California Press, 1995.

Hillman, James, and Michael Ventura. *We've Had a Hundred Years of Psychotherapy and the World's Getting Worse*. San Francisco: HarperSanFrancisco, 1993.

Hobsbawm, Eric. *The Age of Extremes: A History of the World, 1914–1991*. New York: Vintage Books, 1996.

Horvath, Adam, and Lester Luborsky. "The Role of the Therapeutic Alliance in Psychotherapy." *Journal of Consulting and Clinical Psychology* 61, no. 4 (1993): 561–73.

Hughes, John. "Harold Wyndham and Educational Reform in Australia 1925–1968." *Education Research and Perspectives* 29, no. 1 (2002): 1–268.
Illouz, Eva. *Saving the Modern Soul: Therapy, Emotions, and the Culture of Self-Help.* Berkeley: University of California Press, 2008.
Ingleby, David, ed. *Critical Psychiatry: The Politics of Mental Health.* London: Free Association Books, 2004. First published 1980.
Ivison, David J. "Clinical Psychology in Public Service." In *Psychology in Australia: Achievements and Prospects,* edited by Mary Nixon and Ronald Taft, 175–83. Sydney: Pergamon Press, 1977.
Jamieson, Lynn. "Intimacy Transformed? A Critical Look at the 'Pure Relationship.'" *Sociology* 33, no. 3 (1999): 477–94.
Jenkins, Norman. "Training and Work: Inservice Training for Psychologists in State Education Departments." In *Psychology in Australia: Achievements and Prospects,* edited by Mary Nixon and Ronald Taft, 136–47. Sydney: Pergamon Press, 1977.
Johnson, J.A. "The New Psychology and the Schools." Report of the 16th Meeting of the Australasian Association for the Advancement of Science, 696–703. Wellington, NZ: The Association, 1923.
Kaminer, Wendy. *I'm Dysfunctional, You're Dysfunctional: The Recovery Movement and Other Self-Help Fashions.* Reading, MA: Addison-Wesley, 1992.
Kempe, C. Henry, Frederic Silverman, Brant Steele, William Droegemueller, and Henry Silver. "The Battered-Child Syndrome." *Journal of the American Medical Association* 181, no. 1 (1962), 17–24.
Kitzinger, Celia. "Therapy and How It Undermines the Practice of Radical Feminism." In *Radically Speaking: Feminism Reclaimed,* edited by Diane Bell and Renate Klein, 92–101. Melbourne: Spinifex Press, 1996.
Krupnick, Janice, Stuart Sotsky, Irene Elkin, Sam Simmens, Janet Moyer, John Watkins, and Paul Pilkoni. "The Role of the Therapeutic Alliance in Psychotherapy and Pharmacotherapy Outcome: Findings in the National Institute of Mental Health Treatment of Depression Collaborative Research Program." *Focus* 4, no. 2 (2006): 269–77.
Landes, Joan, ed. *Feminism, the Public and the Private.* Oxford: Oxford University Press, 1998.
Lasch, Christopher. *The Culture of Narcissism: American Life in an Age of Diminishing Expectations.* New York: Norton, 1991. First published 1979.
_____. *Haven in a Heartless World: The Family Besieged.* New York: Basic Books, 1977.

———. *The Minimal Self: Psychic Survival in Troubled Times.* New York: Norton, 1984.
Laurie, Henry. "Recent Progress and Present Position of Mental Science." Report of the 5th Meeting of the Australasian Association for the Advancement of Science, 196–206. Adelaide: The Association, 1893.
Laurie, H., J.A. Hartley, H.P. Gill, J.T. Collins, T. Brodribb, and E.F.J. Love. "Report of the Committee on the Best Means of Encouraging Psychophysical and Psychometrical Investigation in Australasia." Report of the 6th Meeting of the Australasian Association for the Advancement of Science, 842–43. Brisbane: The Association, 1895.
Lears, T.J. Jackson. "From Salvation to Self-Realization: Advertising and the Therapeutic Roots of the Consumer Culture, 1880–1930." In *The Culture of Consumption: Critical Essays in American History, 1880–1980*, edited by Richard Wightman Fox and T.J. Jackson Lears, 3–38. New York: Pantheon, 1983.
Lees, Stella, and June Senyard. *The 1950s: How Australia Became a Modern Society, and Everyone Got a House and a Car.* Melbourne: Hyland House, 1987.
Lewis, Milton. *Managing Madness: Psychiatry and Society in Australia 1788–1980.* Canberra: Australian Government Publishing Service, 1988.
Lidwill, M.C. "Some Notes on the Diagnosis and Treatment of the Neuroses." *Medical Journal of Australia* (January 1923): 57–62.
Lifeline Australia. *Annual Report 2009.* http://www.lifeline.org.au
Lovibond, Sidney. "Undergraduate Teaching in Psychology in Australian Universities." In *Psychology in Australia: Achievements and Prospects*, edited by Mary Nixon and Ronald Taft, 100–17. Sydney: Pergamon Press, 1977.
Lowney, Kathleen. *Baring Our Souls: TV Talk Shows and the Religion of Recovery.* New York: Aldine de Gruyter, 1999.
Lukinbeal, Christopher, and Stuart Aitken. "Sex, Violence and the Weather: Male Hysteria, Scale and the Fractal Geographies of Patriarchy." In *Places Through the Body*, edited by Heidi Nast and Steve Pile, 356–80. London: Routledge, 1998.
Mackay, Hugh. "Psychologists in the Age of Discontinuity." *Australian Psychologist* 34, no. 1 (1999): 1–3.
Marano, V. "On Neurasthenia." *Australasian Medical Gazette* (October 1890): 21–24.
Martin, Leonie. "Psychology in the Clinic." *Australian Journal of Psychology* 10, no. 1 (1958): 49–53.
Martyr, Philippa. *Paradise of Quacks: An Alternative History of Medicine in Australia.* Sydney: Macleay Press, 2002.

Matthews, Jill. *Good and Mad Women: The Historical Construction of Femininity in Twentieth Century Australia*. Sydney: Allen & Unwin, 1984.
McAree, J.V. "Notes on Applied Psychology and Suggestive Therapeutics." *Medical Journal of Australia* (April 1920): 355–61.
_____. "Notes on Psycho-therapeutic Practice." *Medical Journal of Australia* (May 1923): 543–47.
McCallum, David. "Educational Expansion, Curriculum Reform and Psychological Theory: Australia in the 1930s." *Australian and New Zealand Journal of Sociology* 22, no. 2 (1986): 225–37.
_____. *The Social Production of Merit: Education, Psychology and Politics in Australia 1900–1950*. London: Falmer Press, 1990.
McGee, Micki. *Self-Help Inc.: Makeover Culture in American Life*. New York: Oxford University Press, 2005.
McLeod, Julie, and Katie Wright. "The Talking Cure in Everyday Life: Gender, Generations and Friendship." *Sociology* 43, no. 1 (2009): 122–39.
McLeod, John. *Narrative and Psychotherapy*. London: Sage, 2004.
McNay, Lois. *Foucault and Feminism: Power, Gender and the Self*. Cambridge: Polity Press, 1992.
Mellor, David P. *The Role of Science and Industry*. Canberra: Australian War Memorial, 1958.
Miller, Nancy. "Introduction." In *An Oral History of Marriage Counselling in Australia: From Meaning Well to Doing Well*, edited by David Fox and Nancy Miller, 5–9. Canberra: Les Harvey Foundation, 2000.
Milligan, E.T.C. "Medical Experiences in the War Zone." *Medical Journal of Australia* (March 1917): 201–03.
Mosher, J. Montgomery. "The Treatment of Mental Disease in the Early Stage." *Australasian Medical Gazette* (February 1912): 153–56.
Moskowitz, Eva. *In Therapy We Trust: America's Obsession with Self-Fulfillment*. Baltimore: Johns Hopkins University Press, 2001.
Murphy, John. *Imagining the Fifties: Private Sentiment and Political Culture in Menzies' Australia*. Sydney: Pluto Press, 2000.
Murray, H.M.L. "Pre-Employment Medical Examination." *Industrial Psychology and Personnel Practice* 2, no. 1 (1946): 33–36.
Muscio, Bernard. *Lectures on Industrial Psychology*. Sydney: Angus & Robertson, 1917.
Nangle, J. "Vocational Guidance." Report of the 17th Meeting of the Australasian Association for the Advancement of Science, 617–27. Adelaide: The Association, 1924.
Neve, Michael. "Public Views of Neurasthenia: Britain, 1880–1930." In *Cultures of Neurasthenia from Beard to the First World War*, edited

by Marijke Gijswijt-Hofstra and Roy Porter, 141–59. Amsterdam: Rodopi, 2001.
New South Wales. Department of Public Instruction. "Report of the Minister of Public Instruction for the Year 1925." Sydney: Government Printer, 1926.
Nixon, Mary, and Ronald Taft, ed. *Psychology in Australia: Achievements and Prospects.* Sydney: Pergamon Press, 1977.
Nolan, James. *The Therapeutic State: Justifying Government at Century's End.* New York: New York University Press, 1998.
North, Maurice. *The Secular Priests.* London: Allen & Unwin, 1972.
Nudelman, Franny. "Beyond the Talking Cure: Listening to Female Testimony on the Oprah Winfrey Show." In *Inventing the Psychological: Towards a Cultural History of Emotional Life in America,* edited by Joel Pfister and Nancy Schnog, 297–315. New Haven, CT: Yale University Press, 1997.
Nurcombe, B. "Neurotic Relationships." *Marriage* (June 1963): 4–5.
O'Grady, Helen. "An Ethics of the Self." In *Feminism and the Final Foucault,* edited by Dianna Taylor and Karen Vintges, 91–117. Urbana: University of Illinois Press, 2004.
O'Neil, W.M. *A Century of Psychology in Australia.* Sydney: Sydney University Press, 1987.
———. *From School to Work: A Plea for Vocational Guidance.* Melbourne: Australian Council for Educational Research, 1944.
O'Neil, W.M., and K.F. Walker. "Psychology in the Universities." *Australian Journal of Psychology* 10, no. 1 (1958): 7–18.
Oppenheim, Janet. *"Shattered Nerves": Doctors, Patients, and Depression in Victorian England.* New York: Oxford University Press, 1991.
Patrick, Jeff. "The Economic Value of Psychology in Australia: 2001." *Australian Psychologist* 40, no. 3 (2005): 149–58.
Pentony, Pat. "Client Centred Therapy and the Communications Analysis Position." *Marriage and Family* (June 1965): 8–9.
Pfohl, Stephen. "The 'Discovery' of Child Abuse." *Social Problems* 24, no. 3 (1977): 310–23.
Polsky, Andrew. *The Rise of the Therapeutic State.* Princeton, NJ: Princeton University Press, 1991.
Porter, Roy. "Nervousness, Eighteenth and Nineteenth Century Style: From Luxury to Labour." In *Cultures of Neurasthenia from Beard to the First World War,* edited by Marijke Gijswijt-Hofstra and Roy Porter, 31–49. Amsterdam: Rodopi, 2001.
Quintrell, Neil, and Margaret Robertson. "Student Counselling in Australian Universities: Forty Years of Development." *International Journal for the Advancement of Counselling* 18 (1996): 203–21.

Reiger, Kerreen. "The Coming of the Counsellers: The Development of Marriage Guidance in Australia." *Australian and New Zealand Journal of Sociology* 23, no. 3 (1987): 375–87.

_____. *The Disenchantment of the Home: Modernizing the Australian Family 1880–1940.* Melbourne: Oxford University Press, 1985.

Rieff, Philip. "The Emergence of Psychological Man." Chapter 10 in *Freud: The Mind of the Moralist.* 3rd ed. Chicago: University of Chicago Press, 1979. First published 1959.

_____. *The Triumph of the Therapeutic: Uses of Faith after Freud.* Chicago: University of Chicago Press, 1987. First published 1966.

Riesman, David, with Nathan Glazer and Reuel Denney. *The Lonely Crowd: A Study of the Changing American Character.* Rev. ed. with a foreword by Todd Gitlin. New Haven, CT: Yale University Press, 2001. First published 1950.

Rose, D.E. "Psychology in the Armed Forces." *Australian Journal of Psychology* 10, no. 1 (1958): 42–48.

Rose, Nikolas. *Governing the Soul: The Shaping of the Private Self.* 2nd ed. London: Free Association Books, 1999.

_____. *Inventing Our Selves: Psychology, Power, and Personhood.* Cambridge: Cambridge University Press, 1996.

_____. *The Psychological Complex: Psychology, Politics, and Society in England, 1869–1939.* London: Routledge & Kegan Paul, 1985.

Rudd, A.W. "The Scientific Study of the Child." Report of the 12th Meeting of the Australasian Association for the Advancement of Science, 763–74. Brisbane: The Association, 1909.

Ryan, Jane, ed. *How Does Psychotherapy Work?* London: Karnac Books, 2005.

Safran, Jeremy, and J. Christopher Muran. *Negotiating the Therapeutic Alliance: A Relational Treatment Guide.* New York: Gilford Press, 2000.

Scanzoni, John. *Designing Families: The Search for Self and Community in the Information Age.* Thousand Oaks, CA: Pine Forge Press, 2000.

Schuster, David. "Neurasthenia and a Modernizing America." *Journal of the American Medical Association* 290 (2003): 2327–28.

_____. "Personalizing Illness and Modernity: S. Weir Mitchell, Literary Women, and Neurasthenia." *Bulletin of the History of Medicine* 79, no. 4 (2005): 695–722.

Sennett, Richard. *The Corrosion of Character: The Personal Consequences of Work in the New Capitalism.* New York: Norton, 1998.

_____. *The Fall of Public Man.* Cambridge: Cambridge University Press, 1977.

Sheehan, Peter. "Anticipations Ahead for Psychology: Looking from Past to Future." *Australian Psychologist* 31, no. 3 (1996): 183–90.

Showalter, Elaine. *The Female Malady: Women, Madness and English Culture 1830–1980*. London: Virago, 1987.
Sigman, Aric. *New, Improved? Exposing the Misuse of Popular Psychology*. London: Simon & Schuster, 1995.
Simmel, Georg. "The Metropolis and Mental Life." In *The Sociology of Georg Simmel*, translated, edited and with an introduction by Kurt H. Wolff, 409–24. New York: Free Press, 1950. First published 1903.
Simmons, Paul. "Relationship and Family Counselling in Australia: A Review of Our History and Current Status." *International Journal of Psychology* 41, no. 3 (2006): 180–88.
Simonds, Wendy. *Women and Self-Help Culture: Reading Between the Lines*. New Brunswick, NJ: Rutgers University Press, 1992.
Small, J., and U. Gault. "Perceptions of Psychologists by the General Public and Three Professional Groups." *Australian Psychologist* 10, no. 1 (1975): 21–31.
Smith, James. *The Nervous System: Its Use and Abuse*. Melbourne: Australian Health Society, 1881.
―――. "Worry as a Factor of Disease." *Victorian Review* (June 1880): 203–12.
Smyth, John. "Five Years' Experience with Testing the Intelligence of New Students at the Teachers' College Melbourne." Report of the 18th Meeting of the Australasian Association for the Advancement of Science, 709–10. Perth: The Association, 1926.
Solomon, Yvette, Jo Warin, Charlie Lewis, and Wendy Langford. "Intimate Talk between Parents and Their Teenage Children: Democratic Openness or Covert Control?" *Sociology* 36, no. 4 (2002): 965–83.
Spearritt, Katie. "New Dawns: First Wave Feminism 1880–1914." In *Gender Relations in Australia: Domination and Negotiation*, edited by Kay Saunders and Raymond Evans, 325–49. Sydney: Harcourt Brace Jovanovich, 1992.
Spillman, Lyn, ed. *Cultural Sociology*. Malden, MA: Blackwell, 2002.
Springthorpe, John W. "The Position, Use, and Abuse of Mental Therapeutics." *Australasian Medical Gazette* (October 1905): 525–27.
―――. "On the Psychological Aspects of Sexual Appetite." *Australasian Medical Gazette* (October 1884): 8–14.
―――. "Psychology: Its Basis and Application." *Medical Journal of Australia* (October 1922): 461–64.
―――. "War Neuroses and Civil Practice." *Medical Journal of Australia* (October 1919): 279–84.
Stoller, Allen. "Sexual Conflict in Marriage." *Marriage and Family* (March 1964): 4–6.
Summons, Walter. "Medical Work Seen in the Australian Military Hospitals." *Medical Journal of Australia* (September 1917): 244–47.

Taft, Ronald. "Psychology and Its History in Australia." *Australian Psychologist* 17, no. 1 (1982): 31–39.
Taft, Ronald, and Ross Day. "Psychology in Australia." *Annual Review of Psychology* 39 (1988): 375–400.
Taksa, Lucy. "The Cultural Diffusion of Scientific Management: The United States and New South Wales." *Journal of Industrial Relations* 37, no. 3 (1995): 427–61.
Taylor, F.W. *The Principles of Scientific Management*. New York: Dover, 1998. First published 1911.
Taylor, Ruth. "The Death of Neurasthenia and Its Psychological Reincarnation." *British Journal of Psychiatry* 179 (2001): 550–57.
Thielking, Monica. "An Investigation of Attitudes Towards the Practice of School-Based Psychological Services." PhD diss. Melbourne: Swinburne University of Technology, 2006.
Thomson, Matthew. "Neurasthenia in Britain: An Overview." In *Cultures of Neurasthenia from Beard to the First World War*, edited by Marijke Gijswijt-Hofstra and Roy Porter, 77–95. Amsterdam: Rodopi, 2001.
———. "The Psychological Body." In *Medicine in the Twentieth Century*, edited by Roger Cooter and John Pickstone, 291–306. Amsterdam: Harwood Academic Publishers, 2000.
Trinca, Helen, and Catherine Fox. *Better Than Sex: How a Whole Generation Got Hooked on Work*. Sydney: Random House Australia, 2004.
Tucker, James. *The Therapeutic Corporation*. New York: Oxford University Press, 1999.
Turner, A. Jefferis. "Medical Gleanings in War Time." *Medical Journal of Australia* (April 1919): 294–97.
Turtle, Alison. "The Development of Institutionalized Psychology in Australia between the Wars: Bibliographical Compendium and Commentary." *Historical Records of Australian Science* 9, no. 3 (1992): 241–56.
———. "Education, Social Science and the 'Common Weal.'" In *The Commonwealth of Science: ANZAAS and the Scientific Enterprise in Australasia, 1888–1988*, edited by Roy MacLeod, 222–46. Melbourne: Oxford University Press, 1988.
———. "The First Women Psychologists in Australia." *Australian Psychologist* 25, no. 3 (1990): 239–55.
———. "Institution, Ideology, Icon: Psychology at Sydney 1921–1996." *Australian Journal of Psychology* 49, no. 3 (1997): 121–27.
———. "Psychology in the Australian Context." In *Psychology Moving East: The Status of Western Psychology in Asia and Oceania*, edited by Geoffrey Blowers and Alison Turtle, 305–24. Sydney: Sydney University Press, 1987.

Tyquin, Michael. *Madness and the Military: Australia's Experience of the Great War*. Loftus: Australian Military History Publications, 2006.
Ussher, Jane. "Are We Medicalizing Women's Misery? A Critical Review of Women's Higher Rates of Reported Depression." *Feminism and Psychology* 20, no. 9 (2010): 9–35.
_____. *Women's Madness: Misogyny or Mental Illness?* Amherst, MA: University of Massachusetts Press, 1992.
van Krieken, Robert. *Children and the State: Social Control and the Formation of Australian Child Welfare*. Sydney: Allen & Unwin, 1992.
Verco, D.J.A. "Psychology in Education Departments." *Australian Journal of Psychology* 10, no. 1 (1958): 19–29.
Walker, David. "Continence for a Nation: Seminal Loss and National Vigour." *Labour History* 48 (May 1985): 1–14.
_____. "Mind and Body." In *Australians 1938*, edited by Bill Gammage and Peter Spearritt, 223–34. Sydney: Fairfax, Syme & Weldon, 1987.
_____. "Modern Nerves, Nervous Moderns: Notes on Male Neurasthenia." In *Australian Cultural History*, edited by S.L. Goldberg and F.B. Smith, 123–37. Cambridge: Cambridge University Press, 1988.
Walker, Ronald. "Some Recent Developments in Industrial Psychology." Report of the 19th Meeting of the Australasian Association for the Advancement of Science, 540–42. Hobart: The Association, 1928.
Weber, Cynthia. *Faking It: U.S. Hegemony in a "Post-Phallic" Era*. Minneapolis: University of Minnesota Press, 1999.
Weeks, Jeffrey. *Invented Moralities: Sexual Values in an Age of Uncertainty*. New York: Columbia University Press, 1995.
_____. *The World We Have Won: The Remaking of Erotic and Intimate Life*. London: Routledge, 2007.
Weeks, Jeffrey, Brian Heaphy, and Catherine Donovan. *Same Sex Intimacies: Families of Choice and Other Life Experiments*. London: Routledge, 2001.
West, Candace, and Don Zimmerman. "Doing Gender." *Gender & Society* 1, no. 2 (1987): 125–51.
Williams, Joan. *Unbending Gender: Why Family and Work Conflict and What to Do About It*. New York: Oxford University Press, 2000.
Wills, George. "A Brief History of Counselling Psychology in Australia." *Australian Journal of Counselling Psychology*, Summer (1999/2000): 21–27.
Wood, Ann Douglas. "'The Fashionable Diseases': Women's Complaints and Their Treatment in Nineteenth Century America." *Journal of Interdisciplinary History* IV, no. 1 (1973): 25–52.
Wood, Helen. *Talking with Television: Women, Talk Shows, and Modern Self-Reflexivity*. Urbana: University of Illinois Press, 2009.

Worell, Judith, and Pamela Remer. *Feminist Perspectives in Therapy: An Empowerment Model for Women*. 2nd ed. New York: Wiley, 2002.
World Health Organization. *The World Health Report 2001: Mental Health: New Understandings, New Hope*. Geneva: World Health Organization, 2001.
Wright, Christopher. *The Management of Labour: A History of Australian Employers*. Melbourne: Oxford University Press, 1995.
Wright, Katie. "Engendering a Therapeutic Ethos: Modernity, Masculinity & Nervousness." *Journal of Historical Sociology* 22, no. 1 (2009): 84–107.
_____. "Theorizing Therapeutic Culture: Past Influences, Future Directions." *Journal of Sociology* 44, no. 4 (2008): 321–36.
_____. "Therapy Culture." In *Reflected Light: La Trobe Essays*, edited by Peter Beilharz and Robert Manne, 302–12. Melbourne: Black Inc., 2006.
Zaretsky, Eli. *Capitalism, the Family, and Personal Life*. London: Pluto Press, 1976.
_____. *Secrets of the Soul: A Social and Cultural History of Psychoanalysis*. New York: Vintage, 2005.

Index

A

advertising: and nerves 50, 58, 60-64, 76-84; and psychology 23, 31, 118-19, 131-35; and the therapeutic 22-23, 84, 120
advice columns 129-31, 139
Allbutt, T.C. 55, 60, 63
Allen, Judith 33
analytic attitude: cultural diffusion of 127-28, 142, 217; and the popular media 129, 135; and work 121-22
anxiety: disorders 166, 173; experiences of 172, 184, 187-88, 224; and modern life 23, 43, 181, 195, 223; and therapy 18, 181, 189, 208
Australasian Association for the Advancement of Science (AAAS) 90, 92, 105, 106, 115
Australian Council for Educational Research (ACER) 101-02
Australian Institute of Industrial Psychology (AIIP) 108, 115, 122
Australian Psychological Society (APS) 10, 94, 96, 152-156, 162
authority 8, 15-19, 38, 47, 149, 222
autonomy: and the family 29, 43; ideal of 40; individual 21, 28, 48, 195, 222; and psychoanalysis 45

B

Barkan, Elazar 220
Barrett-Lennard, Goff 151
Beard, George 52-53, 54-55, 77, 83
Becker, Dana 35-36
behavior: acceptable forms of 173-75; analysis of 7, 17, 130, 137; medical model of 151; modification 131; problems in children 103, 104, 110, 155; psychological explanations of 1, 20, 26, 130, 139; shaping 120, 143, therapy and 191, 192-93, 208, 212
Bellah, Robert 21
Benjamin, Jessica 39, 40-41
Berman, Marshall 177
Beyond Blue 172, 225
Blackburn, Kevin 112
Board, Peter 99
Bourdieu, Pierre 180-81
Bringing Them Home 220-21
British Psychological Society (BPS), Overseas Branch 94, 95

C

Calmus, Bernard 135
capitalism: and the family 19, 41; and the public/private divide 41-42; and therapy 27; and the

Index   271

therapeutic 5, 22-26, 33
capitalist control 9, 14, 26
care: duty of 97, 113, 221; ethos of 63; institutional 110, 221; and intimate life 45; pastoral 146; theorization of 32; and the therapeutic 22; of young people 192, 220
Carlier, Ingrid 69
Carrington, W.L. 144-45
Carroll, John 18, 19, 20
Casey, Michael 18
Catholic Church, child sexual abuse 222
CBT 158, 165, 191, 205, 207
Chesler, Phyllis 33
child abuse: exposure of 167-70, 221-22; Prevention program 149; and the therapeutic 170
child development, knowledge of 91, 169
child guidance clinics 104
child sexual assault 222
child study 91
Chodorow, Nancy 40-41
Cloud, Dana 25, 27, 33, 36, 125
Commonwealth Reconstruction Training Scheme (CRTS) 93
confession, genealogy of 30-31
confessional culture: and celebrity 1; rise of 9, 219; and the therapeutic 3, 10, 46, 47, 218
Connell, R.W. 38, 46
consciousness raising 36, 170
consumer culture 9, 23, 58, 76
Cooke, Simon 93, 96, 117, 153
counseling: advent of 7, 10; critiques of 25, 27, 33, 35; experiences of 192, 196, 198-201, 204, 224-25; and football 171-72; growth of 8, 119, 140, 151, 152, 175, 177; pastoral 143, 145, 146, 149, 150; relationship 145, 148, 184, 204, 210 (*see also* marriage guidance); seeking 181-88, 197, 199 (*see also* therapy); student 105, 108, 110, 150-51, (*see also* vocational guidance); telephone 149, 152; and the therapeutic 1, 6, 14, 128, 150, 173, 216-17
counter-therapeutic ethos 140-41
Crews, Bill 149
Crittenden, Stephen 148
Cunningham, K.S. 101
Cushman, Philip 23

D

Damousi, Joy 129, 136
Davidson, Andrew 74
Davis, Dona 77
democratization 43, 45, 222
depression: and advertising 81, 83-84, 132; epidemic 118; experiences of 185, 187, 224; and nerves 6, 53, 56, 76, 84-85, 136; public revelations of 128, 170-73; rising rates of 1, 173, 189; and the therapeutic 3, 76; and therapy 181, 187, 190; and women 34
Directorate of Manpower 94-95
dignity: struggles for 2, 11, 205, 225; and therapy 194, 204, 216
divorce: prevention of 146; rates 128, 144
domestic realm 42, 143, 218. See *also* private life
domestic violence 150, 152, 167, 170, 222. See *also* family violence
Donzelot, Jacques 28-29, 33, 170
Dowrick, Stephanie: on the media 157, 164-65, 166; on therapy 189-90, 197, 206, 213
Durkheim, Emile 15, 17, 19, 53, 228n8

E

education: children with disabilities 110; and mental testing 100-02, 104, 105; and psychology 6, 87, 88, 89, 90-91, 98-111; school psychology services 100, 110; special schools 103; support services 102, 103-04

efficiency: economic 111-12, 116, 119; national 105, 112; personal 132

Elliott, Anthony 32, 40, 44, 46, 180, 233n95

emotional intelligence (EI) 124, 212

emotional life: and gender 142; increasing concern with 127; public discussion of 173; and reflexive selfhood 131-32; and the therapeutic 5, 174-75, 219

emotional problems 132, 137; and therapists 166; public discussion of 170

emotional realm: ascendancy of 3, 5, 225; and capitalism 124; expansion of 132; focus on 143; legitimizing of 8, 46, 48; sport and 173

emotional suffering: exposure of 167; social management of 218; social recognition of 11; and stoicism 69; and therapy 179, 205

emotions: control of 129, 140; and gender 46, 142; privileging of 131, 132; and the public/private divide 21, 41-42, 46; in the public sphere 149; repression of 140; and the therapeutic 1, 5, 11, 174-75, 218-19, 221-22, 225; and therapy 212, 214; and work 124-25

empathy 22, 206

Ewen, Stuart 23, 26

F

Faludi, Susan 34

family, the: decline of 24; government of 29; patriarchal 39, 41; postwar ideas of 128; upholding 146

family friendly workplaces 125

family life: democratization of 43, 222; expectations of 191; intervention into 96, 169-70; investigation of 167; threats to 144; norms of conduct in 29, 43

family violence 167-70, 223. *See also* domestic violence *and* child abuse

femininity: constructions of 8, 33, 141; and hysteria 64, 71; and neurasthenia 56; and the public/private divide 42

feminism 36-37, 142

footballers, professional: scrutiny of behavior 173-74; and depression 128, 171-72, 173

Forgotten Australians 221

Foucault, Michel 4, 13, 28, 29, 30-31, 32, 36, 40

Fox, Catherine 124

Fraser, A.C. 70-71

freedom, and uncertainty 180, 194-95

Freud, Sigmund: and Australian medical journals 58, 72, 73; common unhappiness 57, 177, 215; cultural influence of 6, 7, 104, 129, 130; and psychology in Australia 93; and therapy 196, 202, 204, 215; and war neuroses 69-70, 72, 114

Furedi, Frank 3, 14, 20-21, 25, 41, 47, 179

G

Garton, Stephen 68, 71, 74, 75
gender: cultural-symbolic logic
    of 45; and marriage guidance
    147-48; and the public/
    private divide 41-42; and the
    therapeutic 7, 8, 38, 85, 141-42
gender difference 131, 141
gender order, the 38, 46, 141, 218, 223
gender relations 5, 47, 194
Gersons, Berthold 69
gestalt therapy 147
Giddens, Anthony:
    democratization 43, 192, 210,
    222; late modernity 43-44, 178,
    181, 233n95; self-identity 43,
    194; therapy 44, 195, 214
Giles, G.R. 106, 108
Gilman, Charlotte Perkins 53
Goleman, Daniel 124
Gordon, Amanda: on the media
    157, 161-64, 166; on therapy 189,
    190, 191, 197, 202
Gosling, F.G. 53
Gross, Martin 18-19, 156-57

H

Hall, John 103
happiness: achieving 128, 131, 132,
    142, 144; and advertising 83-84,
    132; cultural ideals of 26, 146,
    179; and the therapeutic 26, 30,
    47-48, 225; and therapy 177, 178,
    185, 211, 214; and work 107,
    116-17
Herman, Ellen 37
Hillman, James 27-28
Hobsbawm, Eric 127
human relations, at work 113, 123
human resource management 94,
    120-21, 123. *See also* personnel
    management

hysteria: and neurasthenia 53,
    stigma of 57, 64; and war 64, 66,
    67, 68, 71

I

identity: exploration of 209, 213;
    quest for 127-28; and therapy
    44, 179, 183, 194, 214
Illouz, Eva 37
intimacy, transformation of 43, 45,
    222
intimate life, problems of 143, 179,
    210
individual differences, theory of:
    contradictory effects of 105;
    and education 99, 100, 102-03,
    106, 110-11; and management
    of populations 87; and scientific
    management 112; and war
    neuroses 72
individualism 21, 35, 47
industrial hygiene 113-14
industrial psychology 93, 94, 111-
    19, 123
inferiority complex 132-35, 136, 139
Ingleby, David 27
injustice 5, 47, 219-221
intelligence testing 95, 100-
    01, 102-03, 104, 109. *See also*
    psychometrics
Ivison, David 104

J

James, William 53
Johnson, J.A. 105

K

Kaminer, Wendy 26
Kempe, Henry 167
Kidman, Antony: on the media
    157, 158-59, 161, 165-66; on
    therapy 189, 196, 207

Kitzinger, Celia 34

L
Lasch, Christopher: culture of narcissism 3, 14, 19-20, 21, 24-25, 26, 150; critiques of 35, 36, 39, 41; psychological expertise 19, 28
Laurie, Henry 87, 90, 99, 156
Lears, T.J. Jackson 22, 23
Lees, Stella 119
Lemert, Charles 46, 180
Lidwill, M.C. 72
Lifeline Australia 149, 172
Lost Innocents 221
Lowney, Kathleen 26
Lundy, Kate 174

M
Mackay, Hugh 156, 195
Maloney, William 65-66
Marano, V. 58-59
marriage guidance 10, 128, 143-48, 152
masculinity: effeminate 141; and fears about masturbation 58-59, 60; hegemonic 46, 50; and nerves/neurasthenia 6-7, 50-51, 56, 60-64; and self-disclosure 171; and the public/private divide 42, 46; and repression 46, 140; and shell shock 71
Matthews, Jill 33
Mayo, Elton 113
McAree, J.V. 73
McCallum, David 98, 102-03, 111
McDonald, Garry 172, 173
McElwain, Donald 93
McLeod, John 191
McNay, Lois 32, 40
Meade, F.G. 65-66
meaning 3, 164, 205-06, 214

meaninglessness 204, 205
medicalization, of women's unhappiness 34
Medicare 155
Mellor, David 117
mental fitness 91, 114-15, 117, 118
mental health: changing understandings of 48, 56, 74, 84-85, 136; increasing concern with 69; legislative reform 74, 75; as a political issue 26, 27; and psychologists 117-18, 155; and religion 145
mental health care 74-76, 144
mental health problems: destigmatization of 158, 172, 173, 225; economic cost of 118; gendered understandings of 50, 57, 84-85; greater openness about 170-73; and the popular media 139; rising rates of 155; stigma 75; and therapy 1, 11, 224; and treatment 74-76
mental hygiene 101, 116-17
Miller, Nancy 146
modern life: alienation of 5; impact on the self 6, 49, 51; and nervousness 50-57, 77, 83; stimulation of 59-60; stresses and strains of 49, 82, 83, 136; and therapy 11, 179, 214
modernity 5, 44, 49-50, 136, 179, 181
modernization 98, 111-12
moral decline 11, 45, 47, 216
Mosher, J. Montgomery 57
Murphy, John 128, 143
Muscio, Bernard 113

N
Nangle, James 106-07
narcissism: culture of 3, 19-20, 21; and therapy 10, 44, 140

nerves: as a common malady 76; discourse of 6, 50-51, 84-85, 129, 136; and gender 64, 82; "manly" 50; popular cures 60-63, 76-84
nervous health 52, 56, 57, 64
nervous debility 58, 60-61, 71
nervous breakdown 72, 224
nervous disorder: democratization of 55; and masculinity 7, 51; prevalence 6, 52, 76
nervousness: and advertising 82; and male sexuality 51, 58; and modernity 50, 55; and suffering 83, 85; and the therapeutic 6, 50
neurasthenia 50-58, 69, 76; and gender 55-56; sexual 56, 63; and social class 53; symptoms 54-55, 72; treatment 56, 57, 64; and war neuroses 67-68, 69
Neve, Michael 56, 57
newspapers, *see* popular media/press
Nolan, James 14, 17-18, 20, 25
normality: concepts of 139, 151; and mental testing 102; psychological discourse of 88; psychotherapies of 30
normalization: of marginal populations 31; of nervousness 57, 82; of therapy 177
North, Maurice 18
Nudelman, Franny 35
Nurcombe, Barry 147

O
object relations 39-40
O'Connor, Peter: on the media 157-58, 159-61, 166; on therapy 165, 190-91, 212-13
Oedipus complex 39-40
O'Neil, W.M. (Bill) 95, 99, 102, 110
Oppenheim, Janet 50, 53, 54

P
parental authority 19, 43, 192
parental relationships 43, 192-94
parenting: education for 144; permissive 23; style 139
parents: counseling for 149, 169; forced removal from 220-21; issues with 187
paternal authority, breakdown of 8, 29, 39, 43
Perry, William Walter 65-66
personal development 146, 186
personal fulfillment 48, 127-28
personal growth 26, 155
personal problems: attention to 131, 171; psychology and 89, 111, 152, 154; speaking out about 42; and student counseling 151; therapeutic responses to 105; and therapy 182, 224; and vocational guidance 108; and work 120
personality: and culture 16, 18, 20, 23-24; development 39-41, 135, 147; and marriage guidance 145; popular analysis of 120, 135, 137; and relationships 147; tests 122, 137; type 118
personnel management 118, 119. *See also* human resource management
politics: depoliticization 22, 25-26, 35-36, 217, 220; politicization of private life 128, 218, 222, 223; therapeutic form of 175, 219-21
Polsky, Andrew 31
pop psychology: critique of 26-27; quizzes 139, rejection of 201
popular culture 1, 2, 120
popular media/press 128, 143, 171; and nerves 52, 60-62, 82, 83; and psychology 125, 129-40

Porter, Roy 53
positive thinking 26, 142
private life: delicacy of 21, 218; democratization of 43, 209-10; and expert intervention 8, 10, 28, 143; openness about 170, 210; politicization of 10, 128, 218; scrutiny of 166-67, 171
private troubles: public concern with 167, public accounts of 170
Protestant ethic 19, 24
Protestantism: ethos of self-denial 22: secularization of 23
psychiatry: anti-psychiatry 27, 31, 140; developments in 9, 73-76, 84; feminist critique of 33, and the therapeutic 1, 2, 40, 177
psychoanalysis: and culture 7, 45 130, 132, 137; psychoanalytic therapy 70, 177; and war neuroses 69-72
psychological experts: critiques of 18-19; and the media 135, 139, 156-66, 171. *See also* psychological profession
psychological knowledge: critiques of 3, 13, 19, 26, 33; diffusion of 6, 10, 94, 97, 157; and gender 3, 10, 33; legitimation of 5, 73, 87, 88; and medicine 57, 73-74; production of 97; and suffering 5; and the therapeutic 6, 84, 87-89. *See also* psychology
"psychological man" 15, 16, 35
psychological profession: expansion of 93, 95, 154; and identity 94, 154, 156; and the media 153, 156-66; and power 115, 140, 154, 156; and professionalization 92, 94-98; promotion of 10, 87, 153-56; and the therapeutic society 1-2, 17.

See also psychological experts
psychological testing, *see* psychometrics
"psychological woman" 35
psychology: and child welfare 96; and education 87, 88, 89, 90-91, 98-111; and feminism 36-37; growth of 84, 85, 110, 154; industrial 94, 95, 111-18, 122; institutionalization of 9, 88-89; marketing of 128, 153-56, 162; and marriage guidance 143-45, 147; and medicine 69-73; origins of 89-93; and personal problems 89; state support of 1, 88, 98, 111, 155; and the therapeutic 6, 9, 13, 97, 87-89; and the workplace 88-89, 97, 111-25
psychometrics: criticism of 102; and education 91, 98, 101, 102, 106, 111, 151; and marriage guidance 146; popularized forms of 137; promotion of 90-91; and work 118, 122, 124; and World War II 95, 101-02, 117-18
public life 11, 21, 46, 88, 127, 128
public revelations: of personal distress 8; of depression 128, 170-73
public voice 43, 218, 222
public/private divide 41-42, 46, 124-25, 141

R
radio 148-49, 159, 161, 162, 165, 171
Reiger, Kerreen 101, 146
relationships: improving 129, 131, 144; intimate 14, 128; parent-child 43, 192; problems in 143-44, 147, 154-55, 191; public examination of 166; and therapy 195, 199, 208, 209, 214

religion: decline of 15-17, 18, 149; pastoral counseling 143, 145, 150; and therapy 190, 205
reticence 2, 170
Rieff, Philip: psychotherapy 205-06; theorization of the therapeutic vii, 3, 8, 13-14, 15-22, 39, 47, 222
Riesman, David 23-24
Rose, Nikolas 29-30, 31, 97; choice 210, 214; speaking out 170; Taylorism 112; the workplace 116, 122, 124
Royal Commission on Human Relationships 128, 166-70, 171, 223

S

salvation 23, 24, 26
Sane Australia 225
Scanzoni, John 43
scientific management 89, 91, 112-13, 119, 124
secularization 15-16, 23, 206
self, the: constructions of 50, 119; cultural fascination with 1, 177-78; destabilization of 6-7, 38, 88, 142; diminished 45, 178, 179; discourses of 88, 122; preoccupation with 13, 129; reflexive 7, 125, 127, 129, 131, 142; therapeutic understandings of 75, 84; and vulnerability 3, 20, 74, 178
self-absorption 10, 22, 47
self-analysis 122, 129-39, 215. *See also* self-examination
self-change 120, 215
self-development 122, 205
self-disclosure 35, 173
self-esteem 2, 35, 135, 187
self examination 24, 131, 142, 182, 191. *See also* self-analysis
self-expression: curtailing of 195; possibilities of 43, 181, 194; quest for 127
self-help books: advertisements for 132-36; critiques of 26, 34-35, 163; and therapy 201-02, 212; and the therapeutic 3, 35, 142
self-improvement 3, 47, 120, 122, 130
self-reliance 2, 141
Senyard, June 119
sex education 144
sexual assault 174, 175, 222
sexual harassment 125, 174, 175
sexual identity 183, 194, 209
sexual minority groups 125, 167
sexual problems 51, 60-61, 136, 155
sexuality: issues of adjustment 144, 147; liberation of 16; and psychoanalysis 45; regulation of 58; and therapy 183, 184, 194
shame 182, 185, 197, 198, 207
Sheehan, Peter 90, 155, 156
shell shock 51, 67-71, 74
Sigman, Aric 26-27
Simmel, Georg 236n14
Smith, James 51-52
Smyth, John 100
social control 3, 22, 33, 47
social critique, therapeutic as 175
social justice 11, 47, 150, 221
social problems, individualization of 25-28, 215, 224
social work 30, 94, 97
social workers 104, 144
speaking out 42-43, 170-71
Springthorpe, John W. 59, 65, 68, 70, 71, 72, 73, 92
stoicism 69, 140, 141
stolen generations, see *Bringing Them Home*

Stoller, Allen 147
stress: and contemporary life 189; counseling for 152, 154-55; discourse of 26, 76, 84; self-assessment of 139
subjectivity: construction of gendered, 35, 37; government of 3, 5, 30; under liberalism 28; and reflexive selfhood 131; theorization of 32, 40; and work 121, 123-24
suffering: and advertising 63, 77, 83-84, 132; exposing private forms of 166-67, 170; and gender 8, 46; public concern with 10, 84; relief from 85, 181; social recognition of 5, 11, 47, 142-43; and the therapeutic 7-8, 48, 175, 218-21; therapists concern with 162, 166; therapy and 179, 181, 188, 204-05
support groups 1, 21-22

T
talk, as therapeutic 1, 30-31, 173
talk shows 26, 35, 157
Taylor, F.W. 112
Taylorism 112. *See also* scientific management
technological change 23, 25, 102, 217
"technologies of the self" 28, 30-31, 36
television: evangelical 148; reality 3; therapists on 157, 161, 163, 165. *See also* talk shows
therapeutic society 1-2; complexity of 103, 149-50, 175, 219; contradictoriness of 47, 75-76, 105, 111, 125, 141, 217, 224; critiques of 3, 13-14, 15-37; emancipatory potential of 4, 42-43, 219, 223; and marginalized groups 8, 45, 170, 218-21; and social justice 11, 150, 219-21
therapeutic techniques 7, 30, 128, 197, 217
therapy: and adaptation 27-28, 193, 216; and authority 18; and choice 209-10, 214; critiques of 25, 27-28, 34; fees for 202-05; and feminism 36-37; and gender 141, 178, 194; and happiness 177, 179, 211, 214; and modernity 11, 44, 224; narrative 187, 191; seeking 178, 181-88; social acceptability of 182; social stigma 201; therapeutic alliance 195-99; and the therapeutic society 27, 50, 89, 178; and uncertainty 180, 208-10, 224; and unhappiness 177, 180, 186, 215. *See also* counseling
Thompson, Nathan 171-72, 173
transactional analysis 142, 147
trauma: counselors 1; new understandings of 69; public recognition of 219-21; war 64, 67, 69, 127, 143
Trinca, Helen 124
Tucker, James 124
Turner, A. Jefferis 68
Turtle, Alison 91, 96, 101

U
uncertainty 4, 45, 180, 223; and therapy 181, 208-09, 210, 224
unhappiness: common (Freud) 57, 177, 215; medicalization of 34; and therapy 179-80, 186

V
Ventura, Michael 27-28
victim culture 13, 175, 218, 219, 222

victimization 20, 219, 221-22
vocational guidance: establishment of 104, 105-10, 115-16; and psychometrics 101; "Worry Clinic" (AIIP) 108
vulnerability: of children 220-22; cultivation of 14, 20, 223; male 50, 74; and the self 3, 178; of women 77

W
Walker, Rev. Alan 148-49
Walker, David 52, 54, 55, 59, 77
Walker, Ronald 115-16
war, *see* World War I; II
Weber, Max 17, 18, 53
Weeks, Jeffrey 45
wellbeing 1, 48, 84, 131
Williams, Joan 38

Woolf, Virginia 53
women's magazines 129-30, 137, 139
World War I 9, 64-72, 84; and psychological medicine 69-75; shell shock 51, 67-71, 74, 114; social and psychological consequences of 6, 64, 69
World War II: postwar period 127-28, 143-44, 150; and psychological tests 101-02, 117; and psychology 93, 94-95, 117-18
Wright, Chris 119

Z
Zaretsky Eli, 41, 42, 44-45, 206, 233n95

www.ingramcontent.com/pod-product-compliance
Lightning Source LLC
LaVergne TN
LVHW040734250326
834688LV00031B/284